THE PATH TO A LONG AND HEALTHY LIFE

AHMED Y. TATIETA

Tatieta Book Publishing
1760 W. 125th Street, #3
Los Angeles, CA 90047
tatietabookpublishing@yahoo.com
Copyright © 2019 by Ahmed Y. Tatieta

All rights reserved. This book may not be reproduced in whole or in part, stored in a retrieval system, or transmitted in any form or by any means electronic, mechanical, photocopying, recording, translation, duplication, importation, distribution or other without written permission from the publisher, except by a reviewer, who may quote brief passages in a review.

Limits of Liability and Disclaimer of Warranty

This book is solemnly for those who deem it valuable and informative to their well-being; and for people seeking health, peace and happiness. The purpose of this book is to educate and provide valuable information based on a research. The content of the book does not guarantee that anyone following the various techniques, suggestions, tips, ideas, or strategies will immediately become successful in trying to get well, but the truth remains knowledge is power. The result is in your hand. This could make room for positive change and a shift of consciousness.

This is a good faith book; it independently works on a good faith basis. Knowing that knowledge is power, every sentence read in this book can contribute to a peace of mind.

The author is not liable nor responsible to anyone with respect to any loss and damages occurred, or any alleged damages caused, directly or indirectly, by the use of the information contained in this book. With this in mind, when it comes to health, many subjects and disciplines have to be considered. But, at the end, each individual experience is unique and individually lived. This is not a professional advice or service to you.

Health is a constant maintenance and requires daily care and abnegation. My advice to you is to never judge a book by its cover. Only the sick need a doctor. We should pray for each other; the prayer of the righteous one is powerful and more effective. Always remember God will never leave you behind, nor forsake you. Health is everything; all strength is with God; and to live is to forgive.

Printed in the United States of America.

ISBN 978-1-7346773-0-0 (EBook)

ISBN 978-1-7346773-1-7 (Paperback)

ABOUT THE AUTHOR

The author's story is an American one you have heard before. He moved from his loved ones in Africa and transitioned to the United States of America. Leaving his country, BURKINA FASO, at the age of twenty-one, he found himself in a land he had to fight to keep his head out of the quagmire of the city of Los Angeles, during his fifteen years of being a permanent resident.

I learned in life, when we pay attention, it repeats itself. I have had ups and downs; days full of joy and other days with questions on my mind. Just like anybody else, I have had days that I laughed and days that I kept a serious face and demeanor.

I have had some times where money was not an issue, and days that I would just wish someone would show up and say, "Here is some money to take care of your needs." Or, "Here is how you should do things to be productive and successful."

On the other hand, I have also had easy days and happy days that would be remembered just like the days of lack and stress will be remembered, too. Regardless, each day made me who I am today. I always believe in helping my fellow men and women, whenever I can, even when not asked to do so.

I have my strengths and my weaknesses. I believe that everyone should be given and taught the opportunity of reaching his/her goals. Each one of us should be more open-minded and attentive to other people and the knowledge they are bringing to us. I have had different teachers who taught me disciplines that I did not give my full attention to. As a student,

ABOUT THE AUTHOR

I didn't pay full attention to many of the subjects being taught when I was growing up.

Once in a while, I have acted in arrogance, and I have also acted in humility and in respect. All my life, I have considered and respected people, life and my environment. I have been cautious and conscious of my actions and deeds. Even though some events and encounters in my life may have taken me out of my character, I always got my senses back. I regained my self-control and I lived right, after the fact.

I realize that knowledge and education are great sources for personal growth. I truly believe we act based on what we know. We react relatively based on our experiences and life circumstance exposures. So I have read a lot of books with different disciplines. I also believe that a single book read gave me more knowledge, understanding and wisdom, regardless of the subject.

I'm the author of the book, *Soul Pathway to Total Health*. I hope that you will read it, too, with an open mind and heart.

Remember; it could only take one sentence in this book to turn on your light, to put you back on track, or to fill in the missing parts in your life, journey and purpose.

This book gives you a brief understanding of where I have been and what I have learned as an autodidact (self-taught person) and researcher for the past ten years in holistic and alternative medicine at a spiritual level. It has been written, knowing that not everything that I have thought of, read and even meditated on, made it in this book. A lot more will come during my speaking and lectures along the way and as time passes with more personal growth.

I am like you; teaching while still learning. Learning while still teaching as everyone is a teacher and a student at the same time.

ABOUT THE AUTHOR

I have a Master of Laws in American Laws and International Legal Practice from Loyola Law School. I'm also known to be an Herbalist, a medicine man, a wellness coach and a holistic healer. I am a motivational speaker and a good listener underground.

In conclusion, I am your humble servant, still learning and listening. I am an activist for a healthy mind, body and soul, including the well-being of the planet and the universe.

I love everyone and everything in the universe as much as I love God/Goddess. I wish you well and much success on your journey.

"Take the pledge today to tell your daughter that she is equal to her brothers; and tell your sons their sisters are equal to them. Everyone plays the role of having each other's back unconditionally."

Overall, there is no veil, nor a shade, over a star. Show me a man or a woman who has never been criticized. Why should we then vex ourselves at things that do not even care about themselves? The truth remains; one man is born, another is born again. And one man is dead and another is also dead. Look around at the courses of the stars like you were going along with them, by considering the changes of the elements into each other and into one another, without worrying if they would change your fate. That way, you might keep a peace of mind and control your life better.

THE PATH TO A LONG AND HEALTHY LIFE

AHMED Y. TATIETA

TABLE OF CONTENTS

PREFACE xv

PREVIEW 1

INTRODUCTION 16

CHAPTER ONE: Heaven: The Kingdom of God is Within You
 – Meditation 19

CHAPTER TWO: The Different Levels of the Soul in a Man/Woman 27

CHAPTER THREE: As Above, So Below. A Star Above and a Divine Soul Below 31
 – The Cycle of the Night Sun through the Duat 31
 – The Thirty-Six Decads in the Cycle of the Annus Magnus (The Great Year) 33
 – The Primordial Abstract Trinity from the Ancients Egyptians 37

CHAPTER FOUR: Astronomy 101 39
 – Inventory of our Solar System 40
 – The Role of the Sun into our Earth Weather 42

CHAPTER FIVE: The Entanglement Theory or the Superstring Theory 54
 – Human Thought Versus Gravity 55
 – Are your Emotions, a Thought Manifest? 56

CHAPTER SIX: General Knowledge to Know 59

CHAPTER SEVEN: The Fruit that Keeps on Giving Fruit 73

TABLE OF CONTENTS

CHAPTER EIGHT: Brief Anatomy of our Physical Body and Required Vitamins and Minerals **78**
- The Roles of the Organs **78**
- What are the Necessary Vitamins the Body Needs? **81**
- What are the Necessary Minerals the Body Needs? **83**
- Benefits of Eating Liver **84**
- Benefit of Eating Quail Eggs and Meat **85**
- The Benefits of Eating Beef Tallow When Consumed **85**

CHAPTE NINE: Trees/Plants/Herbs and Their Effective Cures **87**
- Antiviral Herbs and their Use **100**
- Recipe Based on chili **104**

CHAPTER TEN: Everyone and Everything, Tangible or not, Breathe and Sustain Life **107**
- What is everybody's Role in the Universe? **108**
- Do you Know who you are? **111**

CHAPTER ELEVEN: Secrets: The Most Shared Qualities of the World **113**
- The Burden of Life on Our Shoulders **114**
- The Forces and Mighty behind Our Thought **115**

CHAPTER TWELVE: What is it That is New under the Sun? **118**

CHAPTER THIRTEEN: Is a Confinement of a Soul Possible? **122**
- Same Tree and yet Different Seeds, Qualities in the Fruits **126**
- Fruit of the Same Tree but Taste yet Different upon a Bite **127**
- Our Destiny is not to Stop Judgment Day, but to Survive it **129**

CHAPTER FOURTEEN: The Art of Eternal Love **135**

CHAPTER FIFTEEN: What is Ritual Abuse and their Consequences on their Victims? **140**

CHAPTER SIXTEEN: Philosophy of Daily Practical Life and Events **144**
- What do we know? What it is that is New? **144**
- Can we Claim to have all Knowledge? **144**
- Can we keep a Promise made to someone else if we cannot keep up with our own? **146**
- The Future is not Set **153**
- Are you or aren't you? **158**

CHAPTER SEVENTEEN: Genesis **161**

CHAPTER EIGHTEEN: The Reincarnation of gods and Mystery Masters **167**

CHAPTER NINETEEN: The Cheating Soul **173**

CHAPTER TWENTY: From one Cycle to Another Borrowed Cycle **177**

CHAPTER TWENTY-ONE: Living Simple And Wise
- Universal Mind and Lifestyle of the Wise **181**

CHAPTER TWENTY-TWO: Race, a Divided and Misunderstood Feather among Humans **192**

CHAPTER TWENTY-THREE: Universal Laws And Rules **195**

CHAPTER TWENTYFOUR: The Illusion of Being the Center of the Universe **201**
- Don't Worry and Stress Over the Small Stuff **206**

CHAPTER TWENTY-FIVE: Enlighten and Saved but Still Struggling **208**

CHAPTER TWENTY-SIX: The Forty Two (42) Ideal Laws Of Ma'at To Live By **211**
- The Seven Principle of Ma'at **214**
- The Seven Hermetic Principles **215**

TABLE OF CONTENTS

CHAPTER TWENTY-SEVEN: Parable And Holy Test   **216**

CHAPTER TWENTY-EIGHT: Love, Relationships And What Not To Expect   **219**

CHAPTER TWENTY-NINE: Happiness and the Secret of Being Present   **225**

CHAPTER THIRTY: The Divine Code Of Human Behavior (77 Commandments)   **233**

CHAPTER THIRTY-ONE: The Power of the Mind and how to Reclaim the Power from Your Mind   **237**

CHAPTER THIRTY-TWO: The Original Sin   **241**

CHAPTER THIRTY-THREE: Daily Proverbs, Thought And Wisdom For The Soul   **245**

CHAPTER THIRTY-FOUR: Alternative Techniques to Improve Energy and Balance Emotions   **253**
  – Reflexology of Fingers and Massage of Hands   **253**
  – Reflexology of the Feet   **254**
  – The Benefits of Drinking Water   **256**
  – The Benefits of Turmeric   **257**
  – The Benefits of Ginseng   **258**
  – The Benefits of keeping your Heart Open at all Times   **259**
  – The Misuse of Time   **260**
  – The Importance Of Sleep And Getting Enough Rest   **261**
  – If you don't Tell me, How would I know?   **263**
  – Balancing of the Chakras   **267**
  – Mucusless Diet Healing System (Dr. Sebi's Sample List)   **270**
  – The Importance Of Breakfast   **272**

TABLE OF CONTENTS

CHAPTER THIRTY-FIVE: Breathing Techniques/ Breach control/ Breath of Life **274**
    Prana Breathing Exercise **275**
    Qi/Energy Breathing Exercise **275**
    A Basic Relaxation Technique **276**
    Tips for Health and Wellness **277**
    A Good Practical Habit to keep **278**
    Daily Exercise while on the bed or on the street (Tatieta Physical Therapy Formula) **280**
    Tatieta Energy Balance Techniques **283**
    What to ask for, the Next time you see Your Physician **285**
    Diabetes Foods and Supplements **287**
    How to Decalcify/Cleanse your Pineal Gland-third eye for Higher Performance **288**
    Tips for Kids **292**
    The Reason why you Should Meditate or Learn How to **295**
    How To Meditate **296**
    What Is Living In The Moment, Being Present? **297**

CHAPTER THIRTY-SIX: It is Okay to Talk about Money in our Families and Communities **300**
    – How can we Move Past the Difficulties and Stigma Surrounding Money? **302**

CHAPTER THIRTY-SEVEN: EGYPTOLOGY 101 **308**

    – Egypt, A Black And Humanity Heritage **310**
    – General Knowledge About A Few African Queens Warriors **315**
    – Egyptians Tips For Your Health **316**

CONCLUSION: *After Being Washed, the Blind Went Home Seeing* **324**

ACKNOWLEDGMENTS

I'm dedicating this book to my ancestors, grandparents, parents, extended families, brothers, sisters and friends. I have written this book while living and sleeping in the wilderness; so I would like to thank everyone who had, or have, opened their doors for me when I knocked. I will not mention any names, but they would recognize themselves. Many thanks to my teachers, professors, mentors, and good Samaritans, including the authors of the books I read for sharing their knowledge and insights. Thanks to those who kept me in prayers and those who assisted me financially and spiritually. You are my angels. A special thanks to my dad, my mom and the mothers of my children.

PREFACE

This book will attempt to provide you with most of the knowledge, wisdom and understanding that can only be found after reading the right books over time with an open mind. Luckily, with only this book, you will have access to thousands of years old knowledge, their ways of understanding of the universe and our role in it. You could also enjoy the knowledge of the "Initiated" and start your own journey.

Most of the subjects and diverse disciplines discussed in this book will afford the mind and the spirit of the reader to grow to a higher level of possible spiritual dimensions, or induce a shift of consciousness.

We also live in a time when self-control, the respect of others and the universe is lacking in many aspects. This book will break down our pure essence role towards ourselves and the world. It will give directives on how to control our emotions such as anger, hate, self-hate. It will show you how to tackle regrets and worries by reminding you, the reader, how you should identify yourself to your true essence, instead of your egoist mind.

It will be primordial for you, the reader, to keep an open mind while reading this book as to try as much as you can to free yourself from your prejudices and presuppositions. Do not assume, nor expect, to read only what you hoped for; instead, just read the book thoroughly and let the truth hit you as you discover new ways. This is a book that still retains its freshness, even after you have read it many times. Just by only reading the preview section of this book is already life changing. The answers to your questions are within the links, gaps and holes.

PREFACE

From Spirituality, Philosophy, Astronomy, Intelligence, Science, History, Psychology, Poetry, Social Science, Human Relationships, Environment, Human Rights, Modern medicine and alternative medicine, this book also provides you the knowledge of the herbs and trees to heal yourself during sickness and stress. While feeding your mind with knowledge and understanding, it empowers your spirit to reach its highest being. Simultaneously, it provides mental health support in assisting you on how to deal with your emotions, feelings and expectations.

A series of breathing control techniques and physical therapy, including how to bring positive energy in your home, or work place, is also included in this book.

This book is written with this in mind; that while addressing the spiritual dimension, the mental and the physical parts also need to be taken into consideration simultaneously, to afford a holistic health/healing. As you cannot only take care of the body without taking care of the mind, you cannot leave out the caring for the soul.

Again, free your mind of your beliefs, prejudices, desires and wishes, while keeping an open mind as you are about to dive into an "Ocean of Bliss."

"To live in a world without understanding it, or without becoming aware of it, even though all we have to do is to pause and look, is like wandering around a great library a thousand times, aisle to aisle, without touching or peeking in a book, to know what else is beyond the covers.

"Just stop and look up inside of you. You will know what the world means to you as each one of us is a cover of a book that needs to be opened. We need to know what is stored within."

- Ahmed Tatieta

PREVIEW

Prayer works all the time. Pray and never cease to pray. Forgive because forgiveness is the key to your health. Life is easy and hard when we know that fingers and toes come in different sizes and lengths. To keep your balance, you will have to find a way to forgive others and yourself. In doing that, it does not mean that you are weak, or too lenient; it simply means that you are ready to grow even bigger to a higher health. You may have forgiven, but don't be mistaking it as giving in, because you will learn from the effects that forgiving holds a key to your health.

People come and go. Every one of us has been given a chance to remediate our failings. You might worry, or overlook other people, simply because you might be in an advanced level, but the truth is that, if you are here on earth, it's because of a reason. A chance to grow again. A chance to learn more and to make a way for freedom of self and thereby, open a better way for others. Think about it. Everyone, regardless of their status, gender or sexual orientation, is already viewed as a role model, or an icon, for the younger generation, even for some old ones. It does not matter what is your level of influence. Someone, somewhere, will look at you, hoping and wishing to be like you. Unless you are a total loser, but considering that there might have been a time when you were shining, chances are, someone envied you in a positive way.

You have probably heard this saying already. "By his stripes, we are healed." So, I say unto you, by your stripes, they are healed. And by your stripes, they could be cursed also. My call to you; try your best to shield the youngest ones. Do not expose them to bad influences because, tomorrow, they will be the ones running, leading society and the world.

Everyone has a job to do. Some like their jobs; others not so much. Try your best to find a job that you will find joy and pleasure in doing. Do not let your job and titles determine your views and thinking when it comes to fair decisions. Try to be as humane as possible. Do not hesitate to lend a hand to a fellow man/woman when he or she seeks your help. Whenever you can, try to intercede and help. Because that's the way the universe works. You could have been one of the last that have made a difference to others' lives.

Of course, people burn their own bridges but remind them of their shortcomings. If you can, put a smile on someone else's face, as that reward I can guarantee you, if done in good faith, it will resonate on heaven's gates. Because that's how and why this universe is intended to be lived. Remember; you have made your own mistakes along the way, and you will wish someone else will overlook those mistakes and still give you a smile, when needed. This life, when really understood fully, is nothing but a laughter. Because it's always a circle and its opposite; things and everything we do that need to be readdressed will always land in our laps for adjustment. This is the chance we have been given to always redeem ourselves and grow higher in the next course of the circle. Remember that even those that have had a total memory loss will always get flashbacks. Some will even still remember, in spite of the memory loss, things that have marked them, or what they wish to see happen in their favor, or others. I prefer memory disconnection from the cognitive mind. Whatever was stored is still there but displaced, or it might just need a new fuse to reconnect the system back together.

Do not expect that people will live up to their words, or extend to you a favor, even when due, and you know that that's the least they could have done. Not everyone will give you the respect when needed, nor will even acknowledge your existence. Just dismiss them and move along with your life, serving your purpose with a smile and no regrets of any good deeds you have ever done to them and for them. Know that when it's cold, everybody is looking for a place that is warm. And when it is warm in your place, and the ideal for the season is to get some air and freshness, the same people will vacate and go where there is air to breathe. We are a survival species and do not most of the time stay loyal or faithful until all our needs and expectations are met. Once you understand the logic of human survival mechanisms, then you will be free from judgments.

Also, remember that each one teach one. What you know that would make it easy for the next fellow, do not hesitate to teach and share your expertise. Because without teachers, I will not be even able to convey this message to you. Because someone had to teach me how to read; how to write; and how to think. Teachers are guided and bearers of light to the least and to the extensive courses; because there are always steps to understand prior to the next lessons.

Always respect your teachers. Give them the chance to coach and teach you. Listen and always ask questions; that's the only way to fully understand and comprehend a subject. The future is nothing more promising than with plenty of teachers. So take heed and pride in teaching as nobody has never made it too far without one.

Water: when you have it abundantly, you may not truly know or feel what is it to thirst. Everyone's thirst is different. Some thirst for fame. Some for glory. Others for wisdom. In some low key way, everyone wants to be known. Everyone wants to be listened to. What you want, everyone else wants. We share the same desires and the same feelings. My emotion is your emotion. We truly are the same. In this cycle and universe, it's either you are making babies, or you are makers of babies. Everyone was and is a baby. Every growth started at the procreation. A mother and a father; then a baby.

It's day time, November 4, 2018, and it's 05:58 a.m. on my computer. We share everything in common. The blind see and the ones with eyes cannot see. The ones walking and running today, could one day be unable to lift a finger. As long as we live, we all have the same life. We even have the same likes. We love the same things and know that we need each other. The lion needs the antelope and the antelope needs herbs to survive. We are at the same time a lion and an antelope. We will run after our food and retreat when we feel threatened. We sit down when we want food, we get up, if needed.

Don't we always remain babies? Baby stages after baby stages. Every step as a baby. Today was yesterday and yesterday was today. Show me a present and I will count your breathing. Where does your breathing start? Is it when it reaches your heart and lungs, or when it first goes through the nose through the mechanism of keeping you alive? Isn't that the same breath been with you from your beginning? In life, we ask so many questions, but do we ever ask the right question? What have I done today to better my life? That question alone will get so many different answers. At the end, the question remains; could we have done anything different than today?

When a baby wants something, the baby cries for it. When the baby also gets wet in his/her pants, the baby cries to be changed and made clean. The baby, even knowing what needs to be done, is incapable of doing the task physically by himself. The mind of the baby is willing but the body is still too weak to perform the required movement at will. So the baby talks in signs and cries sometimes with tears in his eyes. The more the baby keeps crying and showing signs of need of being attended, and there is no one to hear his/her cries and signs; the baby becomes louder and louder till anger and impatience takes place. Every baby wants to be treated with love and respect. The baby is still physically not agile enough to get up and get what he/she needs but remains alert and conscious of the environment as the baby has just come in contact with the people he/she was hearing through (inside) the belly.

When you really think about it, we have been babies and are still babies all the times of our lives because there are still a lot to learn and things to experience and lived through. We grow each single day. Conquering our own emotions and others emotions, we will realize that life is beautiful. When you can always find a laugh in every encounter, we all remain inside the super belly of the universe as children.

Keeping up with our own transportation is hard. It breaks when we least expect it. But by the grace of God, we are always covered and something promising always comes around to intercede on our behalf. You might lose your cool here and there, yell and threaten someone here and there; even get into a fist fight now and then. But, at the end of the day, we fix our own transportation and continue cruising through the streets and boulevards of life.

Every word pronounced has a mass, a form that takes its own course but ends up where it started. Every sound listened to has a created line. It is set for it as there is no such thing as empty. Everything belongs to its place.

A memory is nothing else more than so many creations from us and others. Even when we don't know that we are being watched, every eye looking at you also leaves its own print. No eye is alike just like no fingerprints are alike. Am I wrong? The eye is connected to the thought. This may trigger our imagination for the moment. Do not forget that the eye can also trigger a past life, or experience. Should we underestimate the smell, the hearing and the taste? How many times have a simple touch took you to a past souvenir? A spice could also mean something. Every spice has a taste, an envy to purposely intend to let emotions run our course of life. We have all been there, but we have all also came to control it. Being present at all times is really primordial.

Sometimes I catch myself letting emotions get the best of me. I realize that it is something that can be controlled. We do get angry sometimes, and sometimes, we get extremely angry.

Sometimes, we have an extreme joy to the fullest. Today, we are a good person and tomorrow we are seeking retaliation. Name any emotion and I will give you its opposite. Keep a line straight just to realize that it will come right back to where it started. Choose a direction to end up where you are headed. Any delay is still part of time that never existed as everything remains constant. Yesterday is today and tomorrow. Show me a past and I will take you to the past as nothing ever remains present. Every word I'm typing is inclusive of the past, the present and the future. No distinction. Just as the past conditions the present, the present conditions the past, and vice versa to the future as the future never truly existed. Is it then karma that everything is conditioned by a prior cause?

Are we programmed? Yes. Show me anything that has not been programmed? On your first breath, you are already programmed. At conception, you are already programmed. But one thing we have all in common, is the ability to choose, to think, to taste, to feel, to see, to hear, even to smell. Even reading this book could be by some, a program as you cannot step your foot on the street of life without being conscious.

Just like a habit that we cannot abandon, we even get to the point of no longer trying to leave some habits behind. Deep inside of us, we know exactly what is right and what is wrong. We know that even an egg has protective layers. More than one protection indeed. But throw an egg to the ground and it will burst open, breaking the sensitive protective layer. A female bird conceives with the contact of a male bird. And the egg, or eggs, will grow inside the female bird until maturity, when it is time to be ejected. Now, once the egg is out, the egg still has to be cared for by the female bird and male bird until the baby bird is hatched.

After birth, the baby bird will be fed and taught how to survive. Then comes the final push for the baby bird to start flying on its own, looking for its own food and its best interest. One thing the baby bird and humans have in common is that the baby bird never forgot about its parents. Yes, we are programmed to do what is universally right, and there will always be some habits that we will not be able to leave behind. The main thing is the habit of taking care of our children until adulthood when they are mature enough to continue their journey solo without supervision.

Now we have some type of animal babies that have never known both their parents, and seen them after birth. These animals have to survive on their own from an early age. Survival at first sight without anyone to guide them, but they still remain guided through DNA input, because everything that needed to be known and done was already programmed in the newborn baby. And the babies already know what to do and where to go as soon as they are out of their shells.

We are just like any other animal, or bird, in this universal birth quality. Each birth has its circumstance. A lot of kids had to survive and make it on their own at an early age because of lack of support. But still they rise and will procreate proudly. Still, they rise and will raise their kids proudly. Still they will teach their kids how to fly and catch a fish to survive. Those kids from yesterday are now the guardians of the babies. Now an egg has evolved and a baby bird is saying hello. Would you feed it? Or let it go hungry?

There is a lot more than one thing we share in common. From baby stages, each time, we end up becoming the bigger and the older baby in town. Slowly, we move away and go to our own lane to make room for the other new and younger babies. In the midst of this, we also have new and young babies acting and living like bigger, or older babies just like we do have. At the same time, some bigger and older babies act like they are still new and young babies. One thing that always surprises us is growing up in age. All of a sudden, we really come to the realization that some habits and behaviors are best to let go, even if we really don't want to. Nature will play its course and kick us right back to where we belong. The truth is, that when you realize how people think about you and if they like you or not; you simply withdraw and get new friends or people until then. Because two people with different interests and ambitions will inevitably depart from the same road. But, at the end, everyone wants to be respected and be treated with dignity. We can respect and treat each other with dignity, even though we might have different interests and ambitions.

Think about it. We are one thing and its opposite. Everything comes in duality. We measure and subtract. When it comes to addition, we add and better yet, multiply. Then comes another season to divide because the bell rang and we did hear that one since there is a beginning and an end to all things. I don't believe in stagnation and my belief is not that stagnation does not exist. A circle is a circle. Find the beginning and you will know its end. Now we stay up, trying and wondering, how we are going to make it in the morning when everything is connected. We may have an idea of how tomorrow will look, in an instance. We also find out that not everything planned comes to order as a schedule puzzle. Why stay up truly when we can trust ourselves and everything else to keep its flow? Why worry then about what has not happened anyway? Let tomorrow worry about itself.

Something to hold on to, is what is at hand at any given time; the right now and how we are exercising our power of now makes a difference when life is going on. To the morning, to the afternoon, to the evening; something to hold on to is the actual present time and nothing else. Live and feel your presence and the presence of others. Acknowledge others and your surroundings. Pay attention to the plants and trees. Be conscious of the birds singing, smell and admire a flower, catch the sunset and glance at the stars. Remain in tune with the universe and you will be living in the present.

What is this life without the singing of the birds, the yelling from people, the feeling and touch of the winds, the encounter that you have the choice to make a difference with?

The time allocated passes and not everyone feels it. Every dimension of life is a caption mention and exercises power of autonomy. Is everyone a star? Isn't everyone a star? Same question, different answers; and different question, same answers. That sums up our illusion that we always have time.

The world is an amazing place. A lot of places from the mountains to the hills; from the waters to dry land, this world is amazing. Amazing to the point that everyone has his/her space. Whether you live in a mansion, or on the floor, that does not take any place away for the homeless. There is a place for everyone and everyone has a place to go to. We may not like where we sleep, or where we eat, but we will always close our eyes somewhere. Waking up and being surprised where we have spent the night is another thing. Overall, when the body is tired, our eyes just close and we sleep wherever we are. Home is where we sleep. Show me someone who does not live and sleep on earth? A big house with a solid roof protecting us, provides and produces everything we need to grow to our ultimate purpose. Our home is truly the universe.

Sometimes, we have our eyes fixed to an expected location to rest our head. If that does not work, then where you end up resting your eyes is home at that time. Consider and respect the place where you are laying your head. Everyone is cover, regardless of its strategic location in any parts of the globe. You may even think you are sleeping outside, but there is no such thing. Everyone under the sun is sleeping under the atmospheric cover. That includes everything and everyone. It may be cold or hot, but we just need to cover ourselves from the weather.

Life is beautiful and the world is an amazing place to be. It may not be perfect with our expectations, but, this world is an amazing place. We are covered every time until the next season.

Seasons are signs that rotate in a cyclical manner. As people involved in and within the rotations of cycle by seasons, the rotations of everyone is also primordial. This is a model of life. Everyone has to complete the circle in due season. We have no power to stop the continuation of life whatsoever as there is nothing dead unless it never existed. And there is nothing thought of that does not exist either. Seasons come and go. When the cycle is complete, it moves to the next one. Nothing lasts forever. But nothing else gets lost either. If you are not, then you have never been. And if you can read this, it means that you exist.

Due to seasons, it will rain today and be dry tomorrow. It will be hot today, but tomorrow it could be cold. There will also be seasons when it is not raining, rather snowing; even drought and dry lands will occur until it is time for that portion to be watered and made fruitful again. Every one of us is equipped with the ability to bless, or to curse. Every encounter with someone else is either going to be a blessing, or a curse. The curse could be resentment, disappointment, or loss of interest, or not being able to fully express yourself, etc. We will know the blessing ones when we feel or see them.

We have trained our eyes, our mind, our touch, even our hearing; but can we train our taste and not taste what we are tasting? Or can we decide not to smell what we are smelling at the moment. Even though we have trained our smell sensory to pick and choose what's agreeable to smell, or which ones are toxic and should be avoided, we still will smell it, if we are still breathing naturally with no protective gears.

Now we breathe; can we decide not to take another breath without committing suicide? Is walking even optional? You know there are some who cannot walk. There are even some who cannot hear, see, nor talk. Some other people can represent some of the above symptoms, or all of them at once. But, at the end of the day, everyone expresses himself/herself. Everyone still communicates. We may not understand it then, but there is nothing that does not communicate. Even silence has a sound. When we say nothing, it also means something. Because nothing is something.

Every season has its time. Every cycle will have to run its course, and we are built with options. Options that give us hope because we can still catch up and make everything whole and right respective of one's intent. You can choose to repeat your same old game which in turn rolls in its own season and cycle but not without growth. Seasons like at the baby level to his/her puberty and adulthood because habits might become second nature.

Our own seasons mingle with other people seasons within a giant season that is outside of our control to say the least, but there is no season without control. I have my seasons; you have your seasons; and he/she has his seasons. Each one of our seasons within the big universal Seasons and beyond. When we realize that there are a lot of events and seasons that we can't control, we should just focus on what we can. Meaning focusing on our own self, trying to understand our own seasons. Once we can control ourselves, it will automatically lead a path to others as everyone else also leaves an automatic path to their peers and others in a form of DNA and actions. We are all cells with their specific duties and functions. We have a purpose and a job to do, which is to maintain and sustain the Universe. When a cell fails to do what it was designed to do, it becomes its own enemy. This type of cell, now outside of its system of control, acts like a cancer cell.

For beginners, a cancer is caused by a cell that had escaped from being checked and balanced by the immune system. A cell that once belonged within the immune system cell to protect and fight against diseases and keep its host healthy. Now this cell is free, making its own decisions and multiplying at its own rate. And instead of that cell contributing to keeping its host safe and protected, the cell works now against its master host by being destructive by all means. A cell that has rebelled against its host and started being destructive to its own whole organism that sustains it, is committing suicide. That is a cancer cell, reminding us that we should remain within our lane, within our reach and do what we actually have the ability and the power to do. This way, we will avoid working against our self and the whole organism that sustains all life.

What is life? You can try to define it, but the question is, what is not living? While you down, someone is about to go down. While someone is going down, another is going up. We have all been happy several times. And we have also have times of distress. Today, you feel strong and act strong; another day you feel weak and act more carefully. Some days things get out of hands and some other days everything works according to plans. Who knows his/her beginning from the end? At the same token, who knows his/her end from the beginning? Do we really come on earth with an empty brain? Can you then criticize or mock someone else for being ignorant about something?

Every day, someone else always comes your way for societal interaction. That person is full of his/her own moods and intentions that you cannot control. You cannot act and dictate others' behaviors, or actions, either. That simple fact that others are there, outside of your control, is a determining factor that you should focus on getting yourself ready for others. Once you realize that you are not alone, then life becomes easier. Remember that not everyone knows you, or gives a damn about you. No one knows who you are, or your status in society. Once all that is understood, it becomes easy, then, for you to focus on what is your priority. Not everyone will respect and treat you with dignity. Therefore, stop acting like it is the first time you felt neglected and unappreciated. Both sides of the coin exist and complete the unity of good faith and bad faith. What you don't know makes you an ignorant person, and we are all ignorant. Who among us know everything?

That also could depend on your feelings and moods this very day to answer this question. Your ego may also play a huge role on your decision making. Where there is no line, there will always be inconsistences. As if the power of being present is not resurrected, it becomes hard to be honest to yourself. What is your daily goal and overall plan for the real tomorrow?

We have each a unique destiny and a list of what needs to be taken care of daily. What I need today may differ from what I need tomorrow. Give it ten to twenty years and I will have other needs. Isn't life a beautiful craft that we, at the same time, mold and hold the potter's wand? I cannot even say, my friends, this is what will really happened tomorrow. I live and you live. But we all recognize each other as we are all in the same bubble. Plans don't always work according to schedule and timing. So lift yourself back up and keep your head back up again. Try one more time and again and again.

Each one of us has changed the world already in his/her own way. Have you ever given money to a stranger on the street, reaching his hand to add change? If so, you have changed the world already. Just like feeding the birds in the parks or bushes. Watering a plant to the simple act of returning a lost item to a stranger, you have already changed the world. Every day, we change the world without even knowing it. Even a mere smile, or hello to someone, makes a huge difference. Changing the world, one by one, two by two, three by three, and so on. Numbers go up or down, no less. If a number remains constant, it could mean consistency or there is no more of a growth just like when a number goes down. Now, who said a growth has to always be up and not down? Either way, it is still a growth as nothing remains constant. Up is up more and down is down more. When an egg is mature enough, it bursts to a baby that will need to be fed and guided to survive on its own. Which position of the number are you feeling the most? Up or down equating to what you have done to better yourself each day?

Five plus five equal ten. Still numbers. Programs run in a continuous cycle, internally stimulated and auto adapted; you are perfectly who you are each present time with your fears, anger, joy and ability to decide for yourself. With enough knowledge and drawn experience, you can make wise decisions. Every choice is calculated besides the unattended ones that come as a reflex without our conscious command. I call it beyond.

Sometime, when faced with only two choices, there are days that we guess right, and some others, we miss it. Who else has not yet made a choice with some regrets later? If not regrets, some conscious interpolation of if we have acted right. Or, should we have had a chance, we would have acted otherwise and made it right, or just made another decision that suited us best. There is no way to avoid regrets, but you can just let it go and make peace with yourself. You should forgive yourself by not letting your regrets haunt you. Your dreams and visions never came to reality and you feel like all hope is gone. You can always start something new and make amends to your past dreams. Live in the present by moving pass your past and stop looking over your shoulders. In fact, use your regrets to change your surroundings through changing your actions. In a sense, it is a good thing to remember the past so that we can avoid repeating the past that needed to be changed. I call it the Dance of "Forgive and empower."

If you still have a chance to fix anything that is playing guilt moods on you, then you should reach out to your loved ones, or the persons concerned, and apologize, or make peace with all concerned. A lot of the people you may have hurt might still be alive, or at a phone call reach, so reach out and simply make it right. Even when we think we may have been right, the fact that someone else shows concern or resentment, we should give it a consideration. Just say, "I'm sorry."

Truly, no one is to be blamed for feeling regrets, but once you say that you are sorry, you will move on to forgive yourself and live in the present, healthier and happier with self-love.

Love yourself to the point that you care about the food that you eat and the liquids that you are drinking. Be tolerant to those that act in ignorance. Understand whoever is making that wrong choice makes decisions based on falsified facts without knowing. That's also an essential part of being tolerant. When we remain focused on essentials, we then conserve our energy while focusing on what is our priority, which is to better ourselves each day.

Also, practice some regular exercises daily, physically and mentally. Remember not to use your body on auto pilot, without checking your health status. Do not wait until your body starts hurting to begin the maintenance. Care for it daily and make sure all your joints and ligaments are fit and strong. Make your health a priority again.

Now put ten people in a room and ask them what their priorities are at that actual time, and they will all have different priorities. Or, maybe not for those by coincidence, or conspiring to have the same priorities. Is agreeing with each other another meaning of understanding each other? Every man is best served in his own cattle. Don't get mad or upset just because everyone around you doesn't understand you. Beside no one understands no one. A circle has no beginning nor an end. Because once you find the beginning, you will know the end. Now who is among us that know from his beginning, his end? Then do you know the end of your life from the beginning?

> "For God so loved the world,
> that he gave his only begotten Son, that
> Whosoever believeth in him should not perish,
> but have everlasting life."
>
> John 3:16

INTRODUCTION

People come and go. The world becomes old and gets renewed. The strong man today will grow weak tomorrow. Guns will become obsolete and big mansions vacant. People will feel the need to join forces in due time and will not hesitate to kill each other down the road when there will be no need to stay united. There will be no freedom under any other circumstance beside the freedom of minds. In fact, a physical freedom without a freedom of mind becomes dangerous. Health is the balance and harmony between earth, water, air and fire. The balance adds either minds, intelligence, ether, and false ego.

We know now there is nothing new under the sun. The world of today, with all its pain and joy, reflect the world 1,000, 2,000, or 5,000 years ago, etc. Nothing has changed; still everything has its opposite. One thing that the old generation 10,000 years ago and today's world have in common is that no one is remembered forever by everyone. We live and transit all along and alone.

People crying, running, dying and starving have been a reality throughout mankind since the beginning of consciousness. On the side of it, people happy, newlywed, and a newborn baby are signs of stability are juxtaposed. The only weapon that we need is our mind and spirit strengthening in knowledge, understanding and wisdom in order to keep our generations at flow in the middle of the natural chaos theater, with everything else inclusive.

If one's mind is corrupt, he loses its roots and foundation. He loses gravity to remain stable under its own environment. What is then left is to keep floating on the air like a balloon with no sense of direction, for that man has lost control of his thoughts and his life's purpose. Subsequently, his actions and deeds are mandated and commanded by whoever has control of his mind and thoughts.

Therefore, it would be very wise to start protecting your mind and spirit from the world's powers invasions, because where the balance of power is at play anytime, there is always room for false teachings/influences and forced movements and actions.

Look at the world. Tell me one person who has never lied. Now show me someone who has never told the truth. Show me someone who has never hated. Now tell me who has never loved. Better yet, show me someone who has never been loved. This world is a place to learn and grow. You may have doubt it by bad faith, but aren't you growing in maturity? It doesn't matter who we are, we have always learned from our mistakes and experiences. We have always learned from our own misunderstandings and wisdom.

Everyone grows in maturity. Some people just grow faster than others. We are in a web that keeps weaving; a web that rolls with whatever we do within the Webmaster. But not without consequences; positive or negative, still the same thing. Since everything gets balanced off, it evens up simultaneously.

Always be humble and always do the right thing. Love is prayer and every command should come from within. Be the Which that is. There is nothing to search for, when all we have to do is to "Stop and Look." The answer is within. Acknowledge your gift and be it. And if you are stressed, then sleep better naturally and you will stress less. There is no God but life itself. Do not wait on anyone; act on what needs to be taken care of, without seeking fame. Focus on taking care of yourself and things at hands because tomorrow is for those that will see it. You have the freedom to correct an error and replaced it with the correct one, as it is still your freedom to maintain the error. We have the choice to be good today, or choose to become good tomorrow. But remember that no evil have ever ascended high.

Have you seen or heard about *the Undercover Boss* show on television in the United States of America? Isn't it when the owner of a working mechanisms decides to become a pawn within its own creation to check out how everything he/she had put in place is working? And if there is room for improvements, adjustments are then made. Because of the work of every pawn, the system is continuously running, but each pawn has a purpose and collectively the same purpose; to execute and answer to the Boss.

And in due time, the webmaster will retrieve everything and everyone, for the cycle has reached maturity. This will reopen a new season to each and everything accordingly and proportionally. This test, according to Ancient knowledge when it is all done, is based on how you have improved in your actual existence compared to your last ones? In a way, you reap what you sow.

CHAPTER 1
Heaven: The Kingdom Of God Is Within You

We have all talked about heaven and everyone wants to go there. The question has always remained unanswered; where is heaven? Isn't it true that we commonly think of heaven as a physical tangible place that we will go to after death? If so, is heaven everything that is above us from the planet that we are on, or a special location outside of earth? Our generation calls it earth and you can rest assure this planet has been given so many names since mankind realized its existence. Therefore, so is heaven's name.

Nowadays, it is a common assumption that we can only go to heaven until we are dead. That can only be true if heaven is a location, a place where the soul transits to, after death, upon leaving the body in its spiritual form. In this case, heaven is seen as a different dimension where the soul moves to after death, making everyone able to access it. Eventually, no one remains immortal in this planet earth.

Heaven has also been portrayed as the place where only the good people can have access to upon death, where their souls will go to and live in happily-ever-ending joy and abundance. To make it to this kind of heaven, one has to have lived a righteous and forgiving life before death. In that sense, everyone still has access to heaven, except the ones that just have fallen short to sufficiently satisfy the requirements to see heaven's gates open to them. Yet heaven is available and attainable by anyone

CHAPTER 1

but restricted as to who is qualified to enter through its gates. It is actually not a process of elimination; either you have the password to the gate, or you don't. And the password is only found within you and nowhere else. And because you have to live and act a certain way in order to receive the password, power is within ourselves and only you, can have access to your own inner being to retrieve the keys for the password by conforming to the series of requirements.

We have cultures and languages; each one, at their given time, has forged a way of living and adaptation to survive, based on their actual level of knowledge and on the survival needs for that time. So many wise and smart men have died believing that earth was the center of the universe and some even believed that the earth was flat. Could they have been wrong? Who was to tell them that there would be another time that so many other men would also conclude that earth is no longer the center of the universe. That, in fact, earth was never really flat but round? You simply have to just find a way to access the keys to the kingdom.

Is everything above the planet called Earth, at this moment of time, heaven? Could it be that heaven is a transcendence through different greater dimensions within our own conscious and spirit, one at the time? And if yes, can we put aside the accession and reliability of the mind and soul to have access to different dimensions gradually; making those dimensions a truly other world only worthy for those that have past the tests?

If there are different levels of how you could climb the ladder to the top of your mind, what makes it possible, then if it's not what is within you? To look is to seek. To seek is to visualize. To visualize is to have a goal. To have a goal is to have an objective. A definite point of satisfaction, which is nowhere else but conquering obstacles in life. We face challenges after challenges to reach the highest point of heavens within our own body and mind and spirit.

CHAPTER 1

To have accessed heaven is also considered as having been able to shine the light out from within one's Self, according to some other cultures and traditions. For some, the acquiring of the third eye is simply a sign that you have reached heaven. Thus, you could now see what was hidden in plain sight and have access to heavenly information.

When we need light, we reach out for it. When we need darkness, then we dim the light to the level of darkness. Some prefer light and others feel very comfortable in the darkness.

At all times, light has always chased away darkness. Where there is darkness, when the light shows up, all darkness disappears. Darkness cannot chase darkness. Only light can eliminate and occupy the place of darkness. Where is your light? Why would you then lighten your brightness and hide it under the bed? You have known by now that the body/soul is full of light.

If there is light, you must shine it to every place that darkness exists so that light will shine over all things in earth and heaven. The light is within you.

Light has always made a difference in all places where darkness exist. If you have lightened your light to attract heaven, be of the illuminated and enlightened ones, then light is not a question. Without light, it is impossible to see heaven. And the light is nowhere to be found but within you. Within us, the light resides, waiting to be shined. It will put out every darkness on our path. That's our shield, or our ticket to heaven, and to make it to the kingdoms of light.

A kingdom that no one could conquer or take away from you. A kingdom that will last forever. A kingdom that can be achieved anywhere and at any place. No need for buildings or mountains, even though everything, including us, have a reason to exist. All you need is you and some courage to undertake the journey within yourself. A kingdom that no one else can attain for you, or in substitution to you.

CHAPTER 1

You cannot say, "Hello, my friend, can you go and conquer the kingdom of heaven for me?" Or, "Can I purchase it or rent or lease it?" No. Everyone has to liberate himself/herself. Every man/woman has to achieve freedom for himself/herself. I cannot conquer your kingdom at your place. It's a journey only you can undertake.

MEDITATION

"For You, O God, have tested us;
You have refined us as silver is refined.
You brought us into the net;
You laid affliction on our backs.
You have caused men to ride over our heads;
but You brought us out to rich fulfillment."
Psalm 66:10-12

This is where it becomes tricky. Here we are full of ego. We are holding revenge or resentment for ourselves and others; yet everything around us remind us that there is something that among all of us pre-existed that we owe the first existence and consciousness to.

Should we give it a name? A lot have just settled for an unseen God, or the beginning and the end. Still, the question is infinite. What is it that does not have a beginning?

Well, we all do, even though we don't even remember our very early childhood when we were just babies. Yet, we got taken care of and are now heading to maturity and infinity.

We have scriptures, books, sanctuaries, temples, churches, mosques, cathedrals, places of cults, but, at the end of the day, we each go home to where we belong to get some rest. Regardless of how we may think a home is, every one of us has somewhere we call home.

Look around, and tell me where are you? Can you really go anywhere else but earth to live? You can be angry, mad, revengeful,

CHAPTER 1

loving, caring, but, at the end of the day, we are still here on earth, physically together. As we all know, the physical body stays here on earth as it belongs here after death. Your mind and soul, or your soul and spirit, could travel outside of this sphere call earth in a supernatural manner into other dimensions other than earth's.

We have visited other planets to seek refuge for the body but everywhere we go, we concluded that there cannot be a single Man/woman surviving there because, all those places are not equipped, or yet ready to host a human being really free of movement and dignity.

Every day we leave our house and go somewhere. Another place that we have to take the body to in person to do something. It could be a work place, a school, a market, or to visit the next door neighbor, but, at the end of the day, none of us have yet to leave this sphere call earth. We are just circling around in something that we don't even pay attention to, or even consider its existence to a certain extent.

We live fully without regards to anything else at some point. And a lot of us think, by the same token, we are the center of the universe. Or at least, they are.

Would you have even known about my existence if we had never crossed paths? I don't think so. Maybe through the "Earth" echo, you may have known, or heard of me. Earth is small, yet big. We don't even know how many species reside on it. Every time, we are always surprised to discover something new. Something that could have been in our eyes, straight looking at us, but we still don't see it. We are like children wrapped up on the back of our mothers who kept laughing and smiling at us when we tickled them, or bit them. The mother's love is so strong that they always keep nurturing us to maturity and growth, until we truly know right from wrong, and take our following/remaining steps on our own. This is a journey they will still supervise at distance and always remain there to give a hand and to answer any question. That's what earth represents to us; like a mother.

CHAPTER 1

Earth will teach us everything there is to know, if we start paying attention to its signs and lessons. And Earth will then include everything that resides in it. Because no one escapes its supervision.

Now, look up and tell me what do you see? A cloud, a sun, a star, and a lot of other things that live so far away that we can just wonder what else is there? Obviously, if someone is up there looking down to us, He/She would also wonder what else is going on here on earth. Remember that everything lives and experience existence just like us. We pretend to want to study life from other planets and understand them, when we have not fully understood and yet to know our own. Indeed, an illusion but yet a good thing as we are trying to learn how we can all live in harmony. I hope so.

It is ironic when every time we go to space in someone else's home, we come back and say, "There is no life there." At the same time, we say, "We have seen dry rivers, or salty water buried underground." Just as though that in itself is not life. Like we are the only ones and we just expect to go there and find Tarzan, or King Kong running to welcome us to its jungle. Doesn't everything live and exist? Or, is it that everything has to always fit to our only human conceptions and expectations to earn the qualification of a presence?

We don't even know why some planets are closer to the Sun and some are far out away from the Sun. Yet we know that each planet has its own suitable weather readily equipped proportionally for the needs of its inhabitant. Why should we expect that the planet called Mars will have the same survival needs for humans there? Or in Neptune or Jupiter? Are we one of them? At least not now! I can only guess. And what if, we are not being told the truth anyway? What if different species, intelligent like us, are actually dwelling there with houses and roads?

It is also kind of ironic that a lot of people are still claiming to be the center of the universe, when everything reminds us that behold, humans on earth, you are not alone and will not even survive if you were alone. You don't even know how far your air travel to or how far your oxygen has travel from another place to you. Innocent just still like a baby wrapped up at his/her mother's back, still finding a way to free his/her arms and better position his head while crying when hungry or thirsty.

The "Anthropic Principle" reminds us how everything in the universe is mightily designed and, if there was a little bit of a slight deviation in numbers, life everywhere would have not even been possible. Scientists have concluded when studying the many physical and mathematical subtleties making up our universe that a slight variation in any, would have rendered any life quasi impossible. They continued that if Earth was either closer, or more distant from the sun, or even bigger or smaller than its actual size, life would have been impossible. That's how the "anthropic principle" was coined since it gives the appearance that the universe was carefully molded and designed specifically for men and women.

Now, my question for you is this: what would it take from Earth's distance to, and from the Sun, to change? Would there be a breaking point of a distance that would render life impossible, or difficult on Earth?

Take a look at the Sun's position. It is the light that holds everything else around it. All the planets everywhere, regardless of their sizes or distances, orbit and turn around the Sun. The Sun is indeed in a strategic location and position that it could light up and witness everything around and about anywhere. A good faith judgment would place the Sun as the center of the cosmos. Its light reaches everywhere and gives life to about every existence. It is a source that heals, nourish and provides earth with the heat needed to regenerate. Some have called it the most beautiful temple; some a lantern of the universe. It is called the ruler, or the visible god, seating on a royal throne with an all eye seeing. I cannot imagine how life would be sustained without it as its importance to us remain

CHAPTER 1

a core necessity for survival. Do not put stock on the words/names given to the Sun; the words do not make you. Just continue reading and feel free to give the Sun a different name. Some also have called it the eye of God/Ra.

Now allow me to ask the right question. Who else contributed to the creation of all things? Who is behind all these magnificent order of all the creation? I know we are small lights, small suns and small stars. But not without living inside a huge rock and water (earth) circled themselves within a clear atmospheric sphere. Yet the sunlight millions of miles away still reaches us. Yet the star's light reaches us equally. I have another question. Would a small entity like us survive alone without connecting itself to a bigger and giant entity for a possible communion? Who is GOD and where is the residency of God? Can you set a place where God has no presence, or home?

> "It is the glory of God to conceal a thing, but the honor of kings is to search out a matter."
> Proverbs 25:2

CHAPTER 2
The Different Levels of the Soul in a Man/Woman

Man is composed of three Soul aspects of the divine Man. We have the Divine Soul, the Spiritual Soul and the Terrestrial, or Astral Soul. What this means is that our soul has three aspects of evolution that are accessible to everyone, regardless of their gender, race or tribal affiliation.

First is the astral soul followed by the spiritual soul and third is the divine soul. Each one of the souls aspect is achieved through separate steps and challenges coupled with different experiences gained and mental and spiritual growths. No step could be skipped before moving to the next levels. The ability and the aptitude of each one of us are also tested before continuing to the next level.

To the Egyptians, (Ancient Egyptians, not our modern Egyptians that we know of today, but Egyptians thousands of years before Jesus Christ,) "A Star was/is the phenomenal expression of an atom-shaped sidereal body; a 'Soul' and that the Divine Man/Woman or the incarnate Logos (Ptah) was their symbol of perfection and completion." This could mean that we are just as perfect as the stars and we are alike when we complete all the Soul's aspect to perfection. The stars above us, which have already reached their completions, are the guide to us that we can also achieve the same perfection. And, indeed, once all the Soul's aspects are achieved, then we will be shining as bright as the stars which is commonly known as shinning the light within us.

CHAPTER 2

If the divine Man/Woman is the true symbol of the Star in its final completion, then what is the Divine man/woman anything else than a Star, or Star-like? I'm sure, you have heard and seen people around the world claim that they were stars? And being a star was the end game and meant that you have achieved the highest point of achievement?

Things to say is for those that have ears to hear and eyes to see. Everyone has an ear and an eye, but not all ears could hear the same way, just like not all eyes can see the same things. One blink of an eye and we have missed seeing. But the truth is, that everything is at reach and has been provided. What is it that we see that is not a manifestation of a will, a desire and an objective? Ask and it will be given. Knock and it will be open. Look and you shall find.

Look around you. Any life will lay first vulnerable and yet protected. Then, the infant will slowly grow by wanting to move around for more freedom. Eventually, we will start crawling. When we crawl, we begin to learn, following what we see by visualization of everyone else walking or standing. So, we begin trying to stand and move one foot forward to move as we desired. Then, we stumble and fall back, just to retry again, because it's the way to do and follow suit, based on what is the goal. We then learn that we need balance and we practice it as we continue to stumble and fall to the point of feeling maturity. We gain confidence and take the step. We are surprised that we are now walking. Suddenly, we fall back again for fear, due to the realization of stability achieved. On our next try, we are ready, then mentally we proceed, one foot after another. We start walking, while keeping some balance to the point of perfection. We realize that all along, it was achievable. We just need to want to walk first, then take actions, learn from them and grow to perfection. The divine body/soul that is equal to what stars looked like in their own perfection. This is our calling.

What is it that is new under heaven? Aren't we aware of everything around us?

Again, look around and maybe this time you will see. Maybe this time you will hear.

Time that is prescribed and is nothing but a sensation; a feeling of existence. When do we feel time at most? Is it when we expect something or when we have a time table to meet?

The Three Primary Soul Aspects

It is no news to anyone that we all possess a soul. In this context I will prefer the word Double to make it easy to understand. The soul would then represent our Double (us) in the spiritual world since the physical body (flesh) can only operate on physical earth. So, we are made of spirit and matter just like everything else. Our Double (Ka) is attached to the Astral Soul-Body (Ba) within the evolution of the soul to its divine purpose, represented by the Ancient Egyptians as Lower Egypt. The Astral Soul-Body allows you to dream but within a restricted scope of range. You cannot go pass the Mental plane which is the range of consciousness of the astral soul.

In order for the individual to reach the range of consciousness of the Spiritual soul, the person has to elevate his mental and consciousness from Lower Egypt to Middle Egypt which is the only way to reach the plane of the spiritual soul. The Spiritual Soul-Body (Saha) is where all the fourteen (14) members of Osiris (Our True Self) have been dismembered and thrown into pieces that have to be recovered and put back together by reconstructing ourselves, giving the individual full access to the Spiritual Plane.

From the Plane of the Spiritual Soul, we then must graduate and move up to Upper Egypt, which opens up the worlds of the Spiritual Plane and Semi-divine plane. At that stage of the Upper Egypt, our range of consciousness is of the Semi-divine nature. Thereby, this makes his grand entrance to the Divine Plane. This is the final range of Consciousness, affording that person of the full armor of the Divine Soul-Body.

CHAPTER 2

In conclusion, the Seven Planes of Self-Existence from the Lower Egypt, Middle to Upper Egypt are: The Physical plane, the Astral plane, the Mental plane; the plane of Spiritual Soul, the Spiritual plane, the Semi-Divine plane and the Divine plane.

> "For thus saith the high and lofty One that
> inhabiteth eternity, whose name is Holy:
> "I dwell in the high and holy place,
> with him also that is of a contrite and humble spirit,
> to revive the spirit of the humble,
> and to revive the heart of the contrite ones."
> Isaiah 57:15

CHAPTER 3
As Above So Below.
A Star Above and the Divine Soul Below

The Egyptians' system of states of being is represented by sevenfold in circles. It will be represented here as the cycle of the night Sun through the Duat. The Duat is the underworld, or the realm of the dead. This is what is called in the Bible as Crossing the Valley of death where the Sun god travels through every night, battling the serpent monster and eventually, rising up again every morning, after winning the said battle.

THE CYCLE OF THE NIGHT SUN THROUGH THE DUAT

The seven states of being as one composite is actually comprised of twelve (12) steps or 12 sequential stages of consciousness. And those 12 steps are represented here as 12 hours of the night before sun rise. And it is during those hours of the night that the soul gradually grows from immaturity to maturity; to losing consciousness of its intrinsic Self to gaining knowledge of Self at the 12th hour after achieving and winning all of the obstacles and battles. Thereby, this consolidates the story of the Fall/Fallen downward of angels as astral soul in the underworld and forgetting their identity consistent with the death of god consciousness and temporarily rising back progressively to the top to semi-divine to divine during 12 hours of the night from sun down to sun rise a fact and a true reality.

CHAPTER 3

It is reminding us of the process that we have to go through to regain the kingdom of god from not remembering who we really are/were, nor our purpose to gradually regaining consciousness of Self. Thereby, we win the battle in the underworld, which is earth in this case and rising triumphant just like the Sun god.

So, the first six hours of the night, consists of the soul gradually losing consciousness, which involves a temporary death of the god consciousness; to a complete gradual recovery. The soul gradually scales its way back up for the remaining six hours to rising back up in its divine state on the twelfth hour. Then the Sun is renewed. Remember that the Sun is consider a Star, according to modern science. But the Bhagavad Gita also reminds us that the Sun is not a star and rather is the one that illuminates the stars and all the planets based on its strategic location in between them.

The Egyptians also believe that in a cyclical manner, there will be a cyclical return of a divine "influence" to Earth. There is a seasonally returning of god's cycle, included in the overall universe cycle. The Bhagavad Gita would confirm this as it also emphasizes that God reincarnates back to this world every other Millennium to either protect, save devotees from being destroyed by demons, or to set a new trend for the next generations to be able to be enlightened and reach true liberation by accessing the eternal life.

That's why in the history of mankind even the ancients have regarded the planet earth as complementary to the microcosm of a vast sidereal macrocosm. Everything that exists that we see is nothing but a sidereal of something bigger in its manifestation.

The Annus Magnus like the ancients called it would make it easy to understand how everything is connected and that all things we see on earth are a sidereal of a completed existence, or Being.

To that we would have to explore in comparison of the Annus Magnus versus Earth's, which is called the Sothic cycle.

The Annus Magnus occurs every 25,920 years and the Sothic cycle every 1,460 years.

This is how it works and how it is explained. Imagine two entities both set out at the same speed in space, at exactly the same time but following somewhat different path but remaining in constant focus to each other conjointly as they circle around, shadowing each other. Now one follows the path of the ecliptic and the other a Spiro-elliptical path around it, using the ecliptic path as its focus. I believe the ecliptic path is part of the Annus Magnus line and the Spiro-elliptical path, the one from the Sothic cycle.

There are thirty-six Decads in each cycle of the Annus Magnus (the great year).

THE THIRTY-SIX DECADS IN THE CYCLE OF THE ANNUS MAGNUS

The annus magnus cycle is complete at 36 decads in 360 degree full circle. Each decad from the 36 may take about 720 years to complete a cycle of 1 decad. Meaning, one decad takes about 720 years to complete its turn.

Now our solar system circles constantly around this path (annus magnus) completing one orbit every 1460 years, when the actual Annus Magnus has completed only two (2) decanates; the plural of a decad (720+720=1440). (i.e., 20 degrees) and then finally find himself 20 years behind schedule (1460-1440=20). And it actually takes our solar system 18 orbits to complete a full circle.

By the time our solar system completes its 18 Sothic cycle/orbits which is 36 decads of the Annus Magnus divided by 2 equaling 18, since one orbit, or one Sothic full cycle is equivalent to two (2) decads or decanates, the Annus Magnus has also completed its 36 decads full circle.

CHAPTER 3

1460 multiplied by 18 Sothic full circle equal 26,280. The Earth Sothic cycle twice or two times the Annus Magnus.

Now twenty years behind at every orbit/ every 1460 years; gives 20 multiplied by 18, which equal to 360 years behind schedule. Thereby, completing the full cycle at 26,280 years now minus (–) 360 years (total of 20 years behind each full cycle 18 times) = 25,920 years, the Annus Magnus. A complete full circle of the whole Universe everything inclusive is now whole. The understanding is that in every 25,920 years, everything is set to restart as the old world is now over making ways for a new world, a new earth and a new beginning for all. Complete the whole cycle and a new cycle will begin.

A period of precession of the equinoxes occurs too since there is a period of precession of the equinoxes that occurs every 25,920 years period indeed.

The Ancient Egyptians also determined that there is a periodical returning occurring cycle in a form of cataclysm that literally wiped out all the human race and animals, and such like life in nature, and thereby, changing the world geographical landscapes. The ancients viewed the world cataclysms as associated with astronomical cycles, following the precession of the equinoxes.

We live, and if we are lucky enough, we bury someone else. And someone else will bury us. So is the cycle. We live and we die. But when it is time for a new world, a lot will perish and a few will be saved to continue the cycle as it is a divine covenant to all living. Some living beings always get saved in the midst of the chaos and life goes on after their survival to create a new world until. It does not matter. The strong, the weak, the rich and the needy will perish and only few will remain to help the whole webmaster continue its cycle. No one can stop it and even kings and queens will see their loved ones perish while waiting for their turn. Only a few chosen fortunate ones will carry the torch for all living and procreate when the opportunity is present. Nothing indeed on earth remains eternal. Everything is subject to die and move on to the next experience and living conditions so that everyone gets a fair share of the evaluative cycle. Everyone is condemned to die and there is no way of escaping the cycle of return as no one can live when there is no more breath available for him in that dimension. We live and when our times come, we move on to a greater challenge.

So be it cycles, or a death sentence, once born. We are going to be pushed to the next level, even if we feel that we are not ready, or not expecting it. Life comes when we least expect it; so does death. We can never really be fully ready for it as we never know when it is going to happen. The only way to win is to live and do our best, as if the next seconds in our lives don't matter. Indeed, it doesn't until we wake up in another dimension just like the start, a new baby in a world not really different than the one we just left. Another place to learn, experience and grow to the next, and so forth.

So, my friends, I say unto you, always remain the same in sharp pains and in long illness, even during time of losing a child as we all carry a mask, and the mask need to be dropped down at some point in our lives. Keep in mind that only the webmaster knows the end from the beginning.

The Ancients believe that at the very beginning of the Annus Magnus, the gods themselves would reappear to provide the new impulse and sense of future direction in line, accordingly to Divine Purpose that would set as a road map to all humankind. The gods would begin their cycle of influence until they themselves get replaced by semi-divine kings and leaders followed by "heroes," or spiritual adepts.

What to underscore here is that those spiritual adepts are drawn from the ranks of the most spiritually advanced man and woman evolved and living during that said period of time, according to records.

CHAPTER 3

After the Heroes/spiritual adept independently evolved without a specific training and initiation from the semi-gods, there will take place the Fourth and Final period, when the Heroes and spiritual adepts would slowly withdrew themselves into the background to allow the mass and the rest of all mankind to guide their own destiny. At that period of the cycle, people would be independently selecting their own kings and leaders/rulers, however they wished to rule them.

Those Four Cycles of evolution are depicted by the Ancient Egyptians in an orderly manner as: The Age of Aquarius, which correspond to the god's cycle until the gods yielded sovereignty to "mortal kings" semi-divine beings at the end of the Age of Gemini, or the very start of the Age of Taurus. And the old Age closing the cycle in which spiritually advanced beings/ heroes would withdraw from the mass, leaving them to become materialistic, mentally corrupted and enjoying inhuman behaviors, even bestiality, to the point of denying their own divine parentage.

In the light of what is written above, it would be fair to add that Ancients' records, including the Puranas and the Bible attest and confirmed that long before there were Giants people living on earth before us, the common Men/Women. Those Giants are the Four Original Races that God/Goddess have created and they were the ones that was the very first four races of humanity. Those races colors from then were Black, Red, Yellow and White races equally distributed.

The four races, according to old records, were referred to as "Giants". Those four original races were mortal and before them, they were preceded by three Divine or Semi-Divine races. Those three consisted of gods first, which marked the era of the golden race followed by demi-gods (the silver race) and to end with the "heroes," which made the bronze race. This is consistent with the idea that god's rules earth first at the very beginning of each cycle. And it was after the first three divine, semi-divine races and heroes that the next and first four original giants' races were created, or saw existence millions of years before us. Considering that the world is very old, nothing should surprise us as even the dinosaurs have had their era and are no more today to be seen anywhere.

The Primordial Abstract Trinity from the Ancient Egyptians

AMEN-Ra (Universal Life), MUT (Universal Consciousness), and KHONSU (Universal Creativity) form the Trinity; Life, Consciousness and Creativity.

So our universe progressively unfolded and took on a progressively phenomenal existence depicted in sevenfold terms as various aspect of Ra in his greatest cosmic manifestation.

1. Kheper-Ra – the self-created Demiurge
2. Amen-Ra – the fallen Cosmic Mind principle, or "causeless Cause"
3. Menthu-Ra – the "Breath (or presence) of Ra"
4. Neit/Neith – the "wife," or "ka," of Amen-Ra, or "Eye of Ra"
5. Sebek-Ra – Universal Mentality, creator of diversity and repetition;
6. Khnemu-Ra – the god of the "Waters of Space"; the "desire of Ra" (for objective self-existence)
7. Atum-Ra – the phenomenally manifesting universe.

Since we are made in the image of the trinity and the sevenfold stages of the universe according to ancient records, we are part of the seventh, even though at the last of the steps. Which means that we are Divine just like at the very beginning of the steps. Divine Man/Woman "falling" prey, as one complete hierarchy of the Cosmic Being, into the "underworld" of the World Over-soul below, where there is no other way but to be forced into a cycle of evolutionary differentiation to become divine again. Just like the World was created in seven days and when it was finished, Us, we found ourselves at the bottom of

CHAPTER 3

the creations as a sequence in which there is no other choice than to try to go back to where we started; the Beginning.

The understanding, according to the Ancient Egypt, is that everything that is above is also below and all man/woman is actually a Divine Being but fallen, or on earth as a man/woman flesh, just like in the story of the Garden in heaven of Adam and Eve from the Bible where Adam and Eve were kicked out from the Garden to Earth, after being created on God's Image. The ancients viewed Man/Woman as the essential projection of an ethereal, divine parentage.

Therefore, as above, so below. And there is no God but gods. Nobody can save you, except yourself. You could be protected physically and spiritually from being harmed, but your kingdom rests solemnly at your hands within reach inside yourself and the law of two may apply (teacher- student, master- apprentice, any encounter). And your divine destiny is unique to each others as we individually get born on earth closer, or farther away ,from the general divine purpose, according to our previous life records, which falls under the category of Destiny.

CHAPTER 4
Astronomy 101

"By his knowledge the depths are broken up, and the clouds drop down the dew." Proverbs 3:20

Astronomy is the study of objects existing in the universe/ cosmos, including all the events surrounding them and that have shaped them. It remains part of the unknown until the unknown makes itself visible to us.

The universe/ cosmos is full of stars, planets, galaxies and galaxy clusters. Each one of them and the whole bloc holding everything up is governed by measurable laws and forces.

Our ancestors have always connected the motions of the Sun, Moon and Stars in connection with time and periodic change of seasons or cycles during a year. Our ancestors understood that everything in the universe were connected and full of languages. They understood that even the color of the water in the ocean is conditioned by the lights coming from the Sun, Moon and Stars. So by paying close attention to the universe cycle, we have been able to predict events and even chart celestial motions. Thus, we created timepieces, calendars, clocks and weather watch, even master the Sothic and Annus Magnus cycle through time, etc.

All living existence is directly connected to whatever has created the cosmos, stars, planets, etc. We are the direct result of the processes that started everything. In real words, we are no less than the trees, the stars and the planets. Besides every atom of every being existing anywhere in the cosmos, including earth, originated in space just like already described at the above chapter. The nearest star is 4.2 light years away from us, or four times 9.5 trillion kilometers (km) and 1km is 1000 meters, according to our modern calculations.

When we look at the moon from earth, what our eyes see at that present moment is already old about 1.28 seconds due to the distance stretch range. And we see the Sun as it was 8.3 minutes ago as that is how long it takes the sun light to actually reach us on earth because of the distance difference. It is interesting to know that even the light as we see it is composed of different colors that are: red, orange, violet, yellow, green, blue and indigo. The Seven Fold Aspect of Ra is the Covenant as written in the Bible, concerning the rainbow and the covenant. You can only see a rainbow if only the Sun is behind you and the Rain in front of you. Rainbows appear in seven colors because water droplets break white sunlight into seven colors of the spectrum.

Inventory of Our Solar System

So far, the solar system, until new other discoveries come to light, is composed of one star-Sun, eight planets, ten and counting dwarf planets, 146 and counting moons, four ring systems, countless comets and hundreds of thousands of asteroids.

All the planets of the solar system travel around the Sun, following a path called orbits in an elliptical (slightly flattened circles) manner, already explained in the above chapter about the Sothic cycle as being a microcosm, a sidereal of a macrocosm circling together.

Something to always remember is that the Sun is itself a Star and the biggest source of heat and light in our solar system; but what if the Sun is really not a star and is the one that illuminates also the rest of the Stars like previously stated?

Its heat and light travel throughout the whole solar system and reach all the planets under its dominion. Without the Sun, life is impossible and cannot even exist. The Sun is a big sphere of superheated gas and its color is actually white. We see it as yellow color because the sun-light while passing through our atmosphere, interacts and removes the color blue and red wavelengths from the incoming light, hereby changing the color white to yellow. I'm not sure what will happen to earth and its inhabitants the day the blue and red wavelengths will have access through the atmosphere. Neither do I know what it would take for the atmospheric barrier to give in. Knowing that each wavelength of the sun light carries its own significance and purpose, I doubt that we should be inviting a total new phenomenon to us here on earth, contrary to the original set up of the normal working of the universe.

To come back to our subject, the Sun's heat and light travel through the solar system and it also produces what is called the Solar Wind that reaches earth and beyond. It constantly blows a stream of charged particles and create a huge bubble that surrounds our solar system called Heliopause by modern scientist.

The Sun is part of the Milky Way Galaxy. It is one of the other several hundreds of billion stars in the Milky Way Galaxy. It is just like another Star set against a backdrop of millions of other stars directly facing us here on earth. It is for this reason that ancient belief described it as the Chief of all light. The Bible even proclaims that God created it to rule the days and the Moon, the nights. And since the Sun never really sets, it makes it the ultimate ruler even at night time. In modern scientist views, there is no difference between the stars and the sun.

The only difference is that the sun is the star we live on if we conform to our modern science that the Sun is also a Star. It is the one that has a tremendous influence on our solar system. That's what actually makes the difference and sets it apart from the other stars. We should not misunderstand that the other stars don't actually also play a vital role on our solar

CHAPTER 4

system itself since everything is known to be connected and interdependent working together in a cyclical routine. Some ancient beliefs stated that in fact the Sun is also illuminating the stars, including the moons.

The Role of the Sun into Our Earth Weather

The Sun plays a big role into our earth's weather through the solar wind because of the way it impacts our earth magnetic field, including all the other planets orbiting around it. The charged particles in the form of winds energize the molecules of gas in our upper atmosphere creating like space weather in a form of light that would dictate the course of our earthly weather as well.

In fact, the Sun is the driving force behind all the weathers on all the planets, including Earth. And with the contribution of the earth's winds, air, the ocean currents and the different distribution of mountain chains throughout the world, our weather patterns become more complex based on the solar radiation and its transfer level at each specific part of the continents. Also, relative to the heat, the Earth itself transfers back to the surface of the world after absorbing the said heat from the Sun.

When the Sun outburst its charged particles, we really see the light from the initial outburst 8.3 minutes later and it actually takes one to three days before the masses and particles reach and collide with the earth magnetic field and stir up activities in the ionosphere changing or impacting our seasons here on earth.

Depending on how strong or mild the outburst and collision when it reaches earth will determine how strong or mild, it would impact our earth-space environment (space weather). Subsequently our earth weather will change. A strong and heavy one can even shut down our communication system and satellites, including our electrical power grids and the Global Positioning Systems (GPS).

When a geomagnetic storm occurs from the Sun outburst to earth magnetic field, it increases the number of electrons in our upper-atmosphere. Thereby, blocking signal from GPS (global positioning system) to reach earth in a timely fashion without interference causing loss of data and errors.

A geomagnetic storm is a major temporary disturbance of our planet earth magnetosphere caused by the collision and exchange of energy from the solar winds into earth space. It affects our water sources, air sources and winds flow and directions. The solar flares or solar winds shock wave strike or interact with our earth magnetic field, thereby creating a storm. Therefore, our earth weather and environment, even our seasons, depend on and are directly influenced by the Sun.

For your information, the Sun is so huge that its diameter is about 109 times the diameter of the Earth in comparison. Which means that unbelievably that it will take over one million Earth size to fit into the Sun. To be exact or close enough in number, 1,300.000 Earths should fit inside the Sun according to modern science. The Sun diameter is 1,392,000 km and Earth diameter is only 12756 km.

In fact, the Sun is about 90 percent bigger than all the known Stars in the Milky Way and has about 1000 times the mass of Jupiter. As you keep reading, you will get to the section that describes Jupiter below the lines just like the other planets orbiting around the Sun. There are eight so far and goes as followed plus the Moon:

Mercury

The closest point of Mercury to the sun is 46 million kilometer (km) and its most distant from the sun is 69.8 million km. Mercury has seasons and weather including days and nights just like on earth here. Its length of one year is 88th Earth day. One mercury full day is way more than twenty four hours (24 h). It takes so many days of earth days to make one

CHAPTER 4

(1) day in Mercury. It takes about 59 Earth days to make up for the length of one mercury day. Mercury tilt of axis is 00 and has a 0.38 earth gravity.

Mercury is the closest planet to the Sun. The atmosphere is almost nonexistent and temperatures are very extreme. It goes nearly 610 degrees at its maximum and average at 439 degrees Celsius (C) during the day and drastically drops at night for -183C. Mercury has lost most of its atmosphere due to the constant buffeting from the solar wind. Remember that the solar winds have an influence on all other particles and planets forming the solar system. And at those extreme temperatures, it would be a harsh place for human to live in and any vegetal or animal lives at our actual forms and matter and being too close to the Sun would not help us at all for any life consideration. Let's now take a look at the second closest to the sun that happened to be given a funny and scary surname "the Earth Evil twin"?

Venus, the Earth Evil Twin

At 107.4 million km closer, Venus, at its most distant to the Sun, is 108.9 million km. Venus is the second closest planet to the Sun, according to modern science. Its year makes up to 224.7 Earth days for the length of Venus full year. Venus length of one day is 117 earth days. Meaning, the Sun does not set, nor rises in Venus. Venus tilt of axis is 177.3 degrees and has 0.9 gravity based on Earth's.

Often called the morning or evening Star, Venus remains so bright because of the Sun's reflection through it and because the Sun's never sets. It is almost the same size as earth and have an extreme temperature and atmosphere way extreme for earthly things that makes any life at our actual forms impossible to survive there. It gets really hot at 462 degrees Celsius (C).

Venus, Mercury, Mars, Earth are classified as a "terrestrial" planets under the solar system, according to modern common understanding among scientists, meaning that those planets actually hold a solid ground. The atmosphere in Venus is made of carbon dioxide with sulfuric acid clouds. It has a landscape that is showing traces of previous vast water sources and it is like the ocean water got heated up by the Sun light and water vapor evaporated into space gradually as time passed. We are not so sure why and how Venus had accumulated all this voluminous carbon dioxide due to time and what have caused it but the carbon dioxide level is beyond scary.

Since the carbon dioxide is too much, when exposed to the Sun, it becomes even hotter everywhere the carbon dioxide reaches. Because, when the carbon dioxide is exposed to the Sun, it creates even more heat on contact, making every space available extremely hot.

In my opinion, Venus is an example to Earth as our carbon dioxide emission kept building up over the years. Earth is also building up a great deal of carbon dioxide in our atmosphere. And that could eventually also reach an overwhelming point in our atmosphere that we would have more extra heat than normal that will threatened every existence. Caution should be exercised by earthly occupants to curb our carbon dioxide emission globally to avoid the same sentence as its twin brother/sister.

Venus orbits around the Sun and goes through phases like our moon does when observed over weeks. It goes from a small to full appearance to a quarter phase when it is farther away from the Sun in its orbit. Now let's pay a visit to Venus's twin called Earth.

Earth

Earth observed from the Moon looked like a dot. A tiny pale blue dot away that you could easily put in your pockets or purses. Earth is the third closest planet to the Sun measuring 147 million kilometers closer to the Sun and 152 million km its farthest distance between the earth and the Sun. Earth has

CHAPTER 4

365.25 days for a full year; 23 hours: 56minutes for a full day and its tilt of axis is 23.5 degrees.

The atmosphere of earth is its protective cover and blanket. It absorbs most of the ultraviolet light coming from the Sun, blocking it from harming us. It balances our temperature by warming it. Heat from the sun is then absorbed by gases such as the carbon dioxide and in turn the carbon dioxide radiates that same absorbed heat to the Earth's surface. In its current situation, there would occasion a rising of earth temperature with more heat than usual if we keep adding more carbon dioxide on top of the already existing ones. The greenhouse effect, it is called. Without the effect of the greenhouse effect, life on earth would have been almost impossible. Unfortunately, on earth, we are experiencing a great rise of our carbon dioxide level in an alarming stance that when it absorbs the sun ultraviolet light like it supposed to, the heat that is charged to earth surface also will rise in a continuous basis, leaving us with too much heat than the optimal requirement for a sustainable survival of life. Can you picture what happened to Venus, its twin?

For your information earth is covered by water. Three-fourths of water surround us and the water also rises in temperature when it is hot or hotter, thereby, threatening the livelihood of so many species and fishes living in the water sources, including wild life. And the water could/would eventually evaporate gradually to dryness as the volume of carbon dioxide reaches a level that threatens life for all. At the same time, rising temperature rhymes with a lot of rain also that could submerge life awaiting evaporation.

The importance of the oceans and our water resources in our long term survival are very crucial. When water becomes scarce, life at our actual form would cease too. The ocean traces the long term and foreseeable climates patterns that are they themselves link to our seasons and weather system; all under the influence of the sun light and solar winds. At least here on earth, we are sure about who are those that emit the carbon dioxide into our earth atmosphere? Living beings all-inclusive stationed on earth, especially the human kind are the ones producing more of the carbon dioxide, not limited to the carbon dioxide emitted by our live stocks.

From the moon, earth is so minuscule that you could step on it and not even stumble. How do the moon look like from here on earth?

The Moon

The moon is locked with earth as it orbits around earth. The moon circles around earth as oppose to earth orbiting around the sun. The moon is faithful to earth as it always shows us the same four faces during its cycle without fail. The lunar phases as it is called start with a new moon to a quarter moon and progressively reduce to a slim crescent and close it with a full moon and then repeats the same cycle over and over. It takes 29.5 days for the moon to go through its lunar system phases. The moon completes a full orbit once every 27 days around our own planet earth. It has no atmosphere, which means that the sun's radiation is hitting it raw and straight without a shield like we do have in our earth atmosphere. It is not clear if there was ever an atmospheric system or not. It neither has any source of water or air forcing our astronauts while going there on space expedition to always bring with them all the possible supplies they will need to survive there and make it back to earth.

For your information, the moon viewed from our planet Earth is about 400 times smaller in diameter than the Sun and is at the same time, approximately 400 times closer to Earth, according to science. Because of the strategic locations of the sun and the moon to earth, it mathematically makes our solar eclipse visible from partial to full eclipse making the moon appearing equally as big as the Sun when the Moon is in line with the Sun. The moon is closer to Earth than the Sun, but Earth is still bigger than the Moon. And when/while the Moon orbits around Earth, it takes the moon directly between earth and the Sun, thereby blocking our view of the Sun during its passage and that's what we call an eclipse. Remember here again that Mercury, Venus, Earth and Mars are classified as "terrestrial" planets under the solar system, which places the planet Mars, our very next point of interest.

Mars

The closest point to Sun from Mars is 206.6 million km and it's farthest at 248.2 million km. Its length of year is 1.88 earth year (1 year and 88 days) and 24h 37mns for its length of the day. Slightly over 30 minutes of a full day on earth here. Its tilt of axis is 25 degrees and 0.37 Earth gravity. It takes 687 days for Mars to complete a full orbital around the Sun.

Called the red planet, it is the fourth rock from the sun and the fourth closest to the sun until we get new additions as time goes. It is the second smallest planet in the solar system after Mercury. Mars was viewed and was represented by so many cultures as the god of war and has two moons that orbits around it unlike Earth that so far only has one Moon. There is unlikely any surface water there on Mars, making any life there quasi impossible based on the reports of our recent space expeditions. Even though it may depend on where and how we look for it.

In addition, it has mountains, volcanos, hills, canyons and polar ice caps and a sky as well just like earth, but no life so far detected at the moment. There are signs that water existed in the past because ancient floodplains, riverbeds, shallow oceans and shorelines of ancient lakes can be seen and are now empty based on our actual science and technologies.

To sum it up, our red planet lacks a magnetic field, which has probably caused the atmosphere over time to escape to space, leaving it with a thin one (atmosphere). And there is no telling how and when it lost its magnetic field that was crucial on grounding the atmosphere within since we don't have tools and scientific material to definitely pinpoint when and how planet Mars became at least inhabitable to humans and all lives on Earth included. That could also explain why life ceased to exist there, if there were at least human and earthly beings there in previous existence. But in my opinion, we cannot assumed that there is no life there as I'm sure that there is no such thing as emptiness and lifeless in any planet. As of now, scientists have determine that it does not rain there, but it used to rain in some distant past. The average temperature is about -50/-60 Celsius. Let's now take a look at our next planet which is Jupiter known as the King.

JUPITER, the King of the Planets

Jupiter, like commonly agreed, is a world of superlatives and wonders. It is the largest planet so far discovered in the solar system. Its diameter alone could fit more than eleven sizes of our planet earth. So far, it is the most massive planet as more than 1,300 earths would fit inside Jupiter and still have room to spare. It is a giant planet.

Jupiter takes 12 years alone to go once around the Sun, versus our planet earth that only takes 365 days to circle around the same Sun when observed through time. Its closest point to the sun is 740 million km and the most distant is 816 million km. One year of Jupiter is equal to 11.8 earth years and its days only last 10hours of our time. Its Tilt of axis is 3.13 degrees and 2.64 earth's gravity.

Jupiter rotates faster than earth. Only 10 hours versus earth 24hours making it the planet that have the most magnetic field ever discovered in the solar system. It also has the most planetary atmosphere so far than any other planet in the solar system. It even has three layers of clouds and is orbited by at least 63 known moons so far compared to earth that only have one moon to present.

Jupiter has three rings that surround it in layers. It is commonly called the solar system's vacuum cleaner because it attracts most of the debris falling from the solar system

CHAPTER 4

and deflects comets as well making it a huge part of keeping the whole universe also safe from fallen hazards in the solar system. It is just like Jupiter strategic location and design is purposely engineer to keep us safe from fallen objects in the solar system. Otherwise, all the other planets, including ours, would be frequently hit by rocks, deflects comets, asteroid and a whole number of debris falling down all over from the solar system. Jupiter is well equipped to afford this precious and heavy load task due to its massive size and its strong gravity which is more than two and half times earth gravity at sea level. Remember that more than one thousands Earth could swim in it easily without even touching each other.

I will take the chance here to remind you that Jupiter plays a huge deal in our existence continuity by keeping the solar system safe and free from radical hazards. The internal system of Jupiter is dominated by strong winds. Note that the winds that blow through Jupiter upper cloud tops stir up storms comparative to our cyclones and typhoons at speed toping over 600 km/h in a continuous basis without stops. It is called the Great Red Spot.

SATURN

Saturn has a disk of material around it that is called The Original Ring World. It is covered by gas and makes the whole world of Saturn a giant gas planet. It is so big and massive that 763 Earth size planets could fit inside of it. Saturn rotates on its own axis once every ten and a half hours in Earth time. The closest area of Saturn to the Sun is about 1.3 billion kilometers and it's most distant is set at 1.5 billion kilometers. Saturn day only last for 10h 39mn and it takes 29.4 years on Earth for Saturn to complete a full one year. Saturn is so massive that it has 62 known moons that orbit around it unlike Earth that so far only has one moon. Its temperature is about -178 degrees Celsius, one cool planet. And its temperature variation is due to its own internal processes, not by the Sun or directly from the Sun.

CHAPTER 4

URANUS

Uranus is somewhat the only planet that orbits the Sun on its side because none other planet orbits side ways around the Sun. This way of orbiting always puts one pole or the other on Uranus points toward the Sun during the solstices while at the equinoxes, Uranus equator points toward the Sun. This scenario gives a half a half situation when it comes to days and night as they are equally shared. Each pole therefore gets forty-two (42) earth years of sunlight.

Its closest point to the Sun is 2.7 billion kilometers and 3.0 billion kilometers for the most distant point to the Sun. We should note here that it would take 84 earth's years consequently to make a full one year at planet Uranus and it only takes 17 earth hours to make a full day there. Uranus is also a gas giant, but ice giant mostly, and has 27 known moons that orbit around it in the same plane as Uranus ring system that makes 13 rings so far detected orbiting, just like the moons do.

NEPTUNE

The last of the eight planets in our solar system until any new discovery is another world of superlatives just like Jupiter. It also has ring system like Saturn and Uranus but is the smallest of all the gas giants. Neptune is the farthest planet under the solar system away from the Sun itself at an average of 4.5 billion kilometers distant from it and 4.4 billion kilometers at its closest point. It also takes longer earth years for Neptune to complete a whole circle around the sun once every 165 earth years. Known to be the coldest planet, where temperatures dip down to -221 Celsius or -365.8 Fahrenheit, it takes 16.1 earth hours to make a day.

Neptune has thirteen known moons orbiting around it and happened to have one of the biggest and largest moons that exists nowhere else among the world of planets under the Sun. Oddly, only the largest moon making the thirteen moons

CHAPTER 4

orbits in counter clock wise in retrograde as opposed to the remaining twelve that orbit around Neptune in the same flow at normal universal standard. Which means that the largest moon orbits against Neptune's rotation.

Please notice that Neptune being the last one standing far away happened to be the only planet that has the largest moon ever existed on any other planet and that same moon is orbiting counter clock of it. In my opinion, it couldn't be by chance, and I think it could be to keep a certain balance of the whole solar system. Because it might inevitably, at a certain point, have a solar eclipse. This could be when the structure of the Sun and all the block of the solar system communicate. For that reason, that moon has to be the biggest of all moons farther away from the rest. That could also explain why it rotates against its host planet to absorb the sun's heat/light and redirect it back to the universe as a balance mechanism counter clock wise. The biggest moon has a diameter of about 2700 kilometers and is one of the coolest objects in our solar system.

The whole reason I went to this length to explore the solar system is to bring you more knowledge and stir up your curiosity. Having knowledge in astronomy increases your level of insight and wisdom while taking you close to God/Goddess, the creator. It humbles you and really puts you in the position to acknowledge the greatness and the mightiness of God in all things. And if you are among the ones that look at the same skies and space, wondering if we are alone, I'm sure by now you should have an answer. The answer to that question is that we are truly not alone. I'm pretty sure those planets we just studied are not without inhabitants. We may not have been able to establish any other existence there because we are looking with our naked eyes and less sophisticated scientific tools not equipped to detect them. Life is there; we just can't see it, but our common sense would dictate that different entities, not made of flesh like us, reside in those planets and moons. Besides, the universe is so huge. There are billions of stars in our galaxy alone. Our galaxy is the Milky Way and beside the Milky Way, there are over millions of other galaxies. And each galaxy has its own planets and billions of stars, just like our galaxy (the Milky Way) possesses about 9 and counting planets.

The Bhagavad Gita stretches that mystics, philosophers and those that have attained a great deal of knowledge and wisdom and advanced souls when they die, their souls can reach up to the moon where they would live and remain there for 10,000 years. Those souls have not acquired the eternal life and are subjects to a rebirth again in this world's earth to start another journey in attempt again to pursue a Self-realization and to join the abode of God. Those that once lived here on earth with an advanced soul but died and have fallen short to the real truth liberation to be in communion with the supreme personality of Godhead Krishna consciousness; making them not eligible to the Kingdom of God. It is interesting to note that to reach the moon too after death, one has to have also lived wisely and acquire a higher level of soul growth. Meaning that not every soul even could travel, or reach the moon level upon death. Now can you really be certain that there exist no other Souls or Beings in the different other planets and Stars/Galaxies and even within the Sun itself?

CHAPTER 5
The Entanglement Theory or the Superstring Theory

It is now proven scientifically in a subatomic level that all things in the universe are interconnected as of oneness in all things in a single unity. Another way to say this is that the universe is made up of different dimensions that are connected to each other. The Annus Magnus and the Sothic cycle are two palpable examples of how everything is linked and connected as single but separate independent entities.

It is also known and proven thousands of years ago that there are ten known dimensions in our universe. Those ten dimensions are interacting like vibrating strings similar to resonating violin strings, or parallel wires, that envelop the Universe. In between the ten dimensions, six of them are seen to be entangled and act as one seemingly. Which in my opinion clearly shows us in its own design that beyond the 6th dimension, it is another set of dimensions different from the six with probably a different operational mechanism and engineering system. The ten intertwined dimensions have been given a name and it is called Sephiroth in today's world, but I'm sure they have had other different names given to it in previous life and existence from different generation's far back.

What actually led Dr. Albert Einstein to his "Theory of Relativity" was his discovery of the fourth dimension, adding to the previously misconception that we were living in only three (3) dimensions (Length, Width and height) (up/down, left/right, forward/backward), even though ancient records had already established the number of dimensions we were living in.

Now Time is known to be a physical property and is part of the same dimensionality that gives us mass, including the three spatial dimensions. After Time, then comes Light that is now viewed as a vibration in the fifth (5th) dimension.

And since the universe is based on a binary forces, having each thing and its opposite as opposing forces in nature, the whole universe as a single Web or block is continuously balanced. Therefore, there is no need for any of us to even worry or remain stress over his life circumstances because it looks like things and events in our life could only either be this or that. Always temporary as things quickly move to the next. And we remain, indeed, the master potter's of our destinies, even though also conditioned by our previous dimensional acts.

Would it be safe then to suggest that if we are living in a Universe made of 10 spatial dimensions, that us, too, as living beings could be enveloped and influenced by those said 10 dimensions? As far as each individual entity is concerned, we are also a 10 dimensional projection when access is granted.

Human Thoughts Versus Gravity

Every material, or object, has a mass. Because of the mass, it actually exerts gravity. Any thought, even the tiniest one that we think of, also has a mass. Whenever we think of something, we expressly produce a mass injected into the universe. And since it has a mass, therefore, our thoughts can exert gravity by pulling whatever the thought was closer to realization.

In fact, our thoughts attract what we thought of closer to realization depending of the volume of the mass accumulated for its manifestation. For example, if many people actually focus their thoughts in one similar thing, the accumulation of the mass produced by each mind would merge and grow big into one to bring whatever was thought about to realization. And as a mass, it exerts gravity and would soon move that thing focused on rapidly closer, toward the objective. The thoughts accumulated would then become tangible and bear a powerful force moving matter around. The same applies to human sufferings and struggles everywhere in the world. This also would show the accumulation of the same sufferings and struggles to create a bigger mass shadowing earth.

Each mass accumulated could also have a distinct color as an indication and a differentiation between them, so to speak, like the aura of the human that have different colors. Happy thoughts masses would have different colors than unhappy thoughts masses and so on, with each specific emotion, intention and feeling involved in the process. Some thoughts masses might even be brighter than others, depending on their sources, as far as from whom the thought came from and depending also of the state of minds of the persons, including their spiritual dimensions. The colors of the masses from good intentions would present a different color than a thought originated with bad and negative intentions and the list continues.

Is your Emotions a Thought Manifest?

If so, it also produces a mass that it sends through our mind. The reason why it is known and said that our emotions play a huge role in our health is that our emotional thoughts and feelings produce and create a manifest energy in a form of a mass. The thought focus could be outward, or inward. When it is inward, it enters our energy realm and interferes with the original energy that was in there, thereby, creating a disturbance in the energy field,

This can comply to our existing energy flow where there is no disturbance.

It is known and said that our emotions affect our particular organs, depending on each specific emotional feeling and expression in their respective forms. Anger affects different part of the organs, so does anxiety. Fear affects different part of our organs, so does sadness. Each emotional expression affects a designated organ that it creates an imbalance in their respective energy field.

For example, hate and impatience could affect the heart, including our small intestine. Anger and frustration affect the liver and the gall bladder. Fear, or feeling afraid, affects the kidneys and bladder, just like sadness and depression attack the lungs and the big intestine. Do not forget that worries and anxiety target the stomach, spleen and pancreas, according to Chinese Medicine.

Every emotion expressed manifests itself in a form of a mass/energy that adversely, or positively, affects our body's organs energy system inward, instead of outward, but remains visible on our aura, or through the aura.

It becomes outward when the energy, thought, or feelings, are expressed in a counter clock coming from external source. Supposing it comes as a spiritual attack or spell or from the evil and envious eye. Regardless, it all affects the same locations of the different organs specifically and respectively. Positive thoughts or spells restore health likewise.

In my opinion, our emotions stirred up our specific organ energy already stored within, that was part of the optimal energy balanced within the system of energy. It is not adding any other external energy. Instead, it uses the organ's energy within, but in opposite direction to health. That's why it can be balanced back to its optimal health prerequisite. You should know that balancing in this case is not adding anything else, whatsoever. It is restoring what has been disturbed. Balancing could also mean adding more energy to level the deficiency in a case of depletion after stress, anxiety, depression, or loneliness etc. In that case, the energy has been drawn out and spent on worries.

CHAPTER 5

Thereby, this emphasizes the fact that illnesses, when occurring from internal means, result from the imbalances of the energy within the organs energy system and functions. This concludes the fact that our emotions are indeed inward thoughts manifest in a form of a mass drawn from within.

Can we neglect the fact that our emotions attract also an external energy toward their specific organ that they affect? Thereby, this adds more energy inward that negatively affects the normal energy flow of each organ and their system by upsetting the healthy flow of the energy while adding more energy than required. Too much energy could also damage organs and their flow of energy within.

What about joy, love, peace, happiness and serenity? Aren't they some emotions, too?

These are positive emotions that greatly contribute to health and happiness and only have positive effects on the organs and their energy system of functions. These positive emotions do not upset, nor create any unbalances, within the organs' system of energy.

CHAPTER 6
General Knowledge to Know

"The Cross was not used as a Christian symbol until the fourth century. The cross was used way long before by the Egyptians. And it was representing the intersection of two dimensions: the human and the celestial. As above, so below. It signified visually the representation of the juncture where man and God become one." Because the ancient adepts from the Egyptians understood themselves as divine.

"The Edo people in Benin (West Africa) understood that the physical realm that we see and touch is a mirror image of the spiritual world. And that the Spiritual world is the permanent abode of all living creatures. And it is then recommended that both the spiritual and physical realms be put in harmony according to a divine plan." Another way to remind us to reconcile our physical and spiritual bodies together for positive health.

Now imagine and picture the spirit of the Sun; the spirit of Earth; the spirit of the Stars in their spiritual bodies and how gigantesque they would be. Since everything has a soul and/or a spirit, can you suggest any less that everything else might also have a mind of its own? Possibly thinking also and feeling emotionally? Better yet able to also communicate and process thoughts. Laughter is God's hand for a troubled world where knowledge is no longer equally shared.

"Transformation requires sacrifice and achieving immortality requires a clean break with the material world of male and female. For the sake of becoming immortal, some

CHAPTER 6

people would go as far as castrating themselves to achieve immortality.

Even early Christians heard Jesus Christ Himself extol its virtues in Matthew 19:12, "There are those who have made themselves eunuchs for the sake of the kingdom of heaven, he who is able to accept this, let him accept it."

"In the days of Pythagoras, six centuries before Jesus Christ, the tradition of numerology acknowledge the number 33 as the highest of all the master Numbers. It symbolizes Divine truth."

"Melanin is a complex chemical substance that is omnipotent that cannot be replicated and gives us the ability to communicate with the spiritual world since thanks to the melanin, we can have a higher level of perception. The melanin makes our body whole and a total replica of the universe, galaxies and stars. Melanin gives us a higher intelligence and even of physical strength during extreme living conditions. With the Melanin, our innate intelligence is equal to the geometrical angle of the earth, which is '360 degrees,' according to ancient Afrikans/Khamit/ Ancient Egypt, instead of just 32 degrees commonly understood in the western mystery schools. You can go as high as 360 as long as your brain has the capacity to store knowledge. Melanin heals your body when sick and gives you power."

"Fluoride is a chemical that is added in water, public drinking water, toothpaste, food and beverage with the only intention that fluoride can prevent tooth decay. It has been argued and known that it is a very dangerous chemical to stay away from. There is no disease not even tooth decay that is caused by a fluoride deficiency. The truth is that fluoride can interfere with several important biological processes within your body. When you are healthy enough, your kidneys would excrete 50 to 60% of the fluoride you ingested each day, but the rest stays inside your body and accumulates daily as you keep adding more piles every day that you live and keep consuming fluoride. Scientist have proven that the remainder accumulates in calcifying tissues such as bones and **pineal gland**. Infants only excrete 20% of their fluoride ingested and the rest accumulates in their body."

"Intergenerational trauma happens when trauma, from even beyond 500 years ago, is still transmitted from father to son and mother to daughter and vice versa. The past struggles and sufferings from your ancestors can still get transferred to you via birth. You could be presenting symptoms of anger, depression and stress originated from your great-great-grandparents' traumas. The trauma might lay dormant until a situation or actual life event triggers it. As a result, a person will present deep emotional upsets.

"With this piece of information, it makes it easy to understand why some people might become abruptly aggressive and violent coupled with a deep distrust. The truth is that someone might be lashing out at you without even knowing that the real source of the anger, sadness and despair originated 300 years ago from one of the ancestors."

"Epigenetics is the study of changes in human organisms affected and caused by modification of gene expression. The modification of gene expression can passed down from one person to the next generations. It means that a lot of those that are descendants from people sharing history with wars, crusades, religious persecutions, **slavery**, colonization, segregation, discrimination, racism, extreme/systemic poverty, racialized violence and economic deprivations, etc., are typically born already traumatized when and if those traumas were never addressed or taken care of before their birth. The most important aspect to remember is that the alterations of the genes are biological and it does not actually alters the genetic Code itself. Those alter genes are dormant until something triggers them to wake up and the cycle of transmission of the altered genes continues to the next of

CHAPTER 6

kin. But the good news is that it can be reversed. You can re-alter your genetic code so that you will stop these traumas to continue passing down from one generation to the next. You will need a total shift and transformation of individual mentalities and a lot of rest. While you are resting/sleeping, your body and brain heal themselves. The book also provides a lot of avenues to break the cycle. Stay away from any processed food from now on."

"According to National Research Council (2006), 'It is apparent that fluorides have the ability to interfere with the functions of the brain.'" The US Environmental Protection Agency (EPA) have listed Fluoride among about 100 chemicals for which there is "substantial evidence of developmental neurotoxicity." In short, fluoride can damage your brain and impact your learning and behavior. When the fluoride accumulates in the Pineal Gland, it causes the pineal gland to reduce its **melatonin production** and leads to an earlier onset of puberty. It also affect the thyroid function by lowering its function. Fluoride may cause bone cancer (osteosarcoma), arthritis symptoms; damage bones and may cause reproductive problems; fatigue, headaches, rashes, and stomach and gastro intestinal tract problems. No one would deny that high natural levels of fluoride damage health, how would the chemical one be an exception?"

"The secret is within you. It is the core and roadmap that urge mankind to seek God, not literally in the heavens above, looking up to the sky, but rather within himself/herself. It was the message of all the great mystical teachers. The kingdom of God/Heaven is within you clearly signifies, 'know thyself.' This tells us that the secret hides within us. Even so, mankind continues till these days to look to the heavens, or sky, for the face of God." The only difference between you and God is that you have forgotten that you are divine.

"The **pineal gland** is also known as the **third eye** because it is actually another eye that you have within your brain. The pineal gland contains light sensitive nerve endings, no-visual photoreceptors, which reacts to light, a cornea and a retina. The melatonin secreted by the pineal gland regulates the body biological rhythms such as sleep and wake cycles. And this secretion is inhibited by light and triggered by darkness."

"In African Religion, Virtue is assimilated and often connected to the way someone carries out and adheres to the obligations of the communal aspect of life. This applies to social behaviors, such as the strict respect for parents, respect for elders and raising children appropriately. It also includes providing hospitality, being honest, trustworthy and courageous."

And Morality is associated with obedience, or disobedience to God, concerning the way someone or the community lives. "The living stands between their ancestors and the unborn. And the followers of the traditional religions pray to various spirits including theirs ancestors as well. It is believed that these secondary spirits act as intermediaries between humans and the primary God/ Supreme Deity. They also believe in a single Supreme Being by large, but some societies believe in a dual God and Goddess." Names of God in African languages are Ngai by the Kikuyu; Enkai to the Maasai; Mungo, Murunga/ Mulungu in some part of Zambia; Wenaam in Burkina Faso. African Religions have more similarities than differences in all of theirs aspects and practices. And a person is said to have a good or bad conscience, if or not that person was doing the bidding of God or malevolent spirits.

"Animism is the concept that everything in the universe is alive. The entire universe is alive and this is the central belief of Shamanistic spirituality."

"In an experiment, a dying man offers himself for an experiment to prove the existence of the soul. He was put in a capsule all sealed up that nothing could go in or out when sealed. The man ended up dying inside the capsule. And once the soul left his body, the weight of the dead person went down. The weight of the person after death was slightly lower. The

CHAPTER 6

weight of the person, which was higher, went down after the man was pronounced dead. Thereby, this led to the scientist's conclusion that the human soul does actually have mass.

The experiment lead to the conclusion also that there is indeed an invisible "material" that exits and leaves the human body, right at the moment of death, which is the soul. Therefore, the Soul has to have quantifiable mass that cannot be stopped, or blocked, by physical barriers, "Not even the sealed capsule." The body is just containing it within its cell until the soul free itself after death. And not even the body could hold it hostage from freedom of movement.

"Knowledge and secrets have been hidden from the unworthy people, centuries after centuries. The sages hide them in codes, symbols, on rocks and actually do leave behind the keys to unlocking the mysteries only for the worthy ones. It usually holds the power to lift the darkness and unlock the ancient mysteries, opening them to all human understanding.

"The prophecies about a coming enlightenment, or hero is found in almost all beliefs, faith and cultures. Hindus call it Krita Age and the Jews say it is the Coming of the Messiah. The cosmologists call it Harmonic Convergence. Astrologers call it the Age of Aquarius and the Theosophists call it the New Age. Most cultures call it the coming of the righteous one and healer."

They said, "The mind sits like a golden capstone atop the body; the philosopher's Stone. Through the staircase of the spine, energy ascends and descends, circulating, connecting the heavenly mind to the physical body." This is reiteration that the secrets all-inclusive to heaven/ the kingdom reside nowhere else but within each one of us that has to be climbed up and down like a ladder. Knowing ourselves within is the only way to access heaven.

"WHAT WE HAVE DONE FOR OURSELVES ALONE DIES WITH US; WHAT WE HAVE DONE FOR OTHERS AND THE WORLD REMAINS, AND IS, IMMORTAL UNQUESTIONABLY."

"The ancients had understood that angels and demons were identical. Their difference is all a matter of polarity. They are indeed interchangeable archetypes. Good and evil; light and darkness; the guardian angel who conquered your enemy in battle was also reciprocally viewed and perceived by your enemy as a demon destroyer." Therefore, make no mistake as a coin still will have two sides, just like a broken clock would still tell time twice within every day.

"The gift of fear is shared among Man. Human intuition is more accurate in detecting danger. Either through the guts, nerves, skin or nervous system, we can sense it. Unfortunately, human instinct is afraid of his own fear, including his own mind. Therefore, some people, false teachers and institutions, take advantage of your human gift of fear, shared among all mankind, by using it against you. Against your own mind; against your self-admittance of being afraid. They ultimately hold your fear as a defense and security to their prosperity and survival and you don't even know it."

Take heed and remediate as you own the power to change things accordingly and empower yourself. With fear comes hesitation, followed by procrastination, to end up with a doubt. When in doubt, take a minute and meditate. What's left of a man that doubts his own power and strength? Have you paid close attention to your everyday politician rhetoric? Even some religions and cults nowadays excel by capitalizing on your fear to teach and spread hate and division among societies. Fear leads to stress and excessive, continuous stress leads to sicknesses, even diabetes in the long run.

It is important to know and understand that the Stars and fate are inter-twined. This gives an advantage to whoever pays close attention to the layout of heavens in his life. That person will structure himself/herself a new world/life. The stars and galaxies give us signals and warnings to better ourselves. When was the last time you glanced at the sky, if ever? Just take a good look at it from time to time and learn its signs and

CHAPTER 6

wonders. Gear yourself with a telescope and maybe you are the one to provide us with new discoveries and solve old mysteries.

"Always remember the three prerequisites for an ideology to become a religion from Dan Brown's book, *The Lost Symbol*. 'Assure,' 'Believe,' 'Convert.' In sum, a guaranty of a salvation while believing in a specific theology/teaching and that the only way to reap salvation is through conversion. That without it, there would be no other way to have access to salvation." Only their way, or no other way. Not to target any established religion as each one of them have their reasons to exist and actually contributes to mankind spiritual fulfillment, no jokes aside.

Keep in mind that the accession to the kingdom has no need for belief, nor conversion. In fact, you can access it from where you are reading this book right now, at this moment.

"For centuries, the 'brightest mind on earth' has always found a way to ignore/or have ignored, the Ancient sciences and knowledge, mocking them as ignorant and superstitious, to this day. To then suddenly wake up later, realizing that the more we actually learn from the Ancient mysteries, the more we realize that we did not really know that much either and that actually, the ancient mysteries indeed hold the keys to the future and new enlightenment of generations to come thereafter."

Everyone is a book that only will give access to its reader when trust has been built. Have you finished reading your own book? Isn't the mind resistant to execution sometimes when there is no more energy to think and remain in the present? Once you get the courage to open your personal life book, you will discover the missing pieces that, when addressed, will make you whole again and balanced internally.

The untapped potentials of our human mind is beyond unbelievable to the point that we are not even putting a scratch to it. We have not even put a dent on our mental and spiritual capabilities, to this day. The huge majority are not even using 30 percent of their mind power, or brain capability and potential. I just picked a random number that is not related to any statistic study because the world is big and full of billions of billions of people.

The mind power can be used to achieve anything we want. It is worldwide agreed that most humans only use 10 percent of their brains potentials. So use your mind power wisely and mindfully.

The power of the mind over matter is real as we can change and affect a physical mass/matter at will. Our thoughts have an impact on the physical world as our thoughts interact with it affecting the physical world all the way down even to the subatomic realm reaching beyond the spiritual world."

Consequently, we are the Masters of our own universe with the ability to create and transform the world around us. So, be careful of what you wish for, because everything said and wished for always come back to you with the same intensity in a form of cause and effect.

I just learned that a chicken could live up to twenty years old and a whale up to seventy years (even 200), whereas the giant tortoise even lives longer than a human; a wiping 150 to 300 years old. Some elephants could even go for 200 years, but their average life span is sixty, depending on life circumstances and conditions. Some trees can live up to more than 20,000 years. The Methuselah, (an ancient bristlecone pine), is as old as 5,000 years or more on the world record. The Baobab trees in Africa can live more than 5,000 years and more.

"The seven planes of self-existence or planes of consciousness are: the physical plane, the astral plane, the mental plane, the plane of spiritual soul, the spiritual plane, the semi-divine plane and the divine plane. And the five universal senses are the representation of the five central planes of consciousness from the astral plane to the semi-divine plane within the order. Each plane of consciousness represents a growth and follow up an order that no plane could be skipped

CHAPTER 6

before the next one." A person that elevated himself to the level of just the Mental plane cannot yet reach the Spiritual plane, or the plane of spiritual Soul, until that person passes successfully the required conditions and subsequent tests and so forth to the next levels.

The divine god in mankind has to follow a cycle within each person before it fully manifests itself. That's why, throughout history of mankind, the god within mankind was symbolized as being torn into pieces and scattered in different places. The pieces have to be individually recovered and reunited before the full cycle is complete. The soul world will then gradually reunite in consciousness of the higher orders to become whole again.

What gives us the will to want to grow is our evolving spiritual ego that actually lifts us up way above the elemental world. The spiritual ambition shared in all mankind have paved the way to our evolutionary urges to grow in spirit and reunite with God again just like having been created on God's Image.

"The kingdom of God is within you," said Jesus Christ.

"Know thyself," said Pythagoras.

"Know ye not that ye are gods," said Hermes Trismegistus.

"I have said, ye are gods; and all of you are children of the most high." Psalm 82:6 (KJV)

"At the entrance of Ancient Egyptians Temples, it is written, 'Man, Know thyself'."

"In Ancient Egypt, Osiris is the god of death and rebirth and the father of Horus. The god of the sky is Nut; the god of earth is Geb and the god of the air is Shu. Because there is a parallel underworld and under sky, according to ancient Egypt. Beyond the skies lay the infinite expanse of Nu, the chaos that existed before the creation.

Horus is the Son of Osiris and Seth is the brother of Osiris. After the death of Osiris, Seth and Horus were fighting each other for the inheritance and the throne. Geb, the earth god that happens to be Horus's grandfather, intervenes to solve the issue by convoking the Nine Gods, known as the Great Ennead, to serve as witnesses and moderators. Horus, the rightful son of Osiris, was given sole authority over the whole Egypt and was crowned as the King of Egypt.

It is also said, in the beginning that Seth kills Osiris and takes his crown. Isis, Osiris's wife, wakes up and looks for Osiris and brings him back, but he was inactive and unresponsive. Seth finds Osiris's body again and this time, he cuts Osiris into fourteen pieces at the Lower Egypt. Isis, with the help of Anubis, tracked and found Osiris's body throughout Egypt, and put him together, piece by piece. Isis had put him together, but she is missing the phallus that is buried in the deeps of the Nile fish. Isis made him a new phallus and resurrected Osiris. Later they conceived Horus through the virgin, Isis.

"That's why all men and women have to go through and pass an indefinite series of re-incarnations from the body of one animal to another, until the soul is liberated to immortality. Once at the last step, you will need to find the phallus that resides deep inside of you. Then you will be free from the cycle of birth, death and rebirth, having liberated your soul from the ten chains of the flesh thereby becoming eligible to be accepted to join the circles of God's. The purification of the soul consist of the cultivation of the intellect, with scientific knowledge, knowledge of the nature and plenty of virtue and self-control over mind and emotions. In that note, just like medicine cures the body, music can also be used to heal the soul. Also note that the fourteen pieces of Osiris was also considered to be the fourteen Stars of the Orion constellation in which Osiris was associated as the dying and rising god of Egypt.

"The Solar Winds correspond and represent the Breath of Ra/God, according to the Ancient Egyptians, the Earth ionospheric Sheath is regarded as the world/earth soul. The Sun Spot Cycle with its electromagnetic forces hitting the body of earth at more than 100 miles per second contributes to the

CHAPTER 6

rebirth of earth/**the new earth** in its **annual orbits** in relation to a specific position of Earth to the Sun. Called the aurora borealis effect, these electromagnetic forces/lights in a form of rings ascend and descent from the sun to the earth, charging Earth with **new energies**."

The Bhagavad Gita, while acknowledging the end of the world and the beginning of the new world, emphasizes that, "All beings, enter my lower nature at the End of a World-Age; at the Beginning of a World-Age, again. I Emanate them," said Krishna, which is another word/name for God.

Besides energies dropping and falling onto earth and onto other planets from the Sun, there are also the energies coming from the Black Hole of the very center of the Galaxy, the Milky Way.

Besides the Milky Way Galaxy, there are other and multitudes of Galaxies and each have a black hole in their center/heart as well. Those various cosmic cycles and energies have an impact on our planets and draw a new direction in the course of how earth and other planets should become in the near or far future alternatively cycle after cycle.

The Black Hole in our Galaxy, the Milky Way, is about 26,000/27,000 light years away from earth. Imagine that those energies from there will also have to travel for a very long time before they reach us here on earth. It takes about 26,000 years for each energy to hit earth, and run earth at every second of its course. Coincidently, the star signs known as constellations move forward through the year, making a final and full circle once every 26,000 years.

Most black holes exist and lurk at the centers of most galaxies in the cosmos. And it is scientifically known and determined that the gravitational forces from these cosmic alignment "behemoths" draw in surroundings gas, dusts and objects, possibly falling stars and other particles, into the black hole, at no point of return. No one knows the limits of the Black Holes.

CHAPTER 6

It becomes undeniable that the different cosmic alignments that started way far above our planets determine the way our earth will react and evolve, accordingly. They are there like cosmic post signs, full of meaning, and changing with each new cycle from the latter. We should keep in mind that as our celestial alignment changes poles, so are the constellations, too, accordingly. And some constellation may remain active for over 3500 years, before the next constellation takes place as it replaces each other's by cycles of constellations. Each new constellation has to run its own course until its end before being replaced accordingly, up to their allocated years of duration and back.

There are about eighty-eight (88) known and officially recognized constellations that are covering the entire universe and sky from the northern and southern hemispheres so far. A constellation consist of a group of stars (also called "Ip" in ancient Egypt 3000 B.C.) that forms an image, a design or an imaginary outline, or pattern, that are visible throughout the skies upon connecting the stars together. Each constellation have been given a name from Sagittarius, Orion, Scorpion, Ursa Major, Libra, Taurus, Lyra (the Harp), Ursa Minor, Draco, etc. We also owe our different Zodiac signs to these constellations. So, our star signs were defined by the constellation that happened to be behind the Sun when a person was born but not always necessary. And since we have twelve months in a year, we also have twelve Zodiac signs that is given and distributed to each one of us once born accordingly. Take note that Ancient Egypt have had or may have had different names and constellations different than our modern Scientist. The Sun moves in an ecliptic circle once every 365.256 days. It also takes the Sun 26000 years to move through all of the twelve (12) constellations of the Zodiac.

"The stars complete daily a full circle (360 degrees) every twenty four (24) hours. Note that even during day time, the stars remain still on the sky as usual, and follow their course of rotating. Because of the day-light, it makes it very hard to see the stars with naked eyes when the sun is up."

CHAPTER 6

"We get our oxygen from plants and certain bacteria. They release oxygen during photosynthesis. It is the process they use to transform water and carbon dioxide into sugar that they would use for food later. They reject the oxygen and keep the sugar/glucose. Our human and animal life could not have survived without that oxygen. Oxygen makes up only 21% of the air we breathe.

Again, without the Sun to feed the plants with light, we would not have had breathable air. The mechanism goes like this; we inhale oxygen and exhale carbon dioxide. The plants inhale carbon dioxide and exhale oxygen.

It is obvious and noticeable that plants are also important to us as it feeds us. This includes feeding the animal life that we also cook down the road. Plants helps reduce the level of carbon dioxide, a greenhouse gas in the atmosphere. It also protect the soil from winds and water runoff, helping by this action to control or stop erosion. Plants also release water during their photosynthesis that is later control by the sun to make it rain.

The Sun is responsible for the water evaporation, clouds, rain, air movements, oxygen production, water sources, winds, weather and ocean current."

CHAPTER 7
The Fruit that Keeps on Giving Fruit

Like a seed that is in perfect and good condition to produce, a seed that just need watering, tendering ultimately will only produce good fruits in return by relying also on the soil in which it was sawn to be fertile. What is a fruit? A seed that sprung and grew to a tree till maturity and produced a lovely fruit in return. A fruit that was conditioned to be what it was meant to be.

To be is to know of existence. What exist is conscious and aware of the reality surrounding every aspect of his/ her life. So a tree might as well know of its existence also and aware of its surroundings; observing and expressing itself.

We have different kind of fruits. A sweet and a bitter types of fruits. And by the taste, we can determine what our preference is? Because, we, as humans, can be considered as fruit that also have its own taste. A sweet taste and a bitter taste, we choose. And we have all already the sweet and the bitter.

Since, we have a tremendous power over matter, we can determine the taste of our very own fruits. Either we want it sweet, or we want it bitter. The choice is up to us. Sometimes, we might like it sweet or sour.

Nothing is truly predestined, unless everything is connected and prescribed to the same Law. And if we as human can have choices and have dominion over our actions, deeds, dire, favorites, likes, dislikes; that is an ultimate sign that we also have the power to choose the taste of our own fruits. Sometimes, I might want my fruit sweet today and turn

CHAPTER 7

around making that same fruit sour in a later day given that I could choose the taste of my own fruit.

There are fruits that are passive that still tell everything about us. That we have lived and are still growing. The fruit itself reminds us that we are a design or species that we cannot grow up and become nothing else but what the engineer had programed it to be. Is it really true all the time that we could choose how we are going to act when circumstances could also weigh in?

In fact, what is it that you have learned on your own? Have you read books and took notes? Have you done your own research? Regardless of how one learns, or accesses knowledge, it is always via an intermediary. Seeking knowledge could be another way to spice up your own fruits adding more flavors to it. Therefore, gear up and take your destiny under control.

There is a question that very few ask themselves as far as who they are? Who am 'I? Who are you and why are you running away from yourself? We don't care to ask ourselves this question because we are not ready for the answer. Or simply don't feel like investigating and end up finding the answer that we don't want to know or hear. For instance where in the world do you think you are? By Looking around you, what do you see? Roads, corners, trees, space, moon, sun, water, animal life on air and on sea, earth, stars, mountains, hills, etc. Now tell me what is the difference between you and them? I'm pretty sure they, too, could see you looking at them. You may be down here on earth, yet still connected to heavens, to above as you have never been disconnected from it. In fact, without you, too, something in the universe would be unbalanced or just balanced as you would have never even existed in this case.

As Above, As Below. What exist here, so exists there. too. What exists above in heaven exists over here on earth. There is nothing new under the sun. Cycle after cycle, the universe keeps balancing itself. It keep itself alive independently of our actions. We can well destroy each other here on earth, just to find ourselves exactly where we left ourselves on earth still.

CHAPTER 7

The universe is connected to itself and everything including us. But independently, the universe spiritual and physical body are solid at all time and from the look of it, the order of all-inclusive things is a **must** cycles after cycles even with the slightest small scale and particles. It has sustain itself through time and space and forever eternal. Like a web that restructures itself at a fastest unimaginable rate. The universe is indeed alive and complete each other movements automatically. Springs, Summers, Falls and Winters alternatively year round over and over just like the pure simple effect of raining season and dry season.

As a living entity of the universe, we feel at some point alone and disconnected from everything. But, there is no need to, because the only thing blocking you is not knowing that you are part of it. That you are part of the echo-system. Running is not an option. The only way is to move forward. The only way is to advance. In fact, there is no other place you could go or hide from the all eye seeing; the Universe. Every step of the ladder embedded its unique experience, knowledge and understanding. Anytime that you are a witness to something, know that you are never alone because the universe is already aware of it simultaneously as you realized it since eventually everything happens inside its Belly. You are Its representation, the ambassador.

We are of divine origin. We are spiritual Beings. Our body is a temple. The only fear is not to remember that we are a temple. The only obstacle is to have forgotten that we are a temple. It was designed as if it would not have perished in a sense that we get born, walk, talk, build and leave earth, regardless. But even though we are created like species that will always be as part of the whole Being, we can fall short of recognizing that we are the Generator, Operated, and Destroyer of our lives and we have an impact on everything we see, say and touch. That you are conscious of it or not, you would soon find out, as time will teach you. For instance, we can think. We can change matter into what we want. We have always had an impact over matter, either consciously, or unconsciously, but at the end of

CHAPTER 7

the day, we change things, regardless. We move things around and impact our own course of lives and others.

Do you get it by now that you create as you speak? Speech born from the mind. Speech that is the fruit born from your mind, may be from the ego. The fruit can never be more than what the mind has ordered it to be, to accomplish.

So, in the beginning was the word. The word that spoke everything into existence. From what? From the self-acknowledgement and exercise of inborn authority. Therefore, we are part of it, part of the kingdom and everything that comes with it. Do not sell yourself short.

Nothing can separate us from the all thing. As we are condemned to inhabit it. The word condemn may be harsh but there is no escaping as there is no other place to go and be unless permitted. So far, all mankind have not left this very earth without leaving their flesh back to Mother Earth ultimately just like Dust to Dust. The cool part of it, is that we have a mind. We can make a good use of it to transform our environment surrounding our life, our existence. The mind, a powerful tool that even physical matter Bow down to. So we truly have dominion over the things we can see, touch, feel, smell, taste. We have dominion over our own survival. But it is all linked to the mind on how we are using it and to what extinct we are even aware of the power of our thoughts and intentions. Thinking may be natural, but intentions can be taught and learn. How can we guide intentions without the Know how? And the required knowledge to move along to the progressive line of the circle? Make it easy on yourself by forging good intentions as neither one of us can change tomorrow. Everyone operates on the act of random kindness expressing something that he/she feels satisfied with. So, if you think like a slave, you will act like a slave. If you walk like a stranger in your own town or city, then you are one and most likely will be treated like one too.

In fact, our intentions can be learned and by practice, we can actually reach the true power of the mind. Through focus, concentration, meditation, etc., we can improve the power behind our thoughts to have a great impact over matter. Some people are just different and more gifted than others in controlling intentions at any given time and space, but no one has been shortchanged. Intentions would then mingle and join all other intentions from other different beings, expressing their existence as well. Even though they are different and multiple intentions, they are within the barriers and scopes, still inclusive of the whole Big Web of the universe, intertwined and having impact on each other's intentions. Due to the oneness of the Sole Web, interconnecting everything to the subatomic level of our thoughts and intensions, our collective intentions are just like one. Just like when you fill air to a balloon.

Since intentions can be learn, it means that it is something that could also be taught. We should then emphasize in teaching subjects that are uplifting and healing. Considering that teaching a kid hate versus love produces a different paired intentions instilled in the kid. Therefore, teach the kids love and respect, of the dignity of others to safeguard the equality of mankind. Teach the kids of all skin colors that every skin color deserves to be respected and that black, white, yellow, red... are the same and complementary. If only you could mix all these existing different skin colors into one color, you would discover the beauty of the Creation.

In sum, we are as equal and free like everyone else. We have the same right and deserve to be treated with love and consideration as we all have a mind that shares the same intertwined routes of the universe, dimensions equally without discrimination, or prejudices. We are free to do what we want and move to where we want while being mindful of others. For all humans and existence to auto-respect each other on your behalf, you have to also become a good citizen of the world; not just your country. Get up now and rise as your time has come to start walking the walk and talking the talk. Unity is now and a must, and you are a citizen of the world.

CHAPTER 8
Brief Anatomy of our Physical Body and Required Vitamins and Minerals

- The Roles of the Organs

According to the Chinese Medicine, each organ has a well determined set of functions. Each organ has control of a certain area within the body and a channel or meridian along which acupunctural points are located.

I think it is imperative for us individually to be at least in close contact with our body in order for us to actually become able to take care of the temple. You will not be able to care for the temple if you are not acquainting with those organs that are living inside you working day and night in keeping you moving about your worldly affairs. Being conscious about our organs and their locations is always a plus in self-help. It is also important to know what they like and what they don't like as you are your own guardian when it comes to taking care of you and protecting you from the gates of sicknesses and diseases to open up. Every head of the household should be alert and ready to protect the family against diseases or prevent them. It is part of being the first interceder and the first Samaritan to help your own family.

On a nutshell, the liver helps breakdown the food we eat by secreting a digestive fluid (bile). The bile secreted by the liver is then stored in the Gall Bladder.

The liver produces proteins and stores glycogen, iron and various vitamins. Another big job of the liver is removing toxins

CHAPTER 8

and wastes from the blood and converting the toxins into less harmful substances.

In connection to it, the kidneys filter the waste products contained in the blood, to be pushed out of the body through the urine. Before the urine is excreted out of the body, it has to be stored into the Bladder until the convenient time when we now actually execute the order to go pie through the urethra. You should know that all these movements are part of the involuntary nervous system.

The small intestines help and contribute to the breakdown of the food we eat; also with the help of the pancreas for a good digestion. The small intestines also aid in the absorption of said food, at the same time. While the lungs and large intestines play the major role of elimination by removing waste from the body through the bowels movements and skin pores. The lungs host the air we breathe that goes to the blood vessels deep in our lungs for our oxygen need and take back out the carbon dioxide when we breathe out. I wonder where all these carbon dioxide travel to and their very impact on us.

We should plant more trees and plants to offset the level of carbon dioxide as a solution. And since the Amazon Rain Forest is now mostly destroyed by fires, it becomes even more urgent than before to plant a lot of trees.

The stomach and the spleen are the two considered to actually be the center of the body. Everything we ingest goes straight down to those organs first. The foods and fluids are processed within by the stomach to produce the daily energy and blood needed. The heart pumps the blood throughout the whole body while the pancreas's job is to regulate the blood sugar level. The heart is also referred to as the center of our emotions and responsible for communicating with others as it houses the Soul and our individual consciousness.

Finally, we have the large intestine, which is the final part of the digestive system. Its function is to reabsorb the fluids

CHAPTER 8

from the remaining indigestible food matter and process waste products from the body and prepare for the elimination of all waste through bowel.

A great information to have is to know and remember that all our organs think and are highly intelligent. They make decisions every single second that keep us alive every day. The organs know exactly what we need and what to do in order to keep us alive. They work together without trying to cheat on each other and are faithful to us and to themselves. Each organ with their specific cells contribute to our wellness. In truth, our cells have been outthinking us since the cells already know what to do to keep their host alive so that they also can have a purpose. They have a wisdom and a secret in their commitment to us, as they have no problem working together and fully participating with passion to keep us healthy. The cells defend us while fighting bacteria and viruses and actually die for us to be alive. It is because every cell in our body agreed to work for the welfare of the whole body, regardless if we keep making bad choices of diet or poor judgments. A cell keeps in touch with other cells, sends signals and messages through molecules throughout the whole body; adapt from moment to moment and recognizes each other as equally important because a cell knows that going it alone is not an option. I guess there is a lesson here for us to learn so that humans could become able to work together in the universe body as the cells in our bodies.

We can greatly learn from the cells' mysteries of life as there might be another dimension of life within our bodies that knew knowledge and wisdom prior to us finding out or realizing. We have more than two hundred and fifty types of cells that go to work every day within our body. A liver cell alone performs more than fifty functions and the cool part is that each organ possesses billions of cells with their specific duties but they are not overlapping each other tasks even though dependent to each-others functions to keep the person alive and healthy without complaining. The cells are here to serve and we should live like them without complaining. Serving each other.

CHAPTER 8

What are the Necessary Vitamins the Body Needs?

The daily vitamins that our body needs for a healthy sustainable life are biotin (B-complex), folate (B-complex), vitamin A, vitamin B1 (thiamin), vitamin B2 (riboflavin), vitamin B5 (pantothenic acid), vitamin B12 (cobalamin), vitamin C (ascorbic acid), vitamin D (cholecalciferol), vitamin E (tocopherol), vitamin K.

According to the US Department of Agriculture (USDA) adult Americans practically do not get enough of these vitamins. Vitamin A, C, D and E.

Vitamin A is very important for the body. It is a catalyst for many biochemical processes in the body and extremely essential for nutrient assimilation, bone development and fertility. A deficiency in vitamin A can lead or contribute to poor vision and weakens the immune system. It is associated with cellular growth and maintenance. The foods that are good sources are organ meats such as liver and giblets, vegetables such as sweet potatoes, pumpkin, carrots, spinach, turnip greens and cantaloupe and Bok Choy.

Note that a medium sweet potato provides more than 100% of the daily recommended amount of vitamin A.

Vitamin C, also referred to as ascorbic acid, is required for the collagen, an important structural component of tendons, bones, teeth, blood vessels and muscles. It plays a part in the fat transport system of cells and cholesterol metabolism as it help prevent gallstones. As a powerful antioxidant, vitamin C helps the body fight against viral infections, bacterial infections and toxicity while boosting the immune system. Then the immune system in turn continually and efficiently releases its White Blood Cells to combat diseases and any intruder. Another key is that vitamin C protects carbohydrates, fats, proteins and nucleic acids (DNA and RNA).

Vitamin C deficiency causes bruising, bleeding, skin and hair loss as it contributes to wound healing and ameliorates skin vitality. It is also recommended for those that have colds,

CHAPTER 8

congestive heart failure, high cholesterol, bleeding, high blood pressure, atherosclerosis, angina or scurvy. People that smoke and drink or use contraceptive pills may also benefit from it. The following foods are rich in vitamin C:

In the fruit family, we have guava, oranges, kiwi, strawberries, cantaloupe, papaya, pineapple and mango, lime/lemon etc. In the vegetables family, there is the raw red sweet pepper, raw green sweet Brussels sprouts, broccoli, sweet potato, cauliflower and Bok Choy etc.

It would be wise and a healthy habit to have fresh fruit as a part of every breakfast. One cup of fruit may just be what you need for your daily recommended amount of vitamin C.

Vitamin D is another essential vitamin that our body needs so that the body can absorb calcium to promote bone growth while maintaining strong bones and teeth. It is difficult to get vitamin D based on diet alone because there are not a lot of food choices rich in vitamin D. In fact, most of the food that have Vitamin D have been added (fortified foods). Salmon, swordfish and canned tuna contains some vitamin D. Most of our vitamin D are through exposure to the sunlight. The best source of vitamin D, besides the sun, is lard and Beef Tallow (grass fed). So, I don't know what you are waiting for instead of getting a Sun bath daily with moderation to supply your vitamin D need. Besides, exposing the skin to the sun could also be beneficial for those with high blood pressure. It is proven that exposure to sunlight may help to reduce and lower blood pressure and prevent strokes and heart attacks.

Vitamin E is an antioxidant, which helps fight damage to the cells in the body. These foods are good sources of it. Nuts and seeds such as sunflower seeds, almonds, hazelnuts, pine nuts, peanuts, Brazil nuts, etc. are good sources. We also have turnip greens, peanut butter, spinach, avocado and tomato based product. It is important to know that a small handful of almonds can provide half of our daily recommended amount of vitamin E.

CHAPTER 8

What are the Necessary Minerals the Body Needs?

Daily, the body needs some types of minerals in order to operate efficiently with the goal of affording us our health. They are boron, calcium, chlorine, chromium, copper, fluorine, iodine, iron, magnesium, manganese, molybdenum, nickel, phosphorus, potassium, selenium, sodium, vanadium, and zinc. Choosing foods each day that could provide us with vitamins and minerals are crucial for our overall health. According to the US Department of Agriculture (USDA), adult Americans practically do not get enough of these minerals: calcium, potassium, fiber, and magnesium.

Calcium: Our body needs calcium to build strong bones and teeth in our childhood and adolescent years. As an adult, we need calcium to maintain bone mass. We should get a little bit over 1000 milligrams of calcium daily. The following foods are good sources of calcium: Fish and sea food, pink salmon and ocean perch, beans, spinach, almonds, oatmeal and Bok Choy.

Potassium: Helps the body maintain a healthy balanced blood pressure. It plays a huge role in keeping our blood pressure normal. It is recommended to consume a little bit over 4000 milligrams each day. The following foods are a good source for potassium: potatoes, beans, bananas, peaches, cantaloupe, honeydew melon, fish, halibut, yellow fish tuna, rockfish, cod and tomato based products, including Bok Choy.

Magnesium: This is one of the most essential mineral that helps the body produce energy. It also helps our muscles, arteries, and heart work properly. It would be helpful to have a little bit over 350 milligrams daily. These foods can provide you with some magnesium: Pumpkin, spinach, artichokes, beans, tofu, brown rice, Bok Choy. In the nut family, we have the Brazil nuts, almonds, cashews, beetroot and peanuts. Ginger is also a good source of magnesium. **IRON:** Iron's job is to carry oxygen throughout your body. Iron is also indispensable for the body to create and grow red blood cells.

CHAPTER 8

Iron deficiency causes anemia, dizziness, constant fatigue, shortness of breath and tiredness. You can increase your iron intake daily by the consumption of these foods and legumes: Shellfish is abundant with iron and clams; oysters, including mussels, are expressly great sources to get a good dose of it and some protein. Spinach, rich in vitamin C, possesses also iron. In the legume family, we have beans, lentils, chickpeas, peas and soybeans. Broccoli, kale, Swiss, chard, collard, including beet greens, cabbage, brussels sprouts; pumpkin seed, red meat, eggs, turkey, tofu and quinoa are good sources of iron. Peanuts, pecans, walnuts, pistachios, almond, cashew, sunflower seeds, raisin, peaches and prunes also have iron that we need. Pure raw honey with no additives or antibiotics, sesame, hemp and flaxseed too. We also have potatoes (mostly the skin), tomato, mushrooms, olives, mulberries, whole grains, Amaranth, spelt, oats.

The job that the iron gets done for the health of our body is really important that a daily consumption is a must and express as truly our body cannot produce iron by itself. So strap yourself with iron to boost your oxygen flow and increase the ability for your body to produce more red blood cells at a continuous basis. Especially during menstruation, it becomes a great deal to consume iron-rich foods to compensate any deficiency as it is highly probable you will be losing blood as a result. Please note that the lentils, seeds and nuts rich in iron are also rich in fiber, minerals and vitamins.

Benefits of Eating Liver

Liver contains a huge amount of quality protein, an easily absorbed form of iron, all forms of the B vitamins, including B12 and folic acid in significant amount. Liver possesses a well-balanced quantities of vitamin A, many trace elements and minerals, including copper, zinc, chromium, phosphorous and selenium. It also contains essential fatty acids EPA, DHA and AA as well as the powerful antioxidant CoQ10.

Even though the liver's functions is to act as a filter for toxins. When the toxin is identified by the liver, it is marked to be excreted through the kidneys or the intestines. In the case there is too many toxins to be processed, the toxins generally accumulate in the fatty tissues and nervous system of the animal; the same rule applies to humans too when there is too much toxins in the body to be processed. No toxin actually stays or remains in the liver. Therefore, there should be no second thought about its consumption in small quantities, but please remain civilized and respectful to nature and life. Be aware also of the quality and freshness of the liver before consuming it.

Benefit of Eating Quail Eggs and Meat

Quail meat is a low fat diet due to its low amount of fat and cholesterol. Quail meat may be taken in consideration in diet for prevention of heart diseases because of its high level of C18:1 content.

In addition to the meat, a quail egg is rich in fat soluble vitamins, B-complex; in proteins, amino acids, macro and microelements but above all, quail meat is low in cholesterol triglycerides and saturated fatty acids. The Chinese use quail eggs to help treat tuberculosis, asthma, and even **diabetes**. Its eggs can also help prevent sufferer of kidney, liver or gallbladder stones and even can remove these types of stones. Quail egg is a rich sources of antioxidants, minerals and vitamins. It takes the third place in the Chinese medicine after snake venom and Ginseng.

The Benefits of Eating Beef Tallow When Consumed

Beef tallow is high in Conjugated Linoleic Acid (CLA). It is a type of fat that has been shown to reduce heart disease and reduces the risk of Cancer. Beef Tallow is also high in Vitamin A, D, E and K including a very high level of Omega 3 Fatty Acids. It is rich in antioxidants.

CHAPTER 8

Beef Tallow is protective against metastatic breast tumors (Department of cell Biology and Human Anatomy, University of California, School of Medicine, Davis CA). It has always been ate by our ancestors until refinery oil took over and won the heart of many. Grass fed beef tallow is recommended.

Skin Care recipe: mixture of beef Tallow with the gel from the blue Agave plant.

More Knowledge more health advantage. Cinnamon is antibacterial and antifungal. Tahini is rich in essentials fatty acids. Seaweed is rich in iodine and protein. Tofu boast calcium, magnesium, folic acid and iron. Garlic is a natural antibiotic. Flaxseed oil encourages healing. Walnut should/can be eaten by people who have weaknesses of the lungs, or kidneys, daily on a regular basis. Lemon grass is an herb that is good for digestion and contributes in calming fever and muscles. Dandelion is a good source of rubber. It is also high in vitamin A, C, and iron and calcium.

The Sendha Namak contains calcium, iron, potassium, and magnesium including copper. It is one of the purest rock salt that ever existed. It aids in digestive disorders and removes gas while soothing in a case of a heart burn. Sendha Namak is also good for blood pressure, arthritis and asthma.

Food sources where we can get the mineral called **Vanadium** in largest amounts per serving include Shellfish, Parsley, dill weed and mushrooms; black pepper and spinach. The mineral vanadium helps manage **diabetes** mostly the **Type 2** type of diabetes.

Egg shell powder is a good source of calcium. It consist of 95 percent calcium carbonate that makes it very good to strengthen our bones, and teeth. In fact egg shells composition are as just our body bones and teeth making it probably the first choice or readily available calcium at hands. A powder of half a shell is sufficient for the daily calcium needed when consumed.

CHAPTER 9
Trees, Plants, Herbs and their Effective Cures

Disclaimer

The intent on this chapter is only to present to you with some information about the usage and benefits of herbs and trees. Herbs can be used in moderation and regularly to prevent certain specific diseases, or to cure them. Do not use herbs without your doctor's approval or your Certified Herbalist, or someone that have a great knowledge of herbs. All the information provided is not a prescription for you as you have not been diagnosed. It is best to know the medical history of the patient and of the herbs before taking or prescribing any herbal remedy. In my country, Burkina Faso, we commonly boil the leaves, roots or barks for about 10 to 20 minutes and drink a half cup or full cup a day for three days, sometimes up to a week or two even more, depending on the type of tree and disease. We also use the potion to wash our body simultaneously for the three day and inhale the vapor from the boiled potion each time for about three to five minutes (breathe in and breathe out). Some herbs are just merely use as tea. When it comes to herbs, dosage is very important and you should really consult with your physician, or an herbalist prior to.

Ficus Tree or Ficus Benjamin or Chui Ye Rang

The ficus tree is Anti-bacterial, Aphrodisiac, Maturant tonic, Styptic, vulnerary. The effective cures of the ficus are:

CHAPTER 9

biliousness, bruises, dysentery, headache, inflammation, leprosy, liver diseases and syphilis. The parts of the tree used are the roots, Bark and leaves.

Melisse/ Melissa

Good as honey or queen jelly. The effective cures are: nervousness, anxiety, herpes, digestives troubles, balance the thyroid.

The Olive Tree

The olive tree is anti-bacterial. You can use the bark, leaves and roots. For leaves 100-150 leaves (fresh)/ liter of water or 40-50 leaves when using dry leaves. Boil it and drink with moderation. The effective cures of the olive tree are; HIV/ ARC/ Aids, Urinary tract infections, Tuberculosis, Paludisme/ malaria, zona/ tiredness, Blennoragie, herpes I and II, cold, **diabetes**. It is an anti-oxidant and Improves cardiovascular health and brain functions.

In the ancient time, olive tree was considered a symbol of heavenly power and was called olea eur opaea in those days. It lowers bad cholesterol, lowers blood pressure, prevents cancer, protect against oxidative damage, helps guard against cognitive decline, contains antioxidant, anti-inflammatory and disease fighting characteristics. Improves arterial health, diabetes, cancer, and prevents inflammation in breast cancer, neuro-protection, arthritis, gout, rheumatoid, anti-aging, Alzheimer's, Parkinson's diseases and strokes.

The Magnolia Tree

Magnolia Bark has been used to treat various diseases which are: menstrual cramps, abdominal pain, abdominal bloating and gas, nausea, Indigestion, Abdominal distension, Loss of appetite, Gastro-enteritis, Vomiting, Diarrhea, asthma, coughs with acute phlegm, Anxiety, Weight loss; Alzheimer's disease, Malaria, Rheumatism, Typhoid, Ulcers and stress, bronchitis, amoebic dysentery, including digestive disorder.

The bark of magnolia and flower buds have been used to treat coughs and colds and intestinal problems. The active ingredient or chemical "honokiol" and "magnolol" found in the magnolia are up 1000 times more potent than vitamin E in antioxidant activity. It is anti-allergic, anti-asthmatic, anti-bacterial, anti-fungal, anti-septic, anti-spasmodic, anti-stress, anxiolytic, aphrodisiac, appetizer, and digestive, emmenagogue (a substance stimulation, or increasing menstrual flow), expectorant, ophthalmic, stomachic, tonic and warming.

Beetroot Benefits

It is first a nutritious vegetable that contains numerous vitamins and minerals that contribute to our overall health. Recent studies indicates that drinking beetroot juice can improve certain health conditions and can also improve oxygenation during athletic activities. Beetroot improves blood flow to the brain and can help by slowing down the progress of dementia. It contain potassium, calcium, sodium, magnesium and dietary nitrate.

You should note that potassium lowers the heart rate and regulates the metabolism of the body. Sodium and magnesium help with proper fluid levels well balanced within the body while the dietary nitrate contribute to lower the blood pressure making our heart healthier.

Beetroot is also rich in vitamin A, vitamin C and **Iron**. It contains folates that aid DNA synthesis within the cells. Beetroot becomes an important diet for people with **type-2 diabetes** as its fiber slows down the conversion of beetroot when consumed into glucose. It is also high in anti-oxidants and has anti-inflammatory effects. Beetroot is good for eyes, supports nervous system and beetroot helps build proteins in the body.

CHAPTER 9

Banana Peels

Banana peels are a good source of anti-oxidants. Great for depression, banana peels help you sleep better, lower the cholesterol, are good for skin treatment and teeth whitening, detoxes the body and encourages weight loss. The banana itself is very nutritious and loaded with potassium and magnesium. It moderates blood sugar levels while improving the health of our digestive system. Unripe bananas would even improve **insulin sensitivity**.

Moringa (300+ diseases cure)

Moringa lowers sugar, controls high blood pressure, reduces and regulates inflammation, keeps blood from excessive clotting. It reduces cytokines, Cholera, sore throat, fever, bronchitis, swollen glands; including chest congestion, headaches, ear infection. It also help treat Conjunctivitis (eye infection), high blood pressure and cholesterol. Moringa improves **insulin response** and promotes healthy membranes. It also regulates prostate gland in production.

Moringa is a God-given tree that has been used for centuries, even in the ancient time. It cures more than 300 diseases. The flowers and leaves contain Pterygospermin, a natural antibiotic, antiseptic and anti-fungicide that greatly contribute to your well-being.

Rosemary

The flowers tops contain antibacterial, antioxidant, anti-inflammatory, antifungal and antiseptic substances. Rosemary boosts memory, improves mood, reduces inflammation and relieves pain, strengthens the immune system, stimulates circulation, detoxifies the body of toxins built up over time. It is also good for skin conditions, anti-aging and protects against bacterial infections.

Grape Vine

Its leaves, roots and bark are rich in fiber, vitamin A, K, C, and E, B, minerals antioxidants, Iron, calcium, potassium, and magnesium antioxidant. Grape Vine combats memory loss, Inflammation, Fluid retention, Liver protection, Arthritis, Gastrointestinal diseases, Cancer, Alzheimer, Low glycemic load good for **diabetes patients** and Chronic venous insufficiency. Grape leaves reduce edema in patients with chronic venous insufficiency. It is a condition where the veins have difficulty returning blood in the legs back to the heart. The legs may swell when blood from the legs can-not make it back to the heart for a healthy and normal circulatory procedure causing then Edema. Grape vine can also treat sore throats, fever, headache and rheumatism, diarrhea including hepatitis, stomach ache, pain and thrush. Its leaves can be eaten or use as wrapper or fillings too.

Gumbi-Gumbi

Gumbi is proven to cure Cancer. It works well for all types of cancer. Prostate cancer, breast cancer, etc. As for cholesterol, it lowers cholesterol and triglycerides. It is an immune system booster. Gumbi is an antioxidant, anti-allergic, anti-viral and anti-bacterial. It kills Ecoli and bacilli's subtilis and staph. It is also an antifungal and anti-inflammatory. It eliminates the Candida fungi, lowers fevers, lowers blood pressure, cleanses blood, detoxes, improves the circulatory system, chronic fatigue syndrome, arthritis, skin disease and emphysema. It also improves mood, combats depression and helps treat auto immune disease- GI tract; heals all tissues, IBS (Irritable Bowel Syndrome), cramps and other GI diseases. Gumbi-Gumbi also helps with diverticulosis and the Meniere's disease. The Meniere's disease causes balance problems, vertigo, ringing in ears and hearing problems. (1 1/2 tea spoons of tea from the leaves per quart of water is effective). Drink 120 to 150 mls of the tea daily and there are no known side effect so far. Some people with prostate and breast cancer found that Gumbi worked better than traditional treatment. Always drink it with moderation and, of course, consult with your doctor.

California Pepper Tree

It possesses an anti-inflammatory salve, antimicrobial, antiseptic which protect against bacterial, viral and fungal infections. From candida and yeast infections, to tone balance and even strengthen the heart function. The California pepper tree is efficient for: Mild hypertension; act as regulator for arrhythmia, stops bleeding and heals wounds internally and externally, good for cold, flu, sore throats, upper respiratory infections, bronchitis, constipation, cough, cystitis, depression, diarrhea, eye disease, fever, gonorrhea, heart problems, hemorrhage, inflammation, rheumatism, spasms, tumors, urethritis, lung diseases, asthma, colic, cataract, conjunctivitis, constipation, digestive disorder, foot fungus, mouth sores, tuberculosis, ulcers, warts, uro genital diseases, fractures and venereal disease.

Eucalyptus

It has antimicrobial properties and helps cure those diseases and symptoms: **Diabetes**, colds, respiratory problems, strengthen teeth, treats fungal infections and wounds, Insect repellent, pain relief, stimulates immune system, treats congestion, muscles and joints pain. It also has antioxidants properties that reduces inflammation, cleanses urinary catheters, bronchitis, respiratory tract infections; fights bacteria causing tooth decays, fungal infection, wounds, arthritis. Eucalyptus tree possesses inflammatory properties as well that is good for blocked noses, wounds, and burns, ulcers, cold sores, bladder diseases and infections, diabetes/lowers blood sugar, fever and flu.

Pine Tree

Tea from the pine needles will afford a considerable amount of vitamin C, which is five times higher than the concentration of vitamin C in lemons. Pine tree is good for the treatment of various diseases which are: heart disease, varicose veins, skin complaints, fatigue, rich in antioxidant; reduces inflammation, protects against exercise-induced oxidation, strengthens the immune system, increases the production of white blood cells, vision health (rich in vitamin A,) skin and hair benefits, good for acne, pathogen protection.

It is antiseptic and improves the circulatory system, increases the oxygenation to your body's organs systems, **prevents anemia,** improves the respiratory health, sore throats, reduces and improves inflammation of the respiratory tracts, cough, asthma, excess mucus and phlegm, and neutralize any pathogens, or bacteria, found in your sinus.

Recipe for the tea.

10 needles in hot water for 15 minutes or boiled and drink as tea. Pine needle, cone, bark and resin hold medicinal qualities including the pine essential oil.

Guava Tree

It is one my favorite trees that works wonders and miracles like Iron. Its health benefits are as follow: diarrhea, diabetes and fights cancer, especially breast cancer, oral cancer, gastric cancer, prostate cancer. Guava tree, leaves and barks, boost the immune system, lowers cholesterol, promotes weight loss, normalizes blood pressure, improves the blood circulation in the brain, clears respiratory tracts, throat and lungs, reduces acne, improves skin, good for pain, toothache, swollen gums, oral ulcers, cold, cough, acne and above all promotes a heart health. You can use the leaves and barks at your convenience. Always under the supervision of your herbal specialist.

Lime Tree

The health benefits of the leaves are as follows: promotes oral health, detoxifies the blood, improves the health of hair, reduces stress, boosts immune system, improves digestion, keeps heart health on point, and is mind relaxing. It also lowers inflammation and acts as an antibiotic; it kills bacteria, influenza, is anti-cancerous, heals cough, throat thrush and Sprue (damage to the lining of the small intestine; celiac disease). Lime tree leaves improves hair and skin health. The good news is that we can even eat it just like salad with dressing to relax our mind. The fruits produce the same effects as well and drinking lime with water/or hot water improves your health tremendously and it is something that could be drunken daily with no reason.

Sage

Good for digestive problems, stomach pain (gastritis), bloating, gas (flatulence), diarrhea, loss of appetite and heart burns. It also helps with depression, memory loss, and Alzheimer's. Sage leaves curves the over production of saliva.

Orange Leaves

It improves digestion, boosts immune system, increases the health of the heart, and lowers blood pressure. Orange leaves help treat kidney stone or prevents it, reduces stroke probability and possesses a great amount of vitamin A, C, B1, iron, manganese, potassium, calcium and magnesium. It is anti-aging and you can eat its leaves just like salad and lime leaves. Orange leaves helps treat **diabetes**, flu, influenza and cancer. One orange daily provides the full day vitamin C that the body needs.

Cashew (Anacardium accidentale)

Cashew is a good snack with a lot of healthy ingredients. You can make tea with its barks and leaves to relieve pain and upset stomach. The cocktail is also good when having digestive problems as it treats diarrhea to facilitate a good bowel. You can also enjoy the oil from cashew nuts to remove warts, corns and freckles. Even dysentery stops where there are cashew barks and leaves.

Cassava (Manihot Esculenta)

You can eat cassava leaves as vegetable and as salad when steamed. It is a good source for anti-poison when applied to snake bite. A lot of people also use the leaves for external ulcers, eczema and abscesses. It relieves headache when leaves are applied to the head like a towel.

Kinkeliba (Sekhew/ Combretum)

This is a tree that you will most likely find in West Africa. It is known for its efficiency to treat liver infections and improve its ability to produce the bile for a good digestion. During chronic constipation and gastro-intestinal complications, it is highly recommended as it contributes to a good digestion making the Kinkeliba leaves and barks a good source to cure most of the anomalies that are not favorable to a healthy digestive system. Good in treating patients with high blood pressure; it also helps wounds heal quicker and alleviates pain. It is anti-inflammatory, anti-bacterial, making the tree good for malaria, bloating and obesity as it detoxify the body and increases the volume of piss. 30 g of leaves for a liter of water boiled and drink as tea preferably in early mornings but could be taken at any time of the day. Always consult your doctor too.

Neem tree

Its leaves and barks are used to cure multiple diseases, including leprosy and bloody nose. It takes care of almost all form of eye disorders. It kills intestinal worms and soothes stomach upset. The neem intake improves appetite, addresses skin ulcers issues and reduces fever. It helps cure the diseases of the heart and blood vessels (cardiovascular disease). Treats diabetes, gingivitis, and liver infections and disorder. Neem is a strong anti-inflammatory agent; a strong antioxidant that would neutralize free radicals within the body causing diseases. It fights against bacteria, viruses and the fungi thanks to its antimicrobial properties. Very efficient for malaria disease and

CHAPTER 9

helps protect/strengthen teeth from toothaches. Neem can also be used to neutralize lice when head and scalp are washed from the boiled leaves and barks.

Acacia Tree

Acacia is a good source of fiber. It is good for high cholesterol patients and contributes to weight loss. It relieves pain, stomach pain and irritation while helping wounds heal faster. It also soothes coughs and sore throat while taking care of the overall oral health. Acacia is efficient at removing toxins from the body and as a prebiotic, it promotes "good" bacteria in the intestine. It also would take care of the irritable bowel syndrome (IBS), hemorrhoids and restricts blood loss during cuts or gashes. It promotes a general cardiovascular health.

Mango Tree

High in antioxidants, mango can boost your immune system. It presents a great benefit by improving the digestive system and health. It is good for heart diseases and diabetes. It also strengthen bone health which could be a great benefit for old age people. It regulates and stabilizes the sugar levels in the blood and increases the distribution of glucose making it very efficient for people with **diabetes**. Rich in many nutrients such as pectin, fiber and vitamin C, mango can be consumed daily. It may prevent and helps cure cancer while taking a major role in protecting and guaranteeing the eyes health. It also may improve hair and skin health. It prevents asthma. The juice cocktail made from mango leaves and barks are to be drink with moderation. Enjoy its fruits also and feel free to add it with your salad.

Papaya Tree

Papaya leaves, seeds and fruits contain a powerful antioxidant that kill the free radicals in the body. It is good for the heart and prevents cholesterol from building up in your arteries. Its leaves juice is a good source of fiber, vitamin C, E, A, K, B and beta-carotene that boost the immune system. Good for diabetics as it checks the blood sugar levels and regulates the production of insulin. Papaya protects against arthritis and improves digestion. Papaya fights inflammation and helps ease menstrual pain. It is great for your eyes health and may even help you lose weight. It contains minerals like calcium, magnesium, sodium and iron. It cures the Dengue fever, prevents bloating and other digestive disorders while increasing the platelet count. It is very good against malaria, dengue; papaya cleanse the liver, which means that it would heal many chronic liver diseases, such as jaundice and liver cirrhosis. It would even prevent constipation and clean the colon while preventing stomach ulcers. Papaya leaf juice can also fight liver cancer, lung cancer, pancreatic cancer and breast cancer. It help treat erectile dysfunction. At last, it promotes hair growth and skin health. Enjoy the fruits and make it a habit to eat them constantly.

LOQUAT TREE AND HEALTH BENEFITS

The seed of the loquat crushed with its leaves can be applied to wounds and aches. Loquat Combats pain. The fruit and leaves are a good source of pectin, iron, potassium, vitamin A, C, and fiber. The Loquat tree possesses the very essentials to booster the overall human health. It contains almost all the vitamin B complex vitamins like thiamine, riboflavin, niacin, pyridoxine, folates and folic acid.

It is also a good source of minerals like calcium, manganese, potassium, phosphorous, zinc, copper, selenium and carbohydrates. It even contains the omega 3 and 6 fatty acids. It possesses its own cytokine immune modulation abilities which remains unique in loquat.

Since Loquat in itself possesses its own cytokine immune modulation abilities, it has been proven beneficial in cancer therapy. Its Laetrile is known to be an anti-cancerous agent. Fights against Colon cancer. Indeed its potent pectin retains moisture and helps smooth the colon while protecting the colon mucous membrane by reducing and decreasing the time the toxic substance will remain in the colon thereby banding the cancer causing substance in the colon.

The therapeutic power of loquat is contained in the **green leaves**. It promotes skin, respiratory and intestinal health; weight loss, diabetes and glow the skin. Loquat leaves improves eye vision, controls cancer, maintains blood pressure by facilitating the absorption of nutrients and good for the liver. Eases throat infections. Its seed controls heart rate and is a good source of essential minerals when consumed. It also helps fight memory impairment, neurological and oxidative stress. Loquat is loaded with anti-inflammatory and analgesic properties.

The Health Benefit of Artemisia

Artemisia contains anti-inflammatory, anti-pyretic (reduces fever), properties. It is chemotherapeutic, meaning that Artemisia can kill cancer cells. It also contains anti-microbial and anti-fungal properties that kill bacteria, viruses, and funguses. Artemisia leaves, bark are very good for the treatment of malaria, hepatitis, cancer, inflammation, and menstrual related disorders. It help cure most gastro-intestinal problems, anorexia, indigestion, including our respiratory system problems and liver diseases. Artemisia is also used to kill parasites. In South Africa, it is known as "wilde als" and is used for colds, cough, diabetes, heartburns, bronchitis, asthma and diarrhea including all sort of nervous diseases. Artemisia is also known to be very effective against breast cancer and the Human Immuno-deficiency Virus (HIV) and a paste of the leaves is used externally on skin diseases, cuts, wounds and ringworm. Artemisia plant has been used in ancient times as an anthelmintic, antispasmodic, anti-rheumatic and antibacterial agents.

BENEFIT OF COCONUT OIL

It contains fatty acids with medicinal properties; it can increase fat burning and can help kill harmful microorganisms. Coconut oil can also reduce hunger because it helps you eat less and can even reduce seizures. It also Increases the brain functions and raises the good HDL cholesterol in your blood, thereby, reducing heart disease risk. Coconut oil is very good for providing energy quickly as the special fat that it contains goes straight to the liver and from there the creation of ketones is also good for the brain. Some cancer patients were even advised to ingest couple of spoon of the oil as therapy.

Good for epilepsy and Alzheimer. It has both lauric acid and monolaurin that kill bacteria, viruses, and fungi. It even can kill the Staphylococcus aureus, (a very dangerous pathogen) and the yeast Candida albicans (a yeast infections in humans). It also treats drug resistant epilepsy in children. Protect your skin, hair and dental health. Boost brain function in Alzheimer disease patient. It helps you lose fat especially the harmful Abdominal Fat (belly fat). 2 tablespoon per day for 4 to 12 weeks could help you lose weight. Please choose organic, virgin coconut oil and not the refine ones under the supervision of your physician or herbal doctor.

Here is a generic treatment to revive dead cells or cells that attacks the immune system from an unknown author suggestion yet not a medical prescription for you:

First things first is to categorically stop eating sugar. Second, blend a whole lemon fruit with a cup of hot water and drink it every day/morning for one (1) to three (3) months. And to finish with 3 spoonful of organic coconut oil every morning before food and every night before food.

Prickly Pear, Cactus, Opuntia

Each prickly pear is loaded with high levels of dietary fiber, potassium, Vitamin C, B-family vitamins, calcium, magnesium, copper, taurine, flavanoids, polyphenols and betalains. The fruit upon a bite would afford you with your energy needs for the day. The cactus juice lowers blood pressure, blood sugar, heals wounds and lowers cholesterol. The Nopal cactus and pads prevents so many diseases from forming when consumed regularly. It has antioxidants and anti-inflammatory properties. It is also antiviral, and protects nerve cells, can treat enlarged prostate and eliminate hangovers.

Antiviral Herbs and their Use

Antiviral herbs boost your immune system, fight infection and protect your body from viruses and bacteria.

Elderberry

Elderberry could help treat Influenza A, B, Herpes, viral infections, bacterial infections. The flowers, the barks and roots are what is used, including the leaves. It kills viruses and bacteria causing diseases.

Echinacea

It reduces virus infection and tumors, alleviates pain, and improves skin problems. It helps treat upper respiratory issues and Improves mental health. It is good for cold, flu, controls blood sugar and lowers the blood pressure. Echinacea may help reduced the risk of breast cancer while aiding a healthy cell growth within the body. You can also drink to manage your stress and anxieties.

Licorice Root

It helps cure hepatitis C, HIV and influenza due to its triternoid. Licorice roots possess antioxidant properties providing a free radical scavenging and immuno-stimulating effects that combats Sore throats, Cough; protects against leaky gut signs and symptoms. It helps heal adrenal fatigue and Pain relief.

Oregano

The oil of oregano is proven to be superior to some antibiotics, without the side effects that could be harmful.

It contains two powerful compounds carvacrol and thymol that possess powerful antibacterial and antifungal properties. It's the carvacrol that reverses viral infections, as well as allergies, tumors, parasites and diseases causing inflammation. The leaves can also be used as tea to lower the cholesterol level, to improve Gut health, to help treat Yeast infections, to relieve pain and even help fight cancer.

Ginger (used in Ayurveda medicine)

Ginger warms the body, boosts the immune system and breaks down accumulation of toxins in your organs. It cleanses the lymphatic system, cleanses your body sewage system and prevents the accumulation of toxins. Ginger combats nausea, pain alleviation, anti-inflammation and improves diabetes. It relieves morning sickness, menstrual cramps, muscle pain, soreness, and osteoarthritis and lowers blood sugar.

Cat's Claw

Cat's Claw is known to be effective for: arthritis, ulcer symptoms, herpes, HIV, anti-inflammation, antibacterial, and antifungal, digestives problems such as ulcers, Irritable bowel syndrome, colitis and leaky gut syndrome, gastritis. It is use as a dietary supplement for Alzheimer's disease, cancer, diverticulitis, hemorrhoids, peptic ulcers and parasites. Cat's claw boosts the immune system response and helps calm an overactive immune system.

Olive Leaf

Olive leaf possesses Antiviral properties. It is effective for Cold, Candida symptoms, Meningitis, Pneumonia,

CHAPTER 9

Chronic fatigue syndrome, Hepatitis B, Malaria, Gonorrhea, Tuberculosis, Dental infections, Ear infections, Urinary tracts infections, Shingles, Influenza, Respiratory infections and HIV. I have already provided more detail health information about the olive tree at the beginning of this chapter.

Astragalus Roots

It boosts the immune system, Prevent common flu, Herpes I, Inhibit the growth of coxsackie B virus. It's one of the seven adaptogen herbs to lower Cortisol. The Astragalus roots contribute in balancing and relieving stress level due to the herbs revitalizing and restorative properties thereby enhancing and improving health wholly. Among the remaining seven adaptogen herbs are: Amla, Ashwagandha, Cordyceps, Eleuthero, Holy Basil, Maca and we can add rhodiola, ginseng and ginger. You usually drink these as tea to relieve stress and stress signs. (Use centuries back in Ayurvedic medicine, African and Chinese medicine).

Adaptogens are herbs with stimulant properties that help counteract the effects of stress within our body. Stress damages and causes a real physical changes within the body mostly targeting our neurological, endocrine and immune systems. So the adaptogens herbs help and counteract those harmful effects from stress in our body while lowering the level of Cortisol within the blood.

Cortisol is a steroid hormone secreted by the adrenal glands into the blood. The said hormones help control our body blood sugar levels, blood pressure, regulate metabolism and the immune system response. The most important fact to remember is that Cortisol is release into the body during time of stress. And the more we stress and again and again, chances are we might end up having an elevated cortisol level that might cause blood sugar imbalances (type 2 diabetes), weight gain, obesity, immune system suppression, gastrointestinal problems, cardiovascular disease and fertility problems. The good news is that there is a test now available to determine the level of Cortisol called the Adrenal Stress Index (ASI). There are a salivary test and a blood Cortisol test. Please take note that during chronic stress and long term or prolonged stress and elevated cortisol could lead to insomnia, chronic fatigue syndrome, thyroid disorder, dementia and depression.

Garlic

Garlic intake helps fight a various number of diseases such as: tuberculosis, pneumonia, thrush, herpes, eye infection, and natural ear infection; reduces risk of cancer (lungs, prostate, brain Cancers), Controls hypertension and Boosts cardiovascular health. You can boil it and drink the liquid or crunch it and swallow. Most people just use garlic in their cooking daily and it add a great flavor to any food too. It improves Cholesterol level which reduce the risk of any heart disease and also reduces blood pressure. It has a powerful antibiotic and can be used in Hip osteoarthritis.

Calendula

It protects cells from being damaged by free radicals. It also heals cut faster and treat ear infections. Calendula oil has antifungal, anti-inflammatory and antibacterial properties. The oil can be used in healing wounds, eczema and relieving diaper rash. Its flower is also used to prevent muscle spasms and reduce fever. It can be drunken as tea for cramps, menstrual pain, sore throat, cold and mouth while detoxifying your body and boosting your immune system. So, you should add it to your weekly health regimen. Calendula also eases the hormonal fluctuations during menstruation. Pregnant woman should stay away from drinking it because the tea can induce menstruation as well.

Chili

Chili helps fight cancer, diabetes, arthritis, stomach and digestive system. It is ideal for headache, and weight management. The phytochemicals that it possesses fight diseases and the hotter the better. Adding chili into your diet would benefit your digestive tract and promote a healthy heart. It could even fight common cold, flu and fungal infections. It is good for Quells psoriasis while improving your body metabolism and fight inflammation. If you want to add a little vitamin C in to your chili, just squeeze some lime juice in it. Cayenne pepper has been shown to reduce blood cholesterol, triglyceride levels and platelet aggregation. It would even protect the fats in your blood from damage by free radicals and boost your immune system.

Recipe Based on Chili

Heat up 2 cups of olive oil and ¼ cup of beeswax on low. Stir up the mixture until it is well together, and slowly add 2 tables spoon of chili/ habanero powder. Continue stirring up the mélange until well incorporated. Put the mixture in a jar and regularly use it with your food daily at your convenience. It can even curb diabetes by 24 percent, prevent stomach ulcers, clear congestions and alleviate arthritis. Chili pepper possesses some vitamin E, A, K, B6, B2, B3, fiber, cooper, iron and manganese.

½ teaspoon = 2.5 ml
1 teaspoon = 5ml
½ tablespoon = 7.5ml
1 tablespoon = 15ml

Black Pepper health benefit

The use of black pepper improves the digestive system, lowers blood pressure, protects against cancer and fight infections. Black pepper contains an antioxidant properties and is also antimicrobial with gastro-protective modules. It helps reduce depression, reduce cold and cough while promoting some weight loss. Above all, black pepper is a rich source of calcium making it a perfect match for elderly people with weaker bones. It is known that drinking hot water with black pepper daily for 30 days improves health tremendously in general. It may benefit your brain, improve blood sugar control. It fights free radicals out of your body in protecting the cells from being damage and improve nutrient absorption.

Clove Health benefit

Clove strengthens the immune system, smooth digestion and reduces stomach ulcers. Its intake improves the oral health including gingivitis and strengthen bones. Clove helps regulate blood sugar, improves liver health, kills bacteria and protects against cancer. It is commonly known that clove oil is good for acne and pain reliever. It possesses a great deal of antioxidants, anti-inflammatory and antibacterial effects. Cloves are also rich in vitamins and minerals such as manganese, calcium, fiber, vitamin K, C, E.

Walnut soup is good to promote health and help the womb of pregnant woman that just gave birth. It help the womb recover and shrink. At the same token, rice and milk would promote a healthy production of maternal milk for the baby. (Chinese tradition)

Consuming bananas, oranges and drinking orange juice during the first very two years of life may greatly reduce the risk of developing childhood Leukemia. It is a combination of fiber, chlorine, potassium and plenty of vitamin C which promotes a good heart health.

The Jamaican Chew sticks (Gouania Lupuloides) when used as a toothpaste, or simply chewing removes tartar, stops the gums from bleeding and even kill's bacteria causing tooth decay while tightening any loosen teeth.

Kola Nut is also called bissy in Jamaica. The powder Kola Nut helps heal cuts and bruises when directly applied. It is also used as an antidote against poison. In a small doses, kola nut treats migraine, morning sickness and improves appetite.

CHAPTER 9

The Jamaican Leaf of Life (Bryophyllum Pinatum), also known as love bush, or live forever, is used as a tea for shortness of breath, kidney failure, menstrual problems, asthma, chest colds and bronchitis. It treats intestinal and urinary infections. Good for insect bites, bruises, boils and skin ulcers.

Green onion with their roots soaked in some water overnight is good in helping cure diabetes. Drink it with moderation.

The red kidney beans are rich in healthy fibers which are good for people with diabetes as it moderate blood sugar levels and promote colon health as well. It is a good source of vitamins and minerals such as molybdenum, folate iron, cooper, manganese, potassium, vitamin k1 and phosphorus. Red beans are beneficial to people with diabetes because of its slow nature of release of glucose. The starch takes longer to digest and causes lower and more gradual rise of blood sugar compare to other starch.

Bridelia Ferrugina for diabetes cure. From the West African country Benin. 40 leaves boiled or soaked in 1 Liter of water; drink mornings and evenings for eight weeks. Normalize sugar level.

CHAPTER 10
Everyone and Everything, Tangible or not, Breathe and Sustain Life

One day I went to use the restroom and as I was standing and looking up, I saw a roach in the sink. My first instinct I struck the roach and I missed. The object I used to hit the roach fell in the sink and covered the sink water exit that leads to the underground water pipe where the roach could have escaped through. Now that I have noticed that the roach can no longer run to the sink underworld, I stood now and took a piss as that's why I was in the restroom to start with. When I finished then, and during the time of my peeing, options where running in my mind. Would I kill it? Should I kill it? No. why not? What other solution could I do?

While growing up, grown people struck and killed the roaches with no regard as soon as a roach was sighted. Poom, bang sound you will hear and the rest is history; another roach is dead. The reason we have insects in our houses is because of their migration instincts. Food is the primary reason roaches are in your house and residence as well. Everyone needs food, including the insects and flies. Even insects migrate and stay away from hostile territories and foodless households. Migration is part of life.

The history from any part of the world have always involve migration. People move around for personal needs and self-fulfillments. Birds migrate, too, including all wild life wherever they are. Even plants and trees migrate. When the winds blow

CHAPTER 10

the seed to the next location; when bees, elephants and all other insects transport food/seed and drop it in a disperse manner seemingly, those seeds grow to a tree later after the rain. There is an order in all things even when we think otherwise. Every living being deserves respect and acknowledgment as each one of us has a job to do. Humans cannot do the work of the ants and the ants cannot perform the duties of the bees, either. When you take one or so many species out of existence, the eco-system would become unbalanced. It follows then, that there will be a vacant post, or position, and a necessity task that would not be performed since every species have their specific job assignment embedded in their DNA. An elephant would not be able to replace a crab, or a bird role within the eco-system.

Even rocks become precious metals by changing their molecular structure through time and turn to crystals. Just like some carbons under extreme heat and pressure transform to diamonds and caterpillars evolve to butterflies. Therefore, any life-form wherever they are or their conditions of existence; mineral, vegetal, animal and of course human breathe and sustain life by evolving to become a precious being or enlighten. A Bird could lead you to the Gods just like a man could.

What is everybody's role in the universe?

What is that is created that does not have a role in our existence? You seating imagining things and they materialize but you can dare consume what others have created. Others other than us. Others that exist in communion with us. As nothing exist by himself but who is He. What it is that you are not? Think about it; light, glory, time or space? Inclusive you would remain as none can defy himself. Either way, nature and life takes their courses; Light versus darkness. Sometimes, we see those in the light or darkness, sometimes we don't see them. Sometimes, they can also see us, sometime they don't see us.

CHAPTER 10

The hide and seek game of the dead soul and the living soul is recurrent and no one escapes it. Sometime, the souls from the living share space and even dwell in the same house with the souls of the dead people. This usually happen when people die and their souls are still here on earth. They would live in the same houses that we are living in, in most cases. Their souls could also occupy parks, temples, libraries, museums, street corners, vacant houses, hills, etc. Sometimes, they see us and we don't. People that are yet dead but their souls refused to leave this dimension. Either they could see the light and refused to enter or they cannot yet see, for they are blinded by an unfinished business to handle on this dimension. Each dimension has its inhabitant accordingly.

Wickedness is all about knowing and not taking actions in a positive way. Actions are some fruits we sow and they would grow as if a fruit get the required nutrients and favorable soil, it always grows and becomes a tree that later gives fruits. Upon maturity, all the fruits are then harvested and later will be consumed and digested. If the seed of that same tree harvested is planted and benefits from favorable conditions, it would also become a tree and give fruits like the previous seed and so on.

Not all seed are good. Some seeds don't give fruits. No question asked. Don't ask if a fruit is cursed at its core to start with and cannot become a tree, nor produce fruits. Even the gods have preferences.

We are a result of a creation, or a self-realization. We decide what to do. But, sometimes, it is hard. The heart is willing, but the mind is lacking strength. Sometimes, the mind is alive, vivid and want to be productive, but the heart doesn't feel like it and lacks compassion toward creativity and vitality. Then, we get stuck, battling with our own demons and angels. Forgetting that we are but it shall be realized. If we are not glorious, we can miss the light and darkness will overcome us, with the emphasis that it is just a matter of polarity. Light and darkness could become one when we become able to make up our minds and combine them together.

CHAPTER 10

Cycle after cycle, we progress. Who is the one that does not go through phases? We learn, and we experience. We subtract and add; divide and multiply. We remain neutral often but, most of the time, we puzzle and scramble our way back into the underworld. In fact, many of us started from the underworld before making our way back to divine truth. Was it our choice to start with that there exist an underworld?

No question asked and absolutely not. Because you cannot ask that question until you know and experience something else. A growth indeed. You just become and it is what it is. Your consciousness of being late in life makes it difficult to know exactly what has happened when you were a baby. When your senses were not barely develop according to outsiders. Ready you were, but consciously you were not. Maybe you were, but who else would have known but you? I don't remember but existence knows and can recall the stages of total innocence and the stage of total vulnerability, including the stage of total no self but existence. Present you were. Present we were, but aware? I don't know and I doubt it for a lot of other people. You do realize that someone can be alive, living but lacking consciousness of life? Maybe we were just alert during those stages of life. One thing for sure is that, we could only cry when we need something. We yell and even get angry when what we want is taking longer than we expected, according to our own clock and patience limit. That is what is called the stage of selfishness, the unconscious mind, that is disconnected with the world, or the people around them and the essence of life Itself.

In sum, there is always something that we would not remember. There is also something we hide from the view of others, just as there is always something we don't want others to know, or experience. Strong ones try to hide their feelings and emotions. Weak ones spill it out and express whatever they want with no restrains. Could we really pass a judgment, because there is at least one day that we have acted like a fool with no regards for any consequences, or people around us. I say to you to always try to remain calm and listen to the angel voice as there will always be someone reminding us of the way. To this point, only God knows why we have made it so far without being in trouble. The story of the roach ends with what I call the zigzag. Some get caught committing the same crimes and others don't. Even those that are caught would not benefit a partial judgment. Therefore, my friends, I say into you that there is a laughter of the hands of God. We would not know ourselves until we push ourselves to do better than yesterday. Which means today is the place to make it right. To try it again one more time, even though most people are idiots as we all are, or were idiots at one point. Beat them in their own game. Today, you may have a ride and tomorrow, nobody gives a damn about you. So live today and remain present like tomorrow is never coming.

Do you know who you are?

Settlers; Yes, we are camping and contemplating dominion. We question whether we are truly who we are, realizing by now that there will always be challenges we will face. Even the newborn baby has known challenges, as life in itself, is a burden that one has to cry when the very first breath is taken outside of the womb or shelve. One has to feel the pain of birth as mothers put out tears when delivering a baby. Life is our unique existentiality and we are living, regardless, with no questions asked. No one chooses to come here and no one chooses to be born on this planet called Earth. But really?

If we don't remember what happened when we were babies, how can we remember what we have done and caused our very birth into existence to another dimensions or through whom we were born from. From where, you would asked. Where were we before we got here? But really how can I tell you? Who I am; the know it all? No one ever said that birth only happens in the physical matter. Even in the spirit, we bear children. What do you know about that?

CHAPTER 10

Imagine if we knew it all, our brain would explode. There is a capacity reach for each brain to keep the sanity of the person sustainable. Limits have been placed upon us that forgetting is a must so that we can get an enjoyment of different choices and growth. We live. We grow. We birth, we create and exist. In order for us to live in the present, we have to be able to forget, forgive and leave the past behind. To answer to the question, you are not the voice you hear in your mind. You are not your skin color or belong to a group of race. You are the one that hear and listen to the voices inside your mind. You are the being that is aware of its own essence through awareness and being present. You are here to rediscover your true Self. Your purpose is to be aware of your role in the universe as a pawn and do the will of God by understanding and following the laws.

What do we now do with the Laws? Do you know them?

CHAPTER 11
Secrets: The Most Shared Qualities of the World

What is it that we are all hiding? Our dirty secrets that fade as we deposit more pile of secrets on top of the old ones. Secret after secret, we become unrecognizable even to ourselves. A secret does not necessarily mean a lie. It is just something we prefer to keep away from people, or only sharable with to a select few. With, in mind that once a secret is shared, it ceases to become a secret.

When secrets move to become lies that we are hiding away from the sight and ears from others, then we may end up losing ourselves in our own secrecy. Hoping that our secrets won't be discovered and kicked out to the spotlight. The burden of keeping a really bad secret, or ultimate secret, can put a heavy weight on someone's shoulder. We don't look back, but we are looking over our shoulders because the irony is that someone else may end up finding out about our secret, or knew it from the start.

Some secrets are shared knowledge that only a few people within a circle know about. It could be only the initiated that possesses those secrets and vow to keep silence, even to their most loyal friends and family members.

Secrets, when they are revealed, can be a life saver or a life taker. A secret exposed could lead to war, vengeance, or peace, love and reconciliation. We never can fully foresee what a consequence of a secret, when revealed, could engender. But each one of us may have at least one hanging on our shoulders. And the secret to moving past your secrets is to make peace with yourself. Forgive yourself to stop the mind from reminding you of your dirty secrets, or special secrets. And, if after letting go, your mind keeps trying to play guilt tricks over and over, when it happens, just remind your mind that you have moved on. Forgive and that chapter is closed with no further notice.

The Burden of life on our Shoulders

Each shoulder carries a weight. A weight that we actually don't really be paying mind to. The weight on the shoulders could be balanced, or uneven. Yes, indeed, one might be heavier than the other. But, it is still balanced at some point because of the choices of shoulder that exist. Meaning each shoulder reflects a record, according to our actions. Fears, in general, relative to our brain and neck pull, through our spine. Good deeds might be on the right and bad deeds on the left, or vice-versa. Guilt, remorse, worries, sadness, lack of self-love would each have a specific shoulder to lean on. Thereby, holding and adding unnecessary energies and pressure to the point of blocking the energy from flowing throughout. Who really knows but I leave that task for you to find. Either we are shielding on top of our shoulders, having our head up in normal standard position, or our head on the side on either one of the shoulder. Which side of the shoulder we know only if we take a minute to consider and pay mind to which side our head is mostly leaning to? Who we are and what we have been exposed to, regularly energy wise, or whatever secrets we are hiding away from the world, could also determine the position of our head resting position on our shoulders. Too much societal pressure and too much big responsibilities affect also our standard posture position. Some people would curve forward with a bend forward spine. Some people would curve to the point that their face is now looking down, and they have to make a real effort to look up and keep their head and neck straight.

Our present is the accumulation of what we have done and what has been done to us; what we have heard and how we have handled every aspect of our life; how we dealt with our emotions and how our constant state of mind is. Hopefully, you will make peace with any secrets you are holding and cannot reveal, nonetheless. Do not let the secrets' energies keep you from sleeping or resting, instead forgive yourself and move on.

The Forces and Mighty Behind Our Thoughts

Every writer hesitates. There are days, ideas and creation flow in your mind and you just deliberately say no; I'm not writing right now and hope to remember, just to realize that not all of them, those ideas and thoughts will come back when you are ready. Maybe they do come back in time, during time, as we keep living. Thoughts are like a boomerang. If you throw a thought away, it comes right back at you with the same intensity. The thought has to be covered. It has to be empowered. It has to be dealt with now. Are there any thoughts that has no power?

Every thought from any living being produces a mass, or comes out as a mass, which carries a force. The thought, as a gravitational force, would gravitate towards manifestation of whatever the one that expressed the thought desires it to do/be. The thought could be positive, or negative, depending on which side you are on, or the desired goal for the moment, including your moods. That's why light and darkness as of good and evil forces can be drawn and are equally accessible and at hands. The same person could use the energy to do good today, or use it to do bad tomorrow. Energy follows orders and good and bad reside are only a matter of polarization.

Thoughts and deeds never get lost. They embody themselves through the bloodline as an umbilical cord. Blood, we all share, pay the price, or reap the benefits of our forefathers' thoughts and deeds. The fruits from the tree.

CHAPTER 11

Some would try to neglect the link, but even DNA from science proves such a deep connection between family members.

Survival, imprint; the goodness of the past overshadows and balances off the bad of the present and vise-versa. We can redeem from others. Others can also redeem from us. Your goodness in heart covers a multitude of sin, or evil of others, or loved ones. We heal each other. We curse each other. We rinse the back of each other. If it's not yours, it is mine. If I'm not the one rinsing your back, it is you that is rinsing my back.

Everybody has a keeper. Everybody has an angel and angels, looking out and protecting him/her. Regardless of one's impulse, good or bad in dominion, we are all survival species. We protect what is ours. We protect what we believe, if a reason is there to sympathize and show love and loyalty to, or simply disregard. What is bad for you is not necessarily bad for me. And what is bad for me may not be for you, either. Each one of us on the top of the pyramid feel different vibes, depending on the energy directed to them/us and their/our present state of minds. On that note, it becomes even more difficult to judge people because, truly, we may pretend to know them, but we actually don't know their family tree. The one that predetermined each one of us. Therefore, can I blame you? Can I exclude you? Can I assume things about you? Can I even contemplate knowing my next fellow man and other beings?

I think no. We are who we are. They are who they are. Putting you in a box is a mistake because I don't know you. Because you don't really know yourself either. So how can I know you when you don't even fully know and understand yourself? Let me know you and teach me who you are. I only have an idea of what you are made of, the same atom just like me.

God, you are the most that exist and no one can truly know and see you until you decide to show yourself to him/her.

Ambitious, we are. Rising together, we are. Each one in its own angle. Battling its own mind. Battling its own demons and angels. What if they were the same? Duality, Balance, Yin, yang, would confirm that demons and angels are needed to keep the balance of any organism. Each thing and its opposite? We are indeed in pieces that need to be reassembled at a personal and individual basis. Our mind is torn in pieces. Our soul is in pieces. Unity is the whole global sphere that conclude the circle; a rising sun. Life and death are inseparable as no one can grow without dying just as no one can cease to grow without regressing which is a growth in itself when looking from the other side of the angle. Each angle yet complementary is constantly in orbit with us at a constant basis; a simultaneous end and a beginning. While living leads closer to death inevitably, death, in return is also living closer reciprocally. There is no meaning of life without death. Death actually makes life more exiting and before we grow higher in spirit, something of a lesser has to die.

CHAPTER 12
What is it that is New under the Sun?

We, as human beings, have always transcended humanity to the core of our lungs. Saying this is to say that whatever that is to searched, or looked for, is always a product of a fruit that have matured and then have been consumed just like every other thing coming from the Tree of knowledge. It has had a beginning and an end at a continuous basis. Once something is discovered and made final, what else is left if not improving it, or starting another project? Wasn't that discovery already included of things possible of manifestation? Do we really add anything new on this universe? Can we honestly say with confirmation that anything that we have discovered was never known by the past citizens far long ago? We know that the world is billions of billions years old comparatively to us, yet humans cannot even live up to 200 years old. I believe everything that we do has already been done and was already there as an option. We didn't find that thing up from nowhere. It was already scripted for us. We just chose that route among a multitude of routes to express ourselves. Fornication exists because we each have sexual parts and hormones that want satisfaction; we are able to kill each other because hate and anger want to live also. Now what is end, is it really and if so, where did it began or end the first time?

I don't know but I can guarantee you that we are the product of the seed that is that will always be. Be fruitful, the word says, and one question subsists, fruitful in what? When someone creates you and gives you an order to be fruitful, that person has an intention to His/her creation alive at all time. Right?

CHAPTER 12

Life is a paradox, resting on twanging realities that occurs accordingly thereby giving us options. Choices we are stuck in a place or location, just to realize that we can make good use of every instant passing and going. We are a product of adaptation. Fruitful indeed, we adapt. We change at every constant second and as survivors, we are all instinct to do what is best for us. Put a man in a situation where he has to survive and you will make him a lion. Mankind's preoccupation will depend on the love and sympathy he will feel when in a situation that requires an imminent action to be taken. When you put man in a situation like this, where he is forced to make a choice, different people will always have different reactions.

Some may still posed and wonder what to do? Others would not even hesitate to take action. Same situation different reactions because we have adapted as survivals with different skills, temper and don't always like to do the same things at the same time. That's what we are made of and who we are. Only few are conscious of the sphere (world) that we are living in. They want to ask questions to find out the purpose of life but they lack the courage to do so. They know that they are able to move around freely, able to create but still have not thought pass needing food to eat or wine to drink. Able to breathe into existence life itself for ourselves and others, but still not realizing that we are nothing else than life itself. Life we are, no more, no less. What else can it be if not a product of a junction between what we could see and imagine and the ones that created us?

As above, so below. Everything that we see here and known as knowledge and infinity, are just as above. Creation, we have never cease to create since we were created by Gods. Every day, we create. As we think, so the creation is effective. Reality is our thoughts. Express, and edible, we are our expression and our value is the dividend of how we perceived, want, and need. We are our present action coupled with a constant creativity every second. Choices we have and good ones we have made. Bad ones, we have also made. Who has not took the test and

CHAPTER 12

failed? Therefore, the universe is into us and not the other way around. There is no other reality but the ones we are able to realize and conceptualize.

We have all did fail at some point while taking the test of life. And it is a constant struggle as living in itself requires an effort, know-how and energy. We each wrestling with its own demon. What and which demon, you figure it out. Everyone's has a demon in them that needs to be tamed and subdue. Demons constantly irritate and takes over a person thoughts and dominion to influence that person's own desires and wishes. Just like a demon having a mission to fulfill like an agenda of its own and/or for its peers, we are also victim of the universal manifestation of things and order. Realities of existence that we share roots with. Not realizing what the past was tainted of, we have no clue of the Story of the Keepers or the Watchers from the Book of Enoch.

Now spirits do exist. Demons versus angels, a question of polarity. Which side are you because we have all been on both side when egoism was the center and motivation of our lives? Then it becomes vise-versa, Ying and yang and duality balancing and upholding the survival of humanity. But don't forget in this case that balancing does not means necessarily an equal repartition. Light or darkness are not necessarily in equal proportion. The light could outshine the darkness just like darkness can also take over the light. It is still considered balanced as every sphere of light or darkness occupied a portion within the Sphere. Whichever is in dominion dictates the course of the Sphere and would carry everyone and everything in its path. The reason why I asked you earlier which side you were, is because we are the most contributing factors to light or darkness of the sphere; and each choice we make changes the Tilt of the Sphere. Either way, one of the struggle would always depend of which one is higher at a consistent basis. Which one of the two are our most common action and road map? Because each one of us, as we conduct our survival at the underworld trying to understand our purpose in life, contributes on the Tilt of the Sphere. But at this time, I'm afraid that Darkness has taken over the world and people of light no longer remember who they were and don't even believe when told that they are from the Light. Keep also in mind that overall, this world is full of kind hearted people.

Look around. What else do you see? Is it light or darkness? You decide. And again we end with a choice that we all have to make as there is nothing truly new under the Sun.

CHAPTER 13
Is a Confinement of a Soul Possible?

The phenomena of a soul stolen away is possible. Someone can actually lose his/her soul to a dominion of an outside entity. So many of us that have been lost, stolen and subdued once upon a time know that someone, or outside bigger, or trickier entity could actually hold your soul hostage. The hard part is that so many others don't even know that their souls have been lost/loss and taken to captivity. How hard is it to convince someone that his/her soul is in captivity if the simple notion of it, is relatively new to them or unheard of?

And the new trend now is that there is like some kind of religion or cult that are having people willingly and blindly delivering their own souls to some more advanced Spiritual Beings that they consider their god. And I can assure you that the system of robbing people souls and rerouting them to bondage in some confine places is real and worked for many centuries and is still up to date. As I'm writing these words someone have just gave their soul to a god or some more advanced Souls believed to be a god or higher powers. Those that knowingly joining the occult world or some religions purposely while knowing what to expect are making a conscious and informed decision; thereby assumed to have known that they were giving up their souls to whomever they pray or sacrifice to in return of whatever pact they made and bond themselves to.

In the midst of all this, there are innocent and naïve people that have not done their homework prior to joining any religious, spiritual or occult groups. It is a must to know

CHAPTER 13

which god/God or higher powers you are paying allegiance to or seeking protection from. Because there are gods and a true God of all. There are also angels and rebel angels just as we have demons and Satan. We have good spirits and bad spirits just like in our regular physical world, we have good people and bad people.

Truly knowledge is imperatively being really hidden away from the people ever long. It has gotten to the point that it has had a generational soul loss/lost over the past centuries as most parts of the world were consecutively consumed by darkness and I'm afraid the end will not be near. Too many innocent will follow the footsteps of their parents lost, of their loved ones lost, of their idols lost, and so on. The most difficult part is that a lot of practices are so rooted in a whole lot of people minds and spirits that what they are doing is true and right, without a doubt that they could be in a wrong path for, they grew up in a society already infested by false teachings without their consent or knowledge. How would you know what has not been revealed to you or made known to you through good teachers?

Because of lack of knowledge and understanding or an intent to mislead, many practices have been made official and legalize and totally widely accepted worldwide as a common practice and belief. The truth is, not because a lot of people believe on something that the thing believed on would actually become true. And it does not also matter how long a practice or tradition has been around that it should de facto be accepted as true. In this situation, false remains false regardless of its endurance through time and truth remains truth through time as well. It is a fact that the way we practice religion now is only for a purpose of a mass mind control in order to make the average people more controllable and docile. Not that you would not found the Truth in Religion, but nowadays it has become a blind leading a blind and everyone is obsess with money and power.

CHAPTER 13

In today's world with all these thousands of spiritual, religious, occults and traditional practices, one must do his/her homework and due diligence throughout before joining any group out there for his/her salvation. Those that are fortunate enough to have seen and become the light cannot even contemplate to tell those loss/lost people the truth that they are actually being shipped willingly to the road of spiritual bondage based on today's ways of spiritual worshiping. The same ones on bondage will call you the devil without hesitation once you warn them of the need to being Cautious.

Their eyes have been so blinded by false teachings from their own peers over the years that it almost made it legitimate that they must have some truth in the teachings and that the teachers were indeed right. The scriptures are reel but the intention of the way the message is being taught to the mass is a smooth weapon that their enemies or officials have use against them and have their own peer do the dirty job by spreading the false teachings in disguise with the truth assimilated and they all bought into it whole heartily. This general situation leads to a generational loss/lost souls from great grand-parents to actual grand kids. I call it a total soul loss since it involves a whole lineage of families' souls.

What would you expect someone to suspect something that he/she believes to be true? Something literally widely accepted by their elders, parents and friends? No one second guesses what is accepted everywhere in society besides the few. Besides, the practice of those religions, occults or spiritual sects could give some type of riches and status in society that it clung and fulfill the ego of mankind in general thirsty for recognition, money and power.

Now, let's come back to the many people's souls being stocked in a spiritual land in some four corners, big like warehouses and villages, like first come, first served, willingly, because they were so blind and fooled that they actually thought their souls were going to the so-called heaven, just to find out that it was a trapped all along. But once there, they soon realized that there is no way out easily because every gate is heavily guarded by a fully armed gatekeeper who doesn't hesitate to inflict the maximum pain and shoot whoever is trying to escape, while taking you back to captivity where the attempt to be free fails when caught alive. There are great battles going on at the spiritual levels and realms almost at every dimension, if you want to know.

My brothers and friends, I have seen them with my own eyes. They are trapped and confined that now want to escape but cannot really do so because they have no means.

They have no means to forcibly bust their own escape because they are afraid of the tyranny they would go through upon an unsuccessful plan to escape having witnessed the sentence for those caught trying to be free. It might look like an assumption but like I said earlier I have seen it with my own eyes the gate being open and as soon as so many of them were running out for freedom, they immediately ran back in without a thought when they saw the few armed guards putting their last effort to forfeit the plan of rescue.

But above all this, what I retained was their lack of trust of the rescuers. They were not quite convinced that the rescuers will be up to the task of eliminating all threat to effectively rescue them. To avoid being punished or being harmed, it was easier to run back through the same gate and better yet close the gate behind leaving the rescuers hanging solo. Leaving the rescuers all by themselves to fight all the guards even though the fight was supposed to be a joint effort as before they exited the gate, the rescuers have made them weapons with every scrap of metals and tool readily available at sight and readily transformable to a weapon.

It is indeed true that Souls stealing is real and it is a malicious way that some elites and other evil spirited minds throughout the centuries and ages have used to keep people

CHAPTER 13

at bait to the road of bondage away from the light. Some sell their souls to be rich, and others give theirs away free with a false promise of Salvation.

And most of the time, to achieve their goal, a practice of treacherous spiritual teaching is designed maliciously to lead many in darkness. And once there, every effort is applied to keep them into bondage for a very long time that one would wonder if it will be ever an end to it because every other day, some more lost souls are being redirected to those such prison/soul jail within the spiritual sphere. You should know that before they get you physically in bondage, they must first corrupt your mind in order to strip you away from your soul. Which level of vibrations do you think you are? Are you vibrating High or Low?

Same Tree and yet Different Seeds, Qualities in the Fruits

A fruit is known by its view and its shape. Every fruit comes from a different tree made of the same matter and source. Each fruit starts with a flower. Every cycle of transformation interacts with each other and automatically coexists. A tree may have many fruits but each fruit produces a different seed in design, with each fruit having its own unique taste and texture and flavor having still the same DNA. Some fruits have many other seeds in their respective envelops/shells whereas others just have one seed or two or three, etc.

Every tree is unique and interacts with other trees in their own dimensions and space but yet within the same scope of the whole. There is no other existence visible at bare sight that is not in the spiritual realms. We continuously share dimensions at least in few dimensions so far as I know. But since nothing is outside standing on its sole whole beside the fact that they are all shaped and hold together by an all-knowing all; it becomes contradictory to limiting the trees to lesser dimension because there is nothing that the mighty all is not the precursor. I'm going to end this with a story or a parable.

It was once upon a time, a king did what he wanted to do all the time and one day he decided to interfere with the covenant of God the unseen and he was punished for his evil deeds. That day when the sun came out and it was soon to become dark at 11 hour of the night, the trumpet sounded and he was no more. Taken high to rejoin his ancestors in where many call heaven and from there he rose back up to semi-eternity and started conquering everything and all beings to subdue and to make them slaves at a spiritual level. But, at the end of the day, let me remind you that every tree needs love and compassion. Compassion indeed is what we all need and most of all religions existing today have had their traditions resting and borrowed from a previous one or source that they themselves have to dismiss at all cost as a survival mechanism. Only the honest religions will actually accredit their beliefs, rituals and traditions from whence they came. It should not matter when Love should be the answer to humanity problems.

Fruit of the Same Tree but Taste yet Different Uupon a Bite

One morning, I went to the loquat tree to collect some fruits. From the look at the fruit, I could tell which ones were ready to be picked, by their colors. They were different from the ones that were not yet ready and of those in between. Even though, I could pick only the matured ones. From just the look at the fruits, I could not tell which one of the fruits would be sweeter than the rest of the other fruits. In fact, I could not guarantee that the fruits would indeed be sweet at all.

First, I had to taste it. I opened it and smelled it to see if the texture was looking weird. And once I opened them to eat, each fruit tasted different. Each fruit had its own form, shape and savor to the point that I was sure that of all the many fruits from the same tree, none of them were alike. None of them would taste like the same. Since tasting comes down to individual subjective point of view, we may never really

CHAPTER 13

find out. But for sure I could see that each fruit had different amounts/numbers of seeds within it. The number goes from one to two, from two to three and four even five. Adding to the enigma, even the number of seeds and sizes contained within fruits from the same tree differs.

The point I'm trying to make here is that us humans might be from the same origin but born from different parental lineage and blood. Adding to that, in each family, the kids would come in different sizes, shapes, weights and heights without anyone's control. And within the same family, the kids would have different characters and different inner impulses as good and bad deeds intrinsically will not be equally shared either. Basically, the same kids within a family might have different blessings and favors that cannot be explained, unless you involve a supernatural explanation.

Therefore, stop trying to compare yourself to Joe and Georgette because, just like the fruits, we are different than each other, even though from the same Tree. The Tree that gave us all life. The Tree from which we inherited everything from. The Tree that feeds itself. The Tree that is auto-sufficient.

Talking about trees and you will see the correlation that humans and other living beings are nothing more than a fruit from a tree. From different trees, seemingly indeed, because each species resemble its own kind and tree. To focus on us humans, we will always have different needs and desires; we will be driven differently, just like the fruits of the tree came in different forms and shapes with each fruit tasting differently. We would have mean people on the side of the good ones. We could have killers, robbers and at the side of them, life savers, gatekeepers, gand warriors. Forget about everything generating from the same source for a minute to understand the comparison being done here. There is no guarantee that the fruits would taste the way you expect it, until you actually tasted them. No one ever said that this world would be full of nice people. We have the good and the bad, even the ones in between. Still, it remains true that the Spirit that originated all of us is pure and full of Love.

Residing all within the same incubator that is the ground, we share the same space between the ground and the sky; the void and yet full with living things arranged to keep the incubator at a normal working conditions for all the fruits of the trees, even though different seeds and qualities in each one. The ground also goes deep as high like that is above seemingly at sky level to keep the balance. In a way we are alike all inclusive, form by the same atom and always evolving through time. The trees stick to the ground and remain fixed in one spot until the end of their existence and evolve to something else; whereas the mobile fruits (us) from a different tree (species) could move or run or stop on the same ground, and would also evolve to something else in their own ways. I guess we could be considered somewhat special because we are from a moving tree. A tree that can have access to everything permissible by the main Tree as long as we return to the source of the main Tree. Meaning we are our own limitation as a tree until we decide to join the Tree (main source) which made every tree possible, the mobile and the immobile ones.

Just like a broken clock will give time twice in a day, a mirror would only reflect what is projected to it in accurate manner. Therefore the same tree shall have fruits that will taste different. Equally, the fruits will not mature at the same time nor be picked and eaten at the same time during the same season.

Our Destiny is not to Stop Judgment Day, but to Survive It

The world is populated by human beings and other beings and existence sharing one global unit called earth that revolves around the sun while spinning around, over and over, completing its own cycle. Everything that when look up from earth to the sky seems to be having its own eternal cycle and life and purpose too. We see the Sun, the Moon, the Stars, and

CHAPTER 13

other planets and galaxies above and beyond. In comparison with what we know of the planet Earth having its own cycle by repetition moving around the sun everyday producing changes of time and space; it becomes therefore fair to assume that every other things above and beyond also have their own reasons and importance.

We cannot deny that the moon exerts a great influence in our life. The moon is not a constant thing because it comes and goes in cycles. The moon is the brightest object in the sky after the sun. As the moon goes around the earth, we see the moon from different angles. When we see a full moon, it means that the moon is directly opposite to the sun. And when we see no moon, it's because the moon and the sun are in the same direction. We can only do nothing but to observe and abide our survival according to how the ultimate things that make this whole and massive universe, all things combined function. The question of who put them there and engineered them in such a smart and intelligent manner encompasses one's brain to begin unraveling even. Because from the distance between each planet or things above and their relative and never failed connecting junctions binding and grinding to the Sun and Moons, you would think each planet is disconnected from the rest and only abide to only its laws but truly every move the planets do is closely notice by the rest of the other planets. If there is such a major incident that for example impacted the planet Mars, planet Earth including the rest of the other planets and Sun would also take notice and adjust accordingly. The automatic adjustments are relative to coincide with their final communion to/with the Sun. We know how long it takes for the Annus Magnus to complete from earth to the Sun, but, is the same distance and time applies to the rest of the other planets orbiting also around the same Sun from different galaxies?

Anyway, my eyes were for the one that made everything possible in such with order. You call it mysterious, magic, genius, intelligent, it does not matter. What matters is that there are a lot of things existing in this immense universe that as human, we can always try to understand and explain but we will always fall short of imagination. Can we really explained and understand something that we have not lived or experienced? Maybe that is why we are so eager to go to space and be a witness. What if there are other livings there in the like planets looking down on earth like we are looking up to them wondering if we also exist? Do earth has an owner or a single leader? Who should we address to, if some foreigner from other planets ended up in our planet earth? Who would be our Earth's representative?

Now that it is pretty clear that we know that everything that we see have always had a cycle, that it follows and possibly rendering the same expected results probably conditioned by a prior equilibrium of events in a normal cycle; How about we imagine how would the consequences be in an event something goes wrong within the cycles or their close ramifications of essential elements? Such events would be a catastrophe that would disconnect the orders. But would such events not included of all the possibilities that the universe itself allows? Therefore keep in mind that the world will always survive and everything in it but not without pain and suffering. That leads me to have some questions for you too.

Do we know everything? Can we know everything? Or should we ask, can we remember everything? Can we anticipate or expect something that we don't know or don't see coming?

Can we change what we don't know that is wrong?

Things that will be, will eventually come to pass. Things that are beyond our scope of perception and concession are bind to carry us over in their directions, at their discretions accordingly and to the fullest without any of us being able to stop them or influence them.

Having understood that, it becomes wise to be calm and meditate on this powerful few words. "Our destiny is not to stop judgment day, but to survive it."

CHAPTER 13

Evil and good are not separate forces. They are one energy responding to the same principles, but just being controlled by different minds, different intentions, different desires and wishes. Evil and good are not opposites, they are part of the making of the universe. Just like the day is not an opposite of the night. The same goes with life and death as it is birth and rebirth.

Things that we cannot change only may need to be understood and live without trying to interfere because ultimately, as one gets born, inevitably one dies into another life. Again our destiny is not to stop judgment day, but to survive through it.

Will there be a day when judgment will be rendered? Inevitably every birth, every cycle dies to something new. Eventually there must come a day when judgment will be. Which one? On who? And who will be conducting it? I don't know. Isn't it what being born again means? We don't and can't decide on how we will be born and where? It is decided and sealed for us. Or maybe we do play a huge role on how and where, through whom we get birthed from. Can you tell me what the new born baby is thinking about right now? Then you have your answer.

Now, what if judgment day has something to do with the way the vast and immense universe is drawing from, to, to continue producing a perfect cycle one after another in repetition? It could be like when we reach a time in our human existence that in overall everywhere in earth and oceans including all available water sources, we no longer have enough uncontaminated natural liquid water to evaporate through the sun heat and later make it to the clouds and condense enough to make it rain. Now we will have a serious problem. Earth will run out of drinkable water. I have heard a lot us agreeing that water is life. Then how would life be at that time without water? What would humans die into without water?

Of course, we humans are full of creativity. I'm sure someone will invent another form of water liquid in so call replacing the source of life with something that is now man made. Is water replicable? I probably won't live that long to bring you that answer but we should remember that the goal is not to stop the judgment day from coming, but to live through it.

I strongly believe, it will be important and nice to record today's date and time and the natural event surrounding the day. It's Sunday, November 20[th,] 2016 and it's been raining all day and as of 09:03 p.m. in Los Angeles, it's still raining and the air and the breeze feels rejuvenating and healthful. Funny day to be writing about water not being replicable once we lose it. Right?

Of course, existence is old. Old enough that no one remembers when it started. We only can speculate because records of events and languages died out themselves, leaving no exact trails to where it ended and where it began. This immutable universe as of today reflects the past, the present and will be the future as I blinked my eyes, throwing every breath of mine taken in my lungs into the past as I typed. Nothing is constant. Everything evolves and keep changing status to different status every second away. The world is billion of billions years old.

We all inherit our planet earth as a legacy from everyone and everything that ever contributed to its evolution. From the combined thoughts and feelings and habits, cares and carelessness's, from the collective mixture of things that have happened once happens a time that died up/out to something else; here we are; the actual reflection of what has existed and occurred during time and space long ago. The way the planet earth and all its previous hosts were being treated as a whole summed up giving birth to ours and continuously evolving and changing as we endlessly add into it daily ourselves. There is no single being that have ever lived into this planet without adding his/her prints into the global ball. Where every thoughts and feelings or actions ever transmitted or committed however long are believed to still be in motion, would it be safe to say that at this present time, we are also collectively still being

CHAPTER 13

impacted by them? And to the future, as we will our turn, also keep on adding some more ourselves for the next generations to come. The proof of this, is that we are still being taught wisdoms, traditions, thoughts, religions and cultures that are well over thousands and thousands of years old.

Therefore, we are all at the same time in the same token responsible for whatever this earth would turn out to be and how its hosts will ended up dying into in the future. As a reminder to myself as I'm thinking, my destiny is not to stop judgment day from coming, but to survive it. And throughout the whole book, I have included here and there how you could survive without being judgmental. The main key would be to drop the ego. You will have to forget about the "I", "Mine" and "only me" is right notion. In this way, you will be able to let go of misconceptions, preconceived ideas, beliefs including traditions and what you have already learned from religion and society. Only this way, your yes will be yes and your no, a no.

CHAPTER 14
The Art of Eternal Love

Love; what is love? We have all used it once before. Love is commonly the most used word, but the least understood. I love you could have different meanings. I love you because you are family. I love you because you are my relative. I love you because you are my husband/wife. I love you because I don't know why, I just love people. I love you because I can use you to get what I want. They are all different ways to manifest love, but it is still under the same word, "Love".

Do you want to know if there are different kinds of Love, try testing it first by how far would you put yourself in harm's way to protect your loved ones and guarantee their wellbeing?

It's undeniable that when we love someone, we are ready to do certain things that fall on the categories of things we do when we are in love. When we love, we are eager to be protective and concerned about the object or person our love is projected to. Think of a head of household waking up early every day going to work Monday to Friday, if lucky, on the work schedule just to be able to provide food on the table for the kids/ family and a roof over their heads. That's some form of love. Sacrificing his energy, his time to work in exchange for money, mainly just to keep his loved ones well taken care of. That's a form of showing love.

Another form of love is the single outer love we have towards people we meet and interact with, in a mutual beneficial way that could reflect how we viewed them and how

CHAPTER 14

important they are in our eyes. When people act well towards you, or follow your religion and culture, you tend to also be open to them and show some love. This could be classified as selective love.

There are also cases when we may not dislike someone but, at the same time, we have no love for that person either. And, if we do, that's the kind of love that we are not ready to put as equal energy and sacrifice to, to make them happy or secured, not talking about even putting ourselves in harm's way to protect the person.

We have some other kind of Love such as a love for a nation, love for a country, love for a race or tribe. We have love for the materialistic objects existing in the world. No matter which kind of love we consider, there are always an emotional and feeling attachments towards the person or object being loved. People that love are then ready to protect and defend what they love. They are sometime ready to lay down their own life while protecting what they love. A soldier is ready to die for his country. A father is ready to die for his wife and kids. Even those that are materialistic would die for their possessions or die while trying to get them. In all love situations, the lover has shown willingness to go to the extra mile to comfort the person or object loved.

Writing this is making me believe on the power of love. I can assume that writing is one thing that I love doing and you can see that I'm ready to glue myself in one spot and gather all my thoughts into the computer.

So, if love is the ultimate game changer in what we would not normally achieve with a normal will power, then Love must be the key to survive the judgment day since it is inevitable. A question comes to my head. Where is the love for the nature? Where is the Love for the Universe as a whole? Where is the Love for the most Supreme Being of all beings? Will it be fair to say that base on our irresponsibility and lack of total care nowadays about the natural world around us that we have grown out of Love for the Nature? Otherwise, we would all be joining hands to heal our planet in order to survive through the judgment day together. Keeping in mind that there are a lot more people that still care and are protecting the nature for the next generations.

It's still raining outside and it's almost two in the morning. I must remind you that on the previous chapter, I informed you already that it was raining. Matter of fact, I just got back from outside the balcony and the air and freshness is so pure and clean and it feels nice to be under a rain again.

You must have took notice that I was just talking about the rain earlier and here I'm again mentioning it because the rain is what contributes to growth of plants, trees, herbs. It cleans our pollution and refreshes life by giving it a boost, a push for the continuation of all things that depend on it to rain in order to flourish including our human species. We need for it to continue raining so that we can sustained a favorable condition of existence. It's not like we will not survive through it. A lot will perish upon its extreme absence but as time goes, we will start adapting with whatever conditions we ended up without rain and of course along with all the transformation within not withstanding DNA changes and eventually transforming to another species relative to all combined conditions offer by the universe as a whole. I'm not talking about something that will happen right now but it could be a probability in the far future if we continue destroying the natural life. If that ever happen, humans and other species would be left with no other choice but to adapt and survive. When rain water will transform into sand pouring down, it will be time to use God strength to move forward through God's mercy.

As it is known as a fact, nothing gets lost. Everything gets transformed. A species may vanish from existence or sight but is actually still in existence due to mutation of genes as a survival mechanism. Unless a species is totally exterminated, the species

CHAPTER 14

becomes extinct. Nonetheless, no one can say that an extinct species have never existed or be so sure and certain of their total extinction. Every process takes time and will probably wait on their turn again to materially or physically reemerge in our human conception conformably to our senses or just reappear in great numbers somewhere else hidden from sight.

I was talking about Love earlier, too. Love is a beautiful thing, a beautiful event that can be long, short, permanent, temporary or eternal. Why do we fall for Love if we are not even conscious about its duration? How many of us have ever tried to contemplate about Love and try to understand their relationship with others?

Since when we love, we seem not to have a limit as to how far we could go to protect our beloved, will it not be necessary to share some of that love around to the rain, to clean air, to organic food and healthy choices in our habits and behaviors that could be some key essential elements contributing to our general eco-system survival?

You know my mind just took me back on the crucial message that we are truly not to try to stop judgment day but to live through it. To make it by adapting through changes while conserving our human livelihood and abilities. Perhaps, the guy at the corner street would say it is what it is, but if there exist a way to preserve Mother Nature in her wholeness that you know that is favorable for a healthy existence, why won't you try?

Look at me talking like there is something to fear about. What is it to fear when nothing will be lost but transformed to something else as proportionate to the causes that sprung it?

We may not be able to stop judgment day but we can make the transition easier and safer. Survival through the storming changing of the climate, and their ultimate repercussions on everything on earth including aquatics beings. When we love, we always tend to care. We always tend to be protective and

CHAPTER 14

being anxious about the person or object wellbeing. May be the goal is not only to love the universe as a whole and ensure its wellbeing but to just also develop a love towards our own self. Remembering our self of our being, our existence. May be we would consider then, everything that makes the universe whole favoring human survival through judgment day. Only when we arrive to love ourselves with the same degree and intensity we love someone else, then we might feel the need to also protect our lives by healing the universe.

You noticed I have not mentioned the name of God yet. Because that's whom the eternal Love is drawn from. When we love God and feel the Love of God for us in return, we are guaranteed that we will love everything eternally without discrimination including ourselves. End of temporary and short or long term love. When your Love is directed towards God, the one and only supreme creator, then your roots and all your body parts are touch by the eternal Love making it easier for you to love all people and all things in return. Love does exist, and eternal Love is the key to loving all living in return. Thereby, this makes our survival through the end of time smoother rather than bumpy with uncertain episodes. In this process, you will need to surrender to God by loving all His creation. You cannot say that you love God when you are treating some, or all of His extensions, poorly. Therefore, we all need the Love of God and the Love from God in order to heal ourselves and others. To Love God, you need a cool head. Someone once said.

CHAPTER 15
What is Ritual Abuse and their Consequences on their Victims?

Its 03: 15 a.m. on my computer still the same day briefly after Nov 20[th,] 2016, and I'm burning a rosemary branch that I got from the next door concession next to the side walk on the street a while ago. I sat for a minute watching the rosemary burnt in fire and I have enjoyed every smell and incense that burned out of it. The aroma and flame and the smoke from it being burned reminded me that nothing really gets lost, nothing disappears, everything transforms to something else inevitably. The remaining of the unburned rosemary is left intact conserving its texture and form proportional to its normal exposure to life outside of its main plant nature.

Its 03:32 a.m. and I'm going to bed. Remember to love God, you need to have a cool head.

It's now 07:45 a.m. in my computer and I'm up writing a little bit again about our ritual abuse. I should have just said that I was going to take a long nap but I suppose four hours of sleep could be refreshing. And this is how ritual abuse goes?

I do it. You do it. He does it. We do it. They are doing it. It becomes ritual abuse when in our collective actions, we legalize something that we all do even though the act of doing it, is wrong. It is when a group of people willingly partake to an event that could normally get them in trouble, but yet accepted collectively within that society even though the said events/object could be morally wrong and unacceptable. For example, anybody that owns a car or a motorcycle knows that the carbon dioxide coming out the exhaust is not good for the environment. We know it but we instinctively do not think of it or take it seriously. Because it always feels good to point the finger at somebody else but not at oneself. Ritual abuse is taking place in society when unconsciously or consciously we are legalizing to what extinct we can damage our natural life by deciding which level of toxicity may be allowed to be injected in nature. Other examples are discrimination, slavery and its consequences, such as lynching, rapes and killings without justice, deforestations, abusive animals hunting and pollution of the ocean by toxic chemicals. Every life is threatened on earth. The wild life, the marine life, the forest and people health are threatened by our collective dysfunction ritual abuse.

And, as time goes, and our own kids grow and get to identify themselves with their parents and immediate relatives, they also learn and take habits from the adults and without thinking, they start doing the same things that adults do. Thus, we drive cars, waste water, throw away left over foods, neglect the natural life, buy and possess a lot of objects or toys made of all kind of natural minerals from earth that mostly just sit in the house for our pure satisfaction and materialistic taste. Even though, the majority of the world inhabitant really can't afford to be wasteful, the few that can, are doing it in destabilizing way next to self-destruction.

The nature is not being put in the eyes of young adults that it (nature) also lives. Awareness is growing and taking place as the damages accumulated throughout the centuries is becoming life threatening. I suppose you have just figure out that in this world, we have the ones that care about the nature seeing themselves as fulfill when nature is healed. And we also have the ones that never give a thought about it or considering that nature is even conscious. Least but not last, the ones that do not give a damn about it.

We are collectively abusing this planet without a thought because it's now a necessity. So we think and hopelessly submit.

CHAPTER 15

I drive to work because it's quite a distance. So instinctively I'm looking at it as an action that is beneficial to me. So no question to ask myself what is the level of my only contribution to the ongoing ritual abuse? My selfishness stops me from taking responsible steps to curve and become more conscious of my own personal input into our natural environment. The products and goods we consume comes from big factories that exist all over the world emitting a killing level of carbon dioxide and other toxic chemicals directly infuse into the nature. Now when we add our nuclear waste, industrial waste, air planes, vessels, trains and boats gas emissions and wars, their combination becomes a chocking matter for Earth and its co-habitants. We have already set off a nuclear bomb/atomic bomb during world two and conducted millions of ballistic tests not limiting to missile and other types of bomb that greatly destroyed our environment and the ocean lively wood.

I'm always optimistic and I believe that all people are good, and given the opportunity, they will always try to do the right thing. It is true that our society value less the natural life or even the person's life, instead power and money is the most valued. It's all about control and profit. But life in itself has a way of reminding us our own limits. That we are natural life. That we will perish alongside with what we got left from the environment. Our survival will imbedded in us the need to heal the nature because life without it will be painful/difficult and agonizing.

May be we do not actually impact the natural life more than it is a cycle on its own? But even if it is a cycle on its own only, we do have an impact to it and we are contributing to an accelerated deterioration. The impact is that we as a human, we have an advantage to reflect on it, a compassion of healing. We are apparently the one species that may be questioning with reason the consequences of our own actions. And we have all in common what we never discovered that we are nature and belongs to nature. When we destroy the nature, we are destroying ourselves. I have seen happy people, just like I have also seen people singing unhappy songs. At the end of the day, we move even if the moon is half full. Love, one of hybrid word just like the settlement between time and space since time ceases to exist once in space.

And for the record, all other species from the natural life and mineral life also contribute to healing our planet. They are aware of what is going on and are also taking steps working around the clock to help us remediate our climate upset, sometimes even in anticipation. Until then, the idea that instead of water, the sky could shower us Sand would remain unthinkable and unimaginable.

CHAPTER 16
Philosophy of Daily Practical Life and Events

Today was a good day; it's October 03, 2018. I wake up, breathe and vacate of taking care of my business. I have heard and witnessed a young man talking back to an elderly man without regards. Cursing at him when the old man was just making a productive criticism. The young man replied that he has had enough of him pretty much complaining every time and trying to tell him what to do.

I continued on my journey and went to work. Work was not quite easy because I had to deal with people. Some were nice and respectful, and others not so much. I even dodged a physical confrontation by deescalating the situation. The point to remember is that every-one of us have their road cut off for them every day. It seems we have choices, but every choice made, automatically add to our next day. A day may even be long to be cleared of obstacles because the choice already made immediately conditioned the next second. Whatever that was skip, whatever life events that got delayed will be readdressed in a further occasion. Until then, we always will always have choices. My humble advice to you, make every choice matter. Get it right the first time to avoid repeating a sequence of non-stop choices for the same events.

What do we know? What it is that is new? Can we claim to have all knowledge?

We can know so much and be fulfilled but still know that there is plenty of room in our brain to still fill it up with

CHAPTER 16

knowledge. We live and we learn. We live and we experience. We live and we understand. We make decisions and it's now up to us to stand by our words. We can decree the end of a habit, just to either go back to doing it again or resist or find an alternative way in addressing the said habit. Either way, we are still conscious of what we are doing. Deciding to write today on November 24, 2016 was a choice.

Everything appears far, then close enough to be seen or lived, and continue to past and get buried into the past as time goes. Would we remember it, or is it just a matter of time and consciousness growth? The sooner we start taking responsibility of our actions and deeds, then we are bound to remember our past so that they can be dealt with and learnt from.

We are recycling life and breath as our thoughts assimilate to our presence and make us live through our senses. It is a process of identifying everything, of what has gone around us and what is going on at the present. Time is the essence of awareness. We will then grow from immaturity to maturity, from weak to strong, and from desires and wishes to accomplishing our goal not far from our destiny and purpose. Ups and down, Life is full of mysteries. Not knowing what will happen tomorrow and what would be said tomorrow expose our mental sanity. But we should remain ensure that whatever present we live, is a time to shine. It's the time to make a difference. A time to convert towards something positive and uplifting. We can either chose to remain ourselves with little or no effort to be productive more than what we did yesterday, or we can also cause actions that will enter the eternal life of renowned positive memories. Meaning posing an act of goodness that would forever remind someone of good hospitality. Aren't we all sharing what we all agreed that there is nothing but our own reflections?

Society is the roots of all experience. Where else besides society can we learn so much from everything around us? Got music? Someone will scream out loud; Let me hear it. Now

CHAPTER 16

after hearing it, the singer has to be ready for an appreciation. It could be positive or negative.

Different people accept negative criticism differently. I might perceive it like whoever listened to my music did not understand it or did not relate to it. Someone else might see the negative criticism like a never happened event. While someone else could have took it as jealousy or a lack of compassion. But, what if you just can't sing or suck at singing?

We react from life events based on how we feel, think, and whatever mood we want to be in. because at the end of day, after each reaction, when we are not happy with our reactions, we tell ourselves, I should have acted differently. I should have made a better choice of words or just not let my emotions get the best of me again. I will never do this anymore we promised.

After all, life goes on and one day we decide to bend our own rules. First by convincing our own self about the rules we are about to break. It may take a day or two, maybe more, but when we succeed on fooling our own self in giving in to our desires, wishes and habits, then our first reality check comes with, what was I thinking? For some it's a beginning of life long struggle again to tame a bad habits. Here we go now being reluctant to making promises to our own self ever again.

Can we Keep a Promise made to Someone else, if we Cannot Keep up With our Own?

Life, inevitably is a constant struggle. But really? We live, we plan and we observe. I noticed something while I was sleeping the other day that I was still conscious of my body on the bed even though I was dreaming with the projection of my mind in a different dimension, then reality kicked in upon waking up that I'm still here on earth. I go to sleep, my choice I'm not sure, but I know for a fact that wake ups are not my choices. I go to sleep and then just wake up when my body, mind and spirit want to. In a way it is still my choice as my body, mind and soul belong to me. The only thing that is missing is when did I lose control of the act of waking up? Because it always feels like something else, other than my immediate mind wakes me up. Like hey, wake up now dude. Or it is a combination of both mind and spirit? Or they both look out in alternative manner when the other becomes slower to alert promptly?

Then I remember again that my destiny is not to stop judgment from coming but to survive it. I'm still trying to make sense of that statement. Maybe by the time I finish writing this book, we will figure it out together.

It is 08:14 p.m. on my laptop and I just got back from the echoes I was hearing from the balcony. I was taking a little break. Perceptive and subjective, I'm the only one that can express my experience lived at that balcony during the time there, even if I was sharing it with other people. Our mind is the limit of our perception. Or, should I say that our perceptions are the limit of our mind? What we deduct from our experiences daily is not far from our mental reality of life or the actions and deeds we are trying to give birth to, in the present time. For example, I can sum it up. I will hear a noise of a moving car coming far from hearing to close by and then the noise starts to vanish like a non-event into and away from my hearing reach; then silence as long as the car proceeds to keep moving away. Maybe that's how far I could hear the noise of a moving car until it disappears away.

But does that means someone else is not hearing it anymore, or the moving car has even made it to destination yet? Figure that an elephant could still hear it even up to more than three miles away, but we are equipped with limits naturally.

Everyone's hearing sensibility is different. Other people closer to the moving car would eventually keep hearing that same noise the car makes as it continues rolling. It's a cycle and as long as the car keeps moving, others that are in close proximities are bound to hear the noise that the moving car is emitting. Therefore, we should always remember that things would exist

CHAPTER 16

even out of sight. And depending on our level of consciousness, the events in our life would come back to us in circles until we hear them all. We will always have a replay into our ear and sight in order to make our commune existence better or worse as we desire since we have the Will power to speak and act.

Every day is a new day and must be lived with constant presence like the "I am, then you are."

Choices we have, choices we make. Slight confusion may arise, but we always find a way to battle it within and take responsibility of our actions. Plausible actions; may be not but when encouraging we are silently remaining proud of our self. That's when confidence reigns again, kicking out illusion and uncertainty. We thrive and make each day our best yet and at the same time remaining our own judge. Ritual abuse could also be when we never learn from our mistakes and own up to them to even contemplating another approach to life in general.

Ritual abuse indeed. I have just made a decision to go hang out tonight with a friend and continue writing later even though it's late night. Isn't it my choice? Based on how it goes down will determine how I have lived my time over there. Mostly in comparison with my expectation of how I wanted the night to turn out to be. Then I will either appreciate it or express remorse or regrets. Regardless should I have not been aware that what will happen was independent of only me but the addition of others minds and emotions combined? Why just me. What about the others. We can only know our self, the rest will only be mere speculation as we cannot live and experience their moment for them or dictate their conducts. We can live and share the same events and space but everyone would live it and perceive it differently. Thus it will become difficult to be trying to get everybody on board with us in the same spirit. Because as we rise, we rose alone. We are our own entity and only you can do something for you. Others may influence but only you, choose to express your will into actions. That's why the wise men and women have advise us to leave our preconceptions, such as ideas, cultures including our religious believes behind when dealing with other people and only that way, we would remain present and enjoy every time spent with anybody without judging.

I cannot be you and you cannot be me. But together, we are sharing time and space, learning each other endlessly and making room for improvements daily. Do what you can. Do you and never make any room for regrets by understanding your fellow man, not just you.

Isn't it that our expectations always are the ones that we rely on deciding either a situation or compilation of events was satisfactory or did not live up to the level we did expected? When we meet someone for the first time, what are the qualities that make us being able to pass a judgment and in finish even after a short conversation, we can reliably say that so and so is nice or was very rude. We pass judgment without realizing that our appreciation of an encounter is solely determine by who we are as a person. We always compare others to ourselves for appreciation not forgetting our own expectations that blinded us already making it then impossible to place a good impartial judgment.

Now comes the surprise when things we expected pass the level of our expectations and we are excited and happy when positive, and turn off when negative. We should at least take a minute to realize that we can only be us and us only. The process of being us and us only is very crucial as it helps one to consider that regardless of how others act and react towards humanity and its own kind, individualism in actions and full responsibility still prevails as it takes one to have two and so forth. Someone always has to show the way by knowing that everyone at the same time would live up on their own expectations and place a judgment.

In order to understand people around you, you have to be willing to give each person a chance. Imagine it is 2:00 a.m. and you were sleeping. Then you hear a knock at the door.

CHAPTER 16

"Who is this?" you yell.

"It's Brandon."

"Brandon who?" you murmur. "I don't know anyone named Brandon."

Now depending on who you are and based on your life experiences, instincts and quick reflexes, the other questions become very subjective. "What do you want? Who are you looking for? Is there a problem?" Only a naïve one will just opened the door without doing the safety due diligence check or someone who was expecting a total stranger knocking at his door at 2:00 a.m. in the morning. Again, we are our mirror and no less. Our expectations are our mirrors, too.

I guess, by this time it becomes clear that we are so good on placing ourselves as a measure for comparison to others for our own satisfaction. Because, the end result has always been about nobody else but ourselves. If we don't like it, then we don't want anything to do with it. If we don't appreciate something, then it is easily misplaced, disregarded without care or second thought. Unconsciously, it's like we have a check list for everyone else in our surroundings depending on the situation or occasion. Are we looking for ourselves in others? Are we looking for appreciation from others? When we admit that we can get along with someone, is it because of that person only as a being, or just the person's personal habits and manners that are in concordance to/with ours? Then we simply say, "I have found my match."

In the above situation or scenario, if in the case that you were looking for a mate, your second half, would you say that you Love the person, or you are in love with the expectations you had that turned out satisfactory because that person does and do everything you like? You now like the person because he/she act like manner like you or at least presents favorable traits and character. You graded him/her solemnly in comparison with yourself including your flaws, your good and bad habits, your character etc.

CHAPTER 16

As time goes by, you may realize that there were some more hidden behaviors and talents that you did not get time to select because they occurred later and now there could become a problem if no longer as expected. You no longer like yourself or your expectations since in truth and reality, there is never two people that are alike. We will always be different in our own complementary ways to each other.

It becomes even complicated for people that are constantly changing their characters and their desires and wishes as time goes by. Now what was a perfect match for me yesterday is no more today, because I have different need and different check lists. Life might keep going but not without a scar. Billions of billions of people waking up every day under the same sun, but still cannot seem to find a way to solve their love problems, their relationships issues. Every day, someone will laugh and smile as at the same time someone else is crying or sadden. This is our reality. We can only have the best impact to nothing else but ourselves. Only I can change me. Circumstances may also change me, but the old me always resurrects when the tables are turned around. Whatever I want to do and be, I have the power to do so because it's I that decide my own direction. Maybe when I change, I will then not reflect my expectations to my surrounding and attract or create a bond that will be true of my own true measures; the authentic self. The, I'm that can have an impact on the people living their own false expectations in life through me, the Essence. Consciousness of being is already a step to knowing that what we do affect our friends and family members around. And we are also symmetrically aware of the satisfaction level people grade us because people will always express their feelings and emotions or one way or another to let us know that we stinks or are amiable.

Now, I'm thinking of why I'm always writing about something positive or at least always trying to help and leave a positive impact on others and upon to myself?

CHAPTER 16

Is it that I'm trying to change people and make them a better person that I would appreciate? I have always wonder why I can write down something aimed for nothing. Without an illicit expression of my will and what I'm expecting to see on others? Is the truth, a self-righteous thing? Have you noticed here how the mind works in tricks? Trying to pull a guilt trick on me?

Then, I realize that not everybody likes anything that is positive. Some people just get their pleasure making people unhappy. Going around creating mess and chaos by inflicting pain and agony on their fellow mankind. Then, I came back to my senses that there is nothing wrong, trying the best you can to be positive and stay uplifting with this in mind; no one is holy enough but the God in us.

Imagine someone contemplating and making plans to do harm knowingly. It has happened to a lot of people. Once being on the edge, (or we are probably there right now or been there,) we caught ourselves being in a cycle of up-to-no-good thinking about retaliation or payback without any pity and remorse. You should know that living a shady life, taking advantage of others, also comes with their own mindsets and complications. Those kind of people will have a tendency of not trusting enough. They always have a plan B, or a back-up plan, if things expected don't work out well. Being up to no good leaves someone living his/her life with reserve. It stays in the back of his mind that it's not a permanent reality and he should not be fooled. They remain cautious and always on edge to defend themselves at every little occasion, even if it does not make sense to argue over it. The temptation of quickly assimilating everybody as suspect and untrustworthy is drawn by their own inner self, which is filled with the finest art of deception carefully molded to perfection over time.

Eventually, having no one but themselves as a mirror to place their expectations such as what they want and desire, the beginning of each encounter, relationship or interaction is already being built on foundation with mistrust, calculations, and mainly focus on what they can get away with from you. Not what they can add into your life positively because they must pretend to be someone else that they are not to be able to win confidence and trust from the encountered person. Then proceed into malice actions when time is right. What is to emphasize here is the willful intention of trying to do harm and take advantage of someone else by being malicious and calculative not trying to be caught before passing into action smoothly. Life should not be lived in such with malice calculation or else those that practice this art would always be further away from awakening their highest potential which is the love for the neighbors and self. That which that instructs you to act right and fairly towards your fellow mankind, else, karma would still linger around as each cause will have its effect. Karma would also present itself to us via dreams to convey its message.

In conclusion, when we dream about something in advance about an event that has not occurred, an event that will happened in a short or long future; are we living it in our dreams already in a time that is supposed to have not happened yet? Or is it just a warning about what will happened in the future as predetermined by karma? Have you ever experienced, or paid attention to the Multifaceted Dimensional effect of the Universe?

The Future is Not Set

It is 02:29 a.m. November 28, 2016 and I just got back from outside, from the balcony, of course. The sky is/was beautiful and full of stars as ever that I have not seen or pay attention to since coming to United States. There was three stars that align to each other and the space in between each star is seemingly equal from here and moving together as I have been noticing those three stars in different time and nights located in different directions or positions in the sky for a while now. I'm not sure

CHAPTER 16

if this is because it's been raining consistently the last couple of weeks and recently for the last couple of days back to back that we seem to be able to see more stars than usual since the air and view is pure and clear without the gloomy condense air stock on high having nowhere to go; but the view today of the stars is spectacular.

Do people attract stars? Or do the stars or some stars may follow people or someone around?

It's December 06," 2016. Now, the day slightly after my birthday, which is December 05th or still my birthday because of the time having its own memory and sets. Its 01:43 a.m. and I just watched the three stars aligned again on the sky among other stars even though the weather has been a little cloudy today. The cloud would disperse a little at least on the side and parts of the directions I was observing. You may know, it was at the balcony again facing west side straight to the Pacific Ocean from Western Avenue, Los Angeles. In one minute, as I was observing, I did not see any stars because the sky was covered with thick white condensed cloud. Then, some parts of the sky covering the view to space would slowly dissipate and here is a blue sky like we commonly call it. Few minutes before I started writing, there was a view of some spectacular sighting of stars including the three stars aligning next to each other with space in between them.

I'm now sipping on a tisane I boiled from tree leaves a couple of days ago that I had left sitting on the stove in the pot. Another sip of the drink and I wonder what to write about.

Honesty is what to write about. Honesty is the only thing someone could gift himself. Without it, what's left to offer? You can decide to deprive yourself from your own honesty to one point that inevitably, it would have to come out; otherwise, you may be forced to be under a consent illusion. Who among us do not like honesty? Everyone will prefer honesty in all things, instead of malice and treachery.

CHAPTER 16

Let's overcome pretending and illusion. Pretending may be self-coping to free ourselves from a condemned act, an already thought act, knowingly that it is deceiving. We are deceiving truly no one but our self. We actually master the art of convincing our self to accept a behavior, an act, a choice that we know deep inside of us that it is false or bad. We know we are tricking our self but it give us satisfaction for the moment as we become our own fool. Yet understood as deceiving, yet some of us keep aiming at it, hoping not to miss it. Missing it is not the point. What is there to run away from when we agreeably, consciously plan our fall, our defeat? At the end, illusion takes place if we insist on a constant pace to pretend. Frankly, this world is full of pretenders and fools with in mind that no one is a saint on earth. Put an end to your illusions by recognizing and reminding yourselves that pretending is no longer allowed and needed to face the realities of life.

Is there anyone to blame when in our course of actions, we already accepted whatever consequences thereby following an act knowing already that the actions we did was not ethical? Especially when it seems difficult for the average lay man to control his emotions and feelings including his moods that change like a time clock; then you know that pretending and giving in into illusion is suicidal to your very self. No wonder it become a whole life journey just to find ourselves back again.

Then, we would get angry, bolt ourselves as convincing ourself in a short conversation with our self that today, I do not give a damn whatever consequences my actions would give birth. Too bad if you are in my way. Eventually, we pretend again as we would become a totally different person when the circumstances change. Now. you see how every day, we pretend. Every day we are birthing a new adventure. A new beginning, a new bracket, always in a continuation of one's life unconditionally absent from one's consent. When we wake up, our mind keep going on and on independently of our will. Our mind, having its own mind separate from our mind, keeps

CHAPTER 16

trying to control our thoughts. So we live, we breathe, we work, we do our daily surviving acts presented at each day. Finally, we go to sleep, not fully being masters of our being no more, because during sleep and while at sleep, a lot of things could happened still. For example, dreams, near death experiences, premonitions, visions and after life phenomena such as out of body experience can happen.

Only a few of us take time daily or once in a while to show admiration for another day, once up again from sleep, after which death has given us a pass to see another day. Actually, being present at all times, being conscious through observation of your surroundings, giving your undivided attention to the people present in your life and admiring the landscape will make a good difference in your health and peace of mind. The color of the couch you are sitting on is good to know. Listening to the noise of passing vehicles from the street. The smell of the flowers and the taste of an apple bite would help you live and remain in the present. Quietness also has its own echo. Feeling the wave from the air caressing your skin, when paid attention to, consciously would bring you back to the now present, just like taking a deep breath in/out while focusing on your chest rising up and down.

Can you hear the silence around you? If so, then you are alive. Alive is what I found to describe it. Why? I will let you know.

When two things oppose each other, and a third one show up, what is it to focus on more? Would you take your eyes off the two and look at the third? Or would you if you can, move the three together so you would see all three at once? What if you can't change them and just have to stretch your eye sight to focus on all three things? On that situation, your mind could trick you as it would focus on what it wants to see more. There could be a chance that your mind would attempt to decide for you as usual. So when your mind is playing tricks on you, you need a cool head to know God and focus on your priorities.

CHAPTER 16

It is said that a breath blown out is a job well done. Maybe I'm the one that said it. But when the air brought into the lungs shocked in like we have just had a heart attack, then we are probably on another bracket of life. When we take our last breath, we might be on the verge to step away from this dimension. Which means, we are waking up then on the land of the dead because air is life also and when air stop being utile and don't escape and rejoined the universe once a breath was taken in, while alive, then it would take us to another life. Then, it would escape one way or another as we cannot take anything with us. We might fart out or burp out any remaining air in the body after death. And we leave everything belonging to here on earth and move to somewhere else where survival is somewhat an extension to another universe. So, we fart the air back out or burp it out even after death and actually right after death as soon as the soul exits the body for good after the last breath.

That life ends, I don't think so. Where is your beginning and where is your end when everything is and never gets lost but get transformed?

If you know how you started, then you could potentially know how you will end. What is more than sleeping and waking up? We sleep and we always wake up. There is no eternal sleep. We may remain sleep for a while, even for a good while but we will eventually wake up in due time.

Different appreciation of where we end up waking up may differ but still we cannot sleep indefinitely. I slept yesterday and I woke up today. Now I'm writing and who is to say that I know what would happened as I'm typing? It could be the last type ever. But so far I'm still holding on continuing writing as my mind flows like a river that ends with a fall that encompasses time and space because what is that, that is not? You can imagine everything that humans could perform at a single second, and you will see that someone has took his last breath performing that duty. Everywhere and anywhere is a place to die and rest assure that someone died doing what you are doing right now. Reading; and I know it is not funny either.

You and I and everything are nothing but an extension cord of our source; a source that breathe and contract. And in our course of living, we show signs of wear and tear like the giant globes. What is it that is not? Can you say you are not when you are conscious of your own existence?

You hear yourself and feel yourself. You smell yourself and you can see yourself. Can't you touch yourself? What else is it to exist without knowledge of self? Can you not express your existence? Remind yourself that you are made of God's image. The reason why that you have two separate brain sectors was to equip you with the Will power and the Determined power. The Determined power is the one that still keeps your body alive and functional even when you are in a coma. When in coma, your involuntary brain sector remained in charge, while your Will and voluntary brain cease to function.

Every day we express ourselves even when we are trying not to. Existence is not a choice to be or not to be. You will always be. You cannot try not to be. Where would you be, remains a question that those not aware of their existence but actually living, cannot answer; because of lack of self-acknowledgment. Now have you heard the Silence yet?

Are you, or Aren't you?

If what was said above make sense to you, acknowledge the Creation because you are the creation and part of its Creation. What is it that has been prophesied that did not come to be true? We live, we weave, we remain who we think we are. That you like me, him or her; regardless of one's good intention, you will not be able to hear/listen in one's place. You cannot feel in someone else place. You could feel sympathy, but it is not the real feeling either. You cannot see in one's place or smell in nobody's place also. You might give life through

CHAPTER 16

breathing (mating) from the life you got already here and there but at the end no one can control anyone's thoughts and desires. Just like we cannot stop the winds from blowing.

I might care for you. Taught you the best I can. Be there by example, but when all is said and done, you exist. You existed before I molded you according to cultural requirements and societal recommendations.

Existence, one pill not to swallow. You can decide to end it, cut it short but eventually would soon realize that it was not the solution to commit a suicide because one cannot just simply decide not to live or exist. We simply move to another being in another dimension. I could not guarantee if you will still remember your previous existence in details when the one on Earth is over but I can be confident that it is possible as dead people souls still recognize their loved ones left behind and could even step in once in a while to protect and guide them when extremely needed. Now are you or aren't you? I'm asking the same question again.

I'm about to take a break to eat and get some air. Isn't it my choice? Because I'm in control of my movements, my acts and thought; I'm the master dominating over myself. Execution would take place from the order of movement. Strength would be applied. Will would be applied. Energy would be spent because it's me using my own resources.

The movements and other unconscious actions that I'm not in control of, and yet aware of their necessity preexist beyond my Will. For those ones there is nothing I can do to change them because it's independently out of my Will power. Even though I could interfere with them by living a life that do not respect the laws and principles of always remaining on the middle ground; and not touching the extremes so that I could remain balanced and healthy.

Try holding on, on your breath for minutes. Try not to breathe and tell me how everything in you beyond you want

CHAPTER 16

that crucial air as a survival automatic mechanism? Not just your will depends on it but bigger than you is living. Yes, you are, but there is the one part of you that you cannot change or control; the Being, the Existence. Its needs will always be sustained regardless of how you think or want it otherwise. If you hold your breath longer than normal, you will probably die and Life will still be carrying on without you. You would also continue your own life regardless, but just no longer on earth's Dimension.

That takes me to say that your consciousness in life of your present time does not necessarily reflect your essence. You can decide who to be, but you cannot decide who you are. Because you simply are and are eventually going nowhere that was not set to become.

As long as we become aware that our control is limited, then we grow in appreciating what is, that exist with no one else's instructions or ends. God's presence in all of us.

Life is a beautiful gift. Endless life yet control under its own scope and understanding; but a life without an end since our Being has no end either.

CHAPTER 17
Genesis

Why you are here is an instinctive question and yet deeply misunderstood by everyone. Again pretending gets in the way of the Being. The allocation of time and time sensitive for leniency grow and deepens depending on everyone's impulse. My priorities may not be yours today or tomorrow. Yet we are sharing the same time and space but always inevitably appreciate it our own ways. While I'm up, you may be sleeping or cruising from point A to B. While you are sleeping, I may be sleeping. And while you are up, I may be sleeping, just like we can all be up at the same time. In any sleep, comes eventually a time to wake up. And on any wake up, it also comes a time to sleep or take some rest. A cycle it is. How are we aware of it depends on each individual Will within his/her own master's plan.

Only me can channel what I want and proceed with action as nothing is without the essence which is life itself. The I'm and that is which we can't really control and dominate. The blue print of all things and the reason of existence. It might look like limitations are stopping us from reuniting with the true essence, but we encounter and grow and mature and adopt a philosophy, a way of life that independently would not cease the self to still exist.

It's still Dec 06, 2016 but 09:32 p.m. on my computer and I'm cooking beans (black eye peas) and rice. When I got up to put on the rice at the last minute, my mind took me to the cooking details and processes again. Then I realized that even while cooking, there are still rules and procedures to follow, if you want a decent meal, after the fact.

CHAPTER 17

I had me some beans and rice. We all know that beans takes longer to cook than rice. In the process, I had to first boil the beans for a while to an acceptable readiness before adding the rice so that both of them could finish cooking and be ready at the same time using the same pot. Now before adding the rice, you should also know that beans when cooked can give gas and make you fart a lot. That's why in knowing that, I added a little drop of potassium to eliminate whatever that usually causes our stomach to be bloated with gas.

Technically, this whole process of the cooking reminds me that nothing comes without a plan. If you don't plan, don't expect an unexpected result to offshore you in your laps, like in a make-a-wish movie. Whatever we usually give out is what we get back in return.

You should not also overlook on details because everything in the plan works together as scheduled to ensure the birth of whatever seed you planted. You should not expect oranges when you planted for lemon.

Let me go check on my rice and beans on the stove now as I should remind you that while writing, I'm also cooking. And I almost forgot to tell you that I added a little bit of salt for taste improvement. The food is now ready as I turned the fire off but I will let it sit on there for couple more minutes, then dinner is on me tonight.

What I learn, or pay attention today and took as a lesson in life, is that nothing comes true without an effort. I could have just read the recipe on how to make rice and beans and probably swear I knew how to cook, even before my first try, but until I actually made an effort to go get the beans and rice from the store, I would not have been close to making rice and beans as dinner. And you noticed that just by buying them and actually in possession of what I needed to cook was incomplete. I still had to clean the pot and set a fire. And eventually began the cooking procedure for real to materialize it so that I could have a dinner that I planned for and executed with the plan and would soon enjoy my hard labor as a thank you to myself.

Now I'm thinking why do I even need food? Or who really needed the food? If it's just me, I can play lazy and hope it will go away. But it seems that there are more than just me wanting to eat. More than just me wanting to survive. Now I'm wondering if we are living for ourselves or living for someone else. So far I know if I decide to starve myself, my stomach will start hurting as a result and I would get weaker and weaker as time goes by without me eating a meal. I thought I heard someone whispered to me that I'm the decided of my destiny. That I could do whatever I wanted to do. I could decide not to eat or drink just because. But every time I would decide, it looks like something bigger and stronger than just my Will needed to also survive. Then it hit me on my mind that the body, my body is a host of something else or someone else that really want to live and express itself more than my own choices. Even the mind of my Mind wants to live.

Or, is it that when I decide to not eat and drink for however long, everything that makes me whole and strong with vitality also suffer; and each thing in its own sub body will start acting up and going crazy for not having what they all need and love to survive? Or is it my Ego that needs not to be starved?

By the way while I was cooking and writing, I had in my cup a little drink. As I took my last sip before refilling my glass, I just remembered that there must be some habits and behaviors that my real Being don't like. They are here, built in me, representing everything that makes me whole now without me being able to decide either I want them or not anymore. This is when habits and behaviors transform to addiction or second nature. We simply do and act in auto-pilot without second thought. Habits such us smoking, drinking, drugs and alcohol abuse becomes natural and tolerated. They become part of us and also seem like they also have an urge to exist through us. The only way to combat these bad habits, is to simply hold

CHAPTER 17

the hands and arms that execute their impulses. If I stop reaching out to what my bad habits need, then I would dictate a new order in my life. And by exercising this power, I will have to remain strong during the withdrawal times, too. Meaning that I would have to overcome the urges to go back satisfying those bad habits and behaviors.

We also have habits or tendency that was given to us through inheritance from our family tree. Habits and tendencies that were just there hidden or obvious since I was a baby and grew in size also as I was getting bigger and taller as long as I kept the tendency of continuing with those habits knowingly or unknowingly. Everything making my body, my mind and my soul have always been with me even before I was aware of their existence. Here I realized now that I have never been alone all this along and that my body, mind and soul have been working together to the best they could to survive, to protect themselves, to live, and to deal with whatever circumstances or unwanted events together. Adjusting, coping and improvising at daily basis even way before I knew how to speak, how to walk, and most importantly how to choose my diet. Before I was conscious of my life and self; my body, my mind and my soul were running my life without me having control of my senses. I retain in this entire process of life that it is true that God really provides and protects.

By the way, the rice and beans turned out delicious and reminded me that every aspect of our life is a lesson to learn from. From wiping up ourselves when we finish using the bathroom, to cleaning up our mess and making sure a pot is clean before we put anything we are going to ingest in to. We can learn from anything and everything that we actually do because our daily life routine itself is an assignment. Always remember that no one ever finished learning in life.

It's now 11:51 p.m. on my computer and I'm thinking of silence. Silence, just quietness and not hearing anything but the quietness. Quietness opens a way to hear what is going on in the silence. When you don't hear any noise nearby or far away to the point that you really can't hear nothing but your own single self-remembrance that it is actually quiet, consciously; then it must be really quiet. Silence double checking on itself. Meaning that you are now really listening to yourself in your own silence, endeavor act or echoes as some things cannot be heard unless we put ourselves on silence mode. Silence is golden, we heard; and sometimes, you just have to listen to your own peaceful inner silence to realize that silence really do exist and is accessible to all. So, would you try being quiet and not speaking or listening to nothing for an hour or more? Just for the heck of it; try it and your Self will thank you later.

Then, you look around for a minute and there is no one nearby, or a car passing as you are now alone with yourself. It's just silence. Now, you ended up with yourself by practicing the art of silence. That's when you usually try to think and out of the sudden thoughts start flowing and du coup, you stop yourself from continuing a thought that your other self is trying not to entertain. Sometimes, the thought that we stop from entertaining could be positive or negative or just a lost memory. Leading me to conclude we are still in control of deciding when to block a thought from continuing within our own minds. The mind that exercises the role of checks and balance. The mind that knows wrong from right, good from bad. From practicing silence to finally finding nothing but "emptiness", the True Silence and Light is Golden truly.

You should know that the mind that do the checks and balance is nobody else but our self. Our self, meaning our intentions, our desires, our wishes, our habits, our knowledge, our integrity, our overall daily and everything we put out in the universe. That self is nothing but us. Perfectly showing ourselves our limits or strength and how good or bad of a person we are in the real life. I should remind you that karma plays itself, too, through your mind and makes you hear it.

CHAPTER 17

Those who are living a life of caring and loving would identify themselves in the silence. Those who are attempting to entertain bad thoughts and negative intentions towards anyone or themselves would come back to their senses and try to change a subjects of thought but not necessarily. Where those that manage no effort to giving themselves no boundaries of thinking would keep going and may actually enjoy it until another thought jumped in. The latter, even if a thought is bad or contaminated with bad wishes, bad desires, and negative intentions, would continue entertaining the thought actually without any guilt and could sometimes find satisfaction after the fact.

At the end of the day, thinking is a natural process that could only be slowed down, or stopped through meditation and the art of focusing on our own breathing. And the wise and teachers of the way tell us to become the witness of our own mind. To become the watcher and remain deep behind and don't react to what our mind is telling us, or making us feel. That way, we will be able to control our feelings and emotions. Just like when they said that you should respect the living and respect the dead also; when our feelings and our emotions become One, then we become One with our Self, thereby giving the created power to create and make every prayer and wish come true.

CHAPTER 18
The Reincarnation of gods and Mystery Masters

Today is Sunday March 5, 2017, and it's exactly 3:00 p.m. on my computer. The winds are blowing outside and I could hear birds making noises and singing. The Sun is out and it's nice and beautiful since we had a little bit of rain early this morning in Los Angeles. The trees across the street are swinging back and forth following the direction of the winds just like going with the flow without trying to resist as if the wind is strong enough to move a leaf, so shall it be. The branches are dancing and moving along with the whole tree.

I have not written for a little while and I'm now wondering again what today's effort of trying to commune with my laptop would bring. The air is blowing. Cold, it is; because I can feel it when it hits or touches my skin. I'm seating on the couch while the television (TV) is on but lacking my real attention at the moment.

Even though I could still hear what they are saying or the sounds of the words coming out from the actors mouth, I really cannot understand what the words mean since the movie is in Chinese language. I have the subtitle on, but my eyes are fixed on my key board at the moment.

You may be wondering what kind of movie I'm watching. The movie title is called *IP Man* and it's an art martial film where IP man has to fight with other masters from different schools in order to be accepted as a master within the community. That's

CHAPTER 18

only when IP man proves himself worthy of being called a master that he could eventually open his own art martial school in that community and start accepting new pupils interested in his mastery skills.

What is relevant from this movie is that IP man was actually a master already. He was already known as a master but not in the city or community he had recently moved in to.

As a master already, IP man proceeded directly into getting a place where he will train his new potential students and started handing out flyers to people until he encountered another master that also teaches martial art discipline that actually informed him of the rules and conditions to open an martial art school within the community.

The rule was that in order to be accepted as master in the community, IP man would have to challenge some other known masters and win all the fights. A time and a place was set and after challenging three masters, among the other twenty or thirty remaining, IP man was then accepted and welcomed as master since no other master present wanted to challenge him after his demonstration of his skills and quickness to defend himself. In reality, the master's wont challenge him any longer that day after noticing IP man moves and skills in the art.

I guess the moral of the movie would indicate that we must put ourselves out there and accept to take challenges, even though we may already know who we are and what we can do or contribute; other people need to be convinced that you are who you say that you are.

Once, you have proven yourself worthy of being taken and accepted as who you said you were, then you must keep working on improvement and keeping in mind that every day is a challenge to fight and to win, and that every day brings something new to improve. Always being ready is the key as no challenge knocks on the doors for permission to enter before knocking you out cold to your own floor.

CHAPTER 18

Knowing who you are on a constant basis and staying true to yourself are the best preparations daily before any challenge. Being aware of your impact, your influence, whatsoever in your own life and others and to your community makes you develop an inbuilt readiness line everyday as one should always be prepared for the worst also if it happens.

You have to win if the battle has to take place. You cannot postpone life's struggle. You cannot take a day off of life circumstances. We just have to go with the flow and swing like those branches and leaves from the tree under the influence of the winds directions. Floating back and forth in whatever direction the wind is blowing in life makes us ready daily to take on other challenges.

By the way Wing Chun was the martial art, IP man wanted to teach in the community as a master and had to challenge the already known and registered masters in the neighborhood before he could eventually be authorized to open an art martial school to teach. The master IP man even though as a master already still had to prove that he is a master and he is worthy and deserve to be referred to as Master from other Masters.

Nothing comes easy without an effort. Even basic self-esteem and pride get challenged and have to be refurbished and made new and strong. The old shall become new. And the new shall become old. Endlessly interchanging and interfolding and simultaneously defense and attack.

Wing Chun combines defense and attack. You attack and fight to beat your opponent as quickly as possible.

Simultaneously defending and attacking are ways to be ready on taking any and everything unexpected in our life. You cannot seat and wait on the adversary to attack before making plans and attacking. Once it is clear that you know who you are as an intrinsically awareness, you should know that the world may be full of your opposite. And if so, a daily life is a survival as of any moment you could find yourself in the fight. A fight that

CHAPTER 18

you did not call for or even willing to really take on the challenge, but sometimes who we are intrinsically as a being will often expose us to some uncalled fights or wars that if given a choice, we would have preferred not to fight. But in this fight, there is no other choice but to fight because the opposite of your being may be greedy and won't stop until the last one of you drop dead or is proven no longer worthy of being a master.

Everyone is born with his/her own battle ready at hands. Challenges within families have to be dealt with. Challenges within neighborhood have to be fought. Challenges within society have to be fought. Every challenge we would face depends on the actual accumulation of all circumstances your immediate family members and how society in general welcomes you at hands. Anybody not ready to fight for his and his people will soon realize that he/she could become a statistic. Some battles are not yours directly but belongs to a group of persons or a tribe or a nation or a race etc. But one still have to take on the challenges to make one's life easier and safer and for the next generation.

Circumstances changes one's attitude and one's action. There is no being on earth that is not a fighter. All we know to do is fight. Even when we think, we are peacemaker, we still have to put an effort to convince and conquer peace. And sometimes and most of the time the enemy, your opposite would strike with no hesitation with a fully aware intention to cause you a deadly harm.

Always know your opposite. Always know who your enemy is. And always be prepared for the ultimate fight as it could just start any second. Remember Wing Chun is the combination of defending yourself while attacking your opponent simultaneously.

Everyone needs to choose his own path. But when everyone's life is threatened at once and it's clear that it is in a discriminate manner, the fight must become common. There is

CHAPTER 18

no more room to choose an individual path but to join forces and fight back like one person, one mind, and one soul. It is called a survival act of honor when one drops its own pursuit to contribute to the common fight to guarantee a breath of freedom, liberty, Justice to the offspring's and the young ones. Common causes unite people of all walks of life. They have no boundaries, no borders, no race or gender. If there is a need to unite and fight the same enemy, one should not hesitate. Doing the fight individually, there is a chance of not winning as the enemy might be more armed and possess a great deal of art of war and logistics.

To fight for no reason is totally wrong. To wage war to other people just because you don't like them is evil. To seek or plan the annihilation or elimination of a whole race or group of people or tribe is evil.

That's why everyone has the right to defend himself when his/her very life is at stake. There is no excuse for a Being not preventing itself from being inflicted any pain whatsoever the origin.

Conceding could be a weapon when you are over powered but one should keep in mind that a continual struggle and attempt must be made to reach the level of fire power of the enemy. If it is proven time after time that a battle will not be over soon and it even took and became a generational struggle, people should start organizing themselves to prevent greater harm being inflicted to the up-coming generations.

It is proven by History that the only way to stop your enemy from killing you or your people is to possess as equal force and tactics be it economic, military, logistics, science, technology etc. to counter attack when and if necessary. Then your enemy would then think twice before hazardously trying to conquer and enslave your people.

Be aware of traitors as there is always someone friendly among you that is weak mentally, physically or spiritually that

CHAPTER 18

will not hesitate to go to bed with the enemy for some coins or stature. Again, always know your enemy because everyone has one but not necessarily. Every race has one but not necessarily. Every nation has one but not necessarily. Every tribe has one but not necessarily. Until proven that enemies of today have become friends, do not be a fool because nothing changes until both sides expressly make it clear and underline that a truce, or peace is necessary or has taken place. There should be no complaisance from your part. Always look out over your shoulder; watch your back and shield the young ones. At the worse-case scenario, join your own kind or people with the same values and like-minded that you know are your friends or not dangerous to your very survival.

Ultimately, to sum it up, Life is not fair. This is a jungle until we make it less dangerous to survive as species. You cannot control others actions against you, but you can always protect yourself and always be ready to strike back when necessary with the same fire power. Or else, you will become statistic or your loved ones will. This is not to promote violence under any circumstances but to exercise a right to be able to defend yourself as a self-defense mechanism, when necessary. By the way, why can't we get along and live in peace and harmony together? Whites, blacks, brown, yellow and red skins, etc., living side by side, without greed and malice? Today, would you take the pledge that Violence and Discrimination end with you?

CHAPTER 19
The Cheating Soul

Once upon a time there was a lady called Jeanne. Jeanne was married to John for ten years. During their marriage, John never knew that Jeanne had been cheating on him spiritually until the marriage started going sour.

During their 10 years of marriage, in their union, there was no clear picture as who was truly the head of the household. A clear head of household is the one who would open the door, for instance, if someone knocks at the door bell at late hours while both couples are present. Usually, the one getting the door at those late hours is actually the overseer, the protector, the one ready to fight and defend, if needed. It is the one that you should have to go through first before you could eventually do any harm to the rest of the family in a case of imminent threat. It is understood in a general term but not necessarily. But, I suppose, it will not be wrong to say that the man is usually the head of the family.

So, since there was no clear head in the household, and there was no apparent attempt to establish one, anybody could get the door, even at late hours.

In the spiritual level, a clear knowledge of who is getting the door at late hours also can apply. But in the case of Jeanne and John, it was not clear who answers the door-bell at late hours or so.

So, Jeanne and John would be sleep and the door would ring. Jeanne would usually open it, without consulting with her husband.

CHAPTER 19

One day, the doorbell rang and, as a habit, she went to answer. The difference is this time, she was actually dreaming. So, when she (her soul) got up and opened the door, there was a fine looking gentlemen (also a spirit) at the door who asked to use the restroom that she let in without caring to consult with her husband for safety's concern, or just the respect of family rules. She assumed and didn't see any immediate threat to have a backup.

The gentlemen enters and use the bathroom and immediately Jeanne woke up from her sleep and realized that she was actually dreaming but still have a clear picture of how handsome the man in her dream was.

It was day time, Jeanne and her husband are both getting ready to go to work and they did not have enough time for little chit chat. So, she kept her dream a secret since it was nothing really to tell.

Life went on and one night again, during her sleep while dreaming, she heard the door knock and when she opened it, it was the same man in her previous dream and this time the gentlemen now presented himself as Billy and asked if he could come in for a while holding her favor drink, "Bazooka," as a thank you for letting him use the bathroom the other day.

She hesitated and finally let him in. As soon as she let him in, the alarm clock sounded and she woke up from her sleep and realized that it was actually a dream and that her husband was not near present to even have a slight clue of what had went down during her dream.

It was morning time again and husband and wife were getting ready for work to start their daily routine. As always, everyone was in a hurry. At this point, Jeanne was still keeping her dream secret.

Life was still going on with Jeanne and john and everything was going okay so far until one night, Jeanne, in another

CHAPTER 19

dream, was with Billy and Billy started seducing her. She fell for it. Before you knew it, Jeanne and Billy started being sexual and going out to parties during her sleeps and dreams. Billy would come and take her for a walk and try new adventures. Jeanne felt, at that time, that it was the life she wanted all along. Their spiritual relationship grew stronger so that Billy would actually now move in at her place without her knowledge.

Then the couple, Jeanne and John, started arguing for unnecessary reasons because the presence of Billy's spirit in the house was interfering with Jeanne and John's marriage. They were no longer laughing and codling like they normally did. Jeanne became a little bit distant and would feel comfortable sitting now by herself or sleeping satisfied by her side of the bed, without the flirting and sexual invites as before.

The husband took notice of the changes of behavior and temper but had no clue of what was going on in their relationship.

Jeanne was satisfied now alone physically in the house because Billy's spirit presence comforted her and she would actually be sitting at her corner but with Billy next to her without her even knowing it. Since the husband could not see the spirit of Billy or even know that such a thing could even be possible, John was looking for some physical reasons for their arguing and misunderstanding and disrespect that was going on now.

Jeanne could not also really know that Billy had moved into the house and that it's because of the presence of Billy's spirit that she feels whole, happy being alone but truly not alone and at the same time really not caring any more for what she was bringing into her marriage as far as the lack of attention to her actual husband. Since either way she was satisfied being away from her husband by then now without even fully being aware of it or being present without distraction.

Jeanne failed to see that her behaviors were ruining her marriage because since Billy's spirit is always present with her, even not knowing fully why she fills fulfilled by herself, she

CHAPTER 19

does not feel the need to entertain no other man but Billy in her dream at that point.

John finally got tired of fighting and arguing and filed for a divorce.

And that's how Jeanne destroyed her marriage. By entertaining someone else in her dream and making it a habit until Billy's spirit got connected to her spirit and took control over her and destroyed her marriage purposely, just to keep her to himself. Causing the divorce and now Billy had Jeanne for himself. And Jeanne was now single again in the real physical world, dating and continually dating. She never ever got a serious relationship after the encounter with Billy, the spirit. Because Billy was still around causing issues and contributing to her not being able to have or to keep a man. Billy sees the other men as rivals and acts accordingly to weakened the relationships she has with them. Now, it's been three years and Jeanne is still single.

This scenario goes for both gender and anybody can have a spiritual attachment, a spiritual possession, or a spiritual relationship, blocking the way and success of future relationship with your peers. I just took the example of Jeanne, it could have been John entertaining a female spirit in his dreams.

CHAPTER 20
From One Cycle to another Borrowed Cycle

Life is in itself a learning journey. We appreciate the little second we have as we are taking a small volume of air at a regular basis. Made of a system that need to be sustained at a regular basis, we are forever condemned to attend to our body/health physical daily needs.

We sow seed and wait for harvest. But before harvest, a lot of other things would have to be taken place until the seed sown actually grows and produce fruits/ grains that we later consume as food to stay alive. A survival mechanism that transcend our times that continuously reciprocally inherited and it is the thing to never depart from.

Before we get the food to live, we have to keep the trees/plants etc. alive. We have to keep them alive so that in turn their fruits and grains would keep us also alive. That's what I call the cycle of return.

Everything that exist is correlative and bond to exist with others as none can survive alone without the others. A complete cycle is a combination of a whole lots of small particles that have worked together to keep the big picture grown to maturity. Undertaking the phenomenon to attain or reach the designed architecture definitive goal. Following the design authority that has order and put the system in place, each thing regardless of how big or small is a product that was carefully designed to produce a certain result. A wish and desire from the architect.

CHAPTER 20

When it comes time for each thing to wonder where they have all come from, it becomes a big puzzle.

What even gives us the sense of not being the product of ourselves? We wonder but what about the other living things that surround us? The trees, plants, birds, animal and oceans living fishes and species? Have we made them, too? Did they made themselves too? Do they themselves, the other livings besides humans ever entertained the same questions we have? Like who are they and where do they come from?

I'm going to share a real experience with you. I put couple of apple seeds on a bucket with soil on it. After watering it and letting it get some sunshine, it started pushing out some leaves and before I knew it, the little leaves started being held by the actual plant that the leaves was seating on top of.

Few of the seeds did not start with the leaves first. What was springing out was the straight out roots and the leaves was buried on the soil. I retrieved them and reversed them by putting back the root under the soil leaving out and up the leaves on the surface. The later survived for couple of days but did not make it. Versus the one that started growing in the right way that actually survived.

What I learned and wonder is that it could be a right way to sow and a bad way to sow too.

The seed has to be positioned in a manner that it would grow upward instead of inward.

Now from the little plant, it would grow to a big tree and produce fruits as the required maintenance and nutrition's are met.

In fact, nothing grows without a nurturing. Nothing lives without the requirements set from its architect that it should meet in order to continue its own cycle that it is set to be contained in. An apple seed would not spring out an orange tree and vice-versa. Nothing gets out of proportion.

CHAPTER 20

The mastermind behind the architecture of every living being has put a design forth fact that sustains itself where every need is met. Is it safe to speculate that the mastermind himself lives through what we might see as dispersed design? Co-existing together and yet intertwined and interacting between each other is not just a mere coincidence. Is the whole thing actually also living along with us and we are the ones also responsible to keep it alive as well? As we should know by now that every existence needs nurturing and required ingredients to grow and flourish?

Closed in, in a sphere that produces everything we need as supplies to be alive, we tend to think of since we are the ones to undertake the necessary effort to obtain what we need that we are the central focus point of our own existence. Forgetting that alongside us, some other small entities and species have also contributed to us getting what we needed. The ants played their roles. The elephants played their roles including the bees and butterflies even the roaches and spiders, etc. Would you not acknowledge our weather and seasons that keep the eco-system balance too? At the end, would it not be then fair to consider other living being as equally important like us with a right to live?

Knowing that each one of us, left alone would pass a mere lifetime seeking and trying to find out what we need; everything around us is a ready built organism that auto-fulfilled itself and provides the needs for its guests.

Something produce the water that is essential to us for survival. Something else produces oxygen that is equally essential for our survival. The sunshine we enjoy that actually is the core of all living organism is produced by something else. The food we eat is borrowed from the plants/trees and animal life.

Nothing is to be minimized because each thing no matter how small we think or perceive it to be, plays a huge and necessary role in our very existence and considering that this big

CHAPTER 20

sphere we are living in is also connected and sustained by other spheres outside of our sphere.

Our planet earth orbits around the sun. The moon we see at night orbits around our planet earth and actually regulates earth tilt from far.

Could it have been any other way different than what the mastermind intended it to be so? And who is to say that the moons do not also orbit around all the living beings including the sun, stars, galaxies and every other planet and beyond? Isn't the space and distances calculated and balanced? Doesn't the sun light strength balanced among planets?

The gravity from our planet keeps us stable so that we can walk and remain straight. In comparison with the moon that has low gravity, when the few astronauts landed there, they were jumping like kangaroos from a point A to B because they could not walk and be stable on there because of lack of enough gravity to hold them down. It is said that once at the moon, anyone could pick up even a hill and jump with it like the hill was a piece of paper.

All this, is to emphasize the fact that everything has its place built especially and specifically so that it could readily have all the necessary survival tools and ingredients to continue affording living beings. Every planet is conditioned to its hosts. And adaptation is possible but when survival conditions become too extreme, life in general could also be threatened. Therefore, you should help take care of the planet we depend on to grow to old age healthily.

CHAPTER 21
Living Simple and Wise

We are living in a society where it is easy for us to be confused because of lack of insight and knowledge to determine what other people are doing better than us so that they could have everything they want as far as material life. It really comes a time when you start wondering if what you are doing isn't as worthy or not as profitable financially mostly with someone's else numbers in mind.

Not necessarily being jealous of others success, but wondering why them and not you yet?

Even to the point at now measuring/comparing apples and oranges to find out what went wrong that things are not looking promising at your end.

At the end, it is wise to retain that not all wealth and richness are blessed. People gets their wealth in so many different ways. Some from good and some from bad sources. Some from the right hand, some from the left. Others are profiting because of a system that facilitates their financial prosperity and some because of humanity exploitation.

Modern world and its vision of wealth has changed throughout the years. Wealth is no longer resumed to having food to eat, clean water to drink, and financial means just to tackle life surprising monetary needs here and there. Nowadays, everybody wants to own a luxurious car, a boat or a yacht couple with a mansion. And wealth is no longer knowledge, wisdom or intelligence. Few people care for wisdom and

CHAPTER 21

understanding these days. Everyone wants to be rich in cash money.

Unfortunately, it cannot be possible for everyone. Just like our fingers are not the same length, in real life, prosperity would be as our fingers. Just like people will always have different health issues, we will always have different financial needs and means.

Besides, isn't the financial system an illusion? A system that makes you believe that Paul is doing better than you. And that you might be better financially than Peter. It is a system and everyone cannot be successful at once in a pyramid scale. It is the reality of each society. Some would have a lot and some would have less. Some would have abundantly and some would not have nothing at all. Just like some people are sick and others healthy.

It is a world of contradiction when we always believe that others are doing better than us when in reality, it is comparing apples to oranges. If you don't have the same jobs and getting paid at the same rate, then why compare something that you don't know? Isn't it superficial judgment?

Everyone have different responsibilities and different needs. Everyone has its own hustle separate from their daily work. We have different expenses and different family size and different priorities.

Therefore, it will always remain an illusion to compare yourself to others because it comes with different measurements tools. No one is late in life. Everything is accordingly in its own timing. At least if we consider the natural way of how the nature and universe work.

Therefore, my friend, cool down and hold your heart. No need to be alarmed or panic. Yours is on the way and you already have what you actually need at the present time.

Look around. Aren't others envying you too? Even though they should not but you know it is a natural thing to

CHAPTER 21

do especially when we become desperate in life and wish things would just speed up and make you rich. Does being rich in money truly means you are wealthy?

One more thing to consider here is the sources of the money or wealth. Some are rich by stealing, robbing, killing. While some others are rich by inheritance. And we also have some that have made some pacts with spirits or other Beings to be rich and in return by giving those entities their souls as collaterals or the life of their off springs. Some others it is hard work or just pure luck and coincidence; being at the right place at the right time and having the spirit of recognizing the opportunity.

At that token, would it have just been a test with two choices leading to different paths? Since, so far every decision that we have ever made can no longer be reversed. Try next time to recognize the opportunities knocking at your door. Acknowledge people around you because you don't know who among them would have the keys to open the doors for you to succeed.

So my friend, ease up and focus. Yours is also on the way and perhaps you already have what you actually need and need to watch on your spending and investment habits. Some people may just need to reduce their over-head spending to fit their incomes. Do not live beyond your means and spend your money on things that you need instead things that you want.

Never look up to the rich nor look down to the poor. Treat the rich and the poor the same way with respect and kindness. Be satisfied with your share of the world and let others enjoy theirs too. Love yourself enough, and be too brave to lie, while uprightly making it a habit to be too generous to cheat. When it is your turn to win, don't brag about it. And always respect and show more consideration to women, children and elderly people. Help one another with sincerity.

CHAPTER 21

Universal Mind and Life Style of the Wise

Life is in itself a gift from high powers. What we actually witness and perceive in life is a fact that we coexist with them (high powers). The awareness of something is actually a perception of a reality that our mind or brain or subconscious recognizes.

I chose today to write before I go to work. My choice after all to do whatever I want. But not without hesitations. I wondered for a minute if I would start work earlier or write. After couple of jogging within my mind, the writing won and here I'm.

This is how it went down. I work for myself and I can decide when to start work and when to finish. Since I have that flexibility to choose my time to start work, I, therefore, decided that I could always go to work after I finish writing.

I also leaned toward the writing because I know that writing sometime and most of the time requires the writer to listen to his/her intuitions when the urge of writing is present. Write it down now or you may lose your ideas later. So, I decided to write.

The importance of me telling you this story is because of the fact that I had to listen to all the convincing suggestions and ideas within my own head. Before I decided to write I had to choose what was best for me and what made more sense. Since I could still go to work after all when I'm done writing, it shouldn't be a problem. It is just like hitting two birds with one stone.

The mind is a powerful tool and means to convey what we settle for as a final thought. When we think before we speak or write, the one that comes out is the one we settled for, based on a lot of criteria. When the mind has the accessibility to tap into our knowledge and understanding baggage in a flip second; and come out with something that fit and addresses the situation, it is a beautiful thing. When the mind has access to different perspectives and views or facts, it serves better the person that owns it by providing the person the ability to juxtapose and alternate different ideas, and realities to fit to his/her present needs at a quicker rate. Everything begins and starts in the mind. What you entertained within is your own warfare within. The mind needs to be fed with knowledge, stories, true facts, wisdom, in order for the person to enjoy that flexibility to be agile with controlling the thought to fit to the present situation or issue. Just like to do better, you have to know better; then act better.

Past experiences also strengthen the mind in making quick decisions based on a precedent event with similarities or slight nuances to the present. But make no mistake, because our experiences can lead us to make a wrong decision too. It is dangerous to live in the past.

The growth of the mind is relative to what the person learned and has been taught throughout his past to present time. Whatever the mind has been exposed to, would always have an impact somewhat in the way we might interact or counteract with the immediate or far future just like our previous experiences.

The mind in part or all contributes to us making decisions. It also help us judge and address issues in pretty much any given situation. Even without having all the facts, the mind tend and will render a partial or final decision based on its understanding and available sources of knowledge or insight it draws from.

Everyone has a mind. Everyone is in tune with the reality and mechanism operating within his/her own mind. Different people put in the same situation and issue will not necessarily react and behave the same way. We are equipped with the ammunitions of our own knowledge, understanding and wisdom to shoot at life events and difficulties. Everyone with their own separate experience and ability to handle what the world throws at him/her. Nobody said life would have ever been easy.

Now when we add personal feelings and emotions plus desires and wishes, we are taking the mind to another level, to another dimension where only the person posing an act as a reaction to what the person perceived as his/her reality at that present time; only to those facts and personal realities would dictate ones behavior or action.

We have those that can control some or all those feelings and emotions and those that cannot or not even trying to. The mind, a powerful tool is at the same time a liberator and a prison cell. We can use it to be free or we can let it take over our life when we let it get filled with junk and insecurities.

We should not neglect the fact that the mind could also be victim of an outside influence. Be it spiritual, physical or intentionally done, the mind can be corrupt and kidnap by other people or beings. The mind which is intangible is also a receptor of signal sent by other people different minds. We receive messages by telepathy from other minds in a form of energy and sometimes we do act on it without knowing or knowingly execute someone else's plan and thought or emotions.

Our mind as a receptor also attracts what it wants and needs like a magnet. When we want something and think about it, we send out a message to the universe web of thoughts as a mass, and in return the mass would travel to others that would receive it through their mind signal receptors and a link is made. Now since the mind is also equip to attract as a magnet, it will then pull the links back to its path to make contact and enter possession of what it needed. Thereby, growing in strength and more determined in applying the laws of attraction.

Finally, we can meet people with different minds and backgrounds that end up being the puzzle solvers of our situations or difficulties or needs. Therefore, do not overlooked no-one.

Sometimes, we do miss the opportunities by simply not acting on them or letting our mind again intrude and make us miss what needed to solve our puzzle by being judgmental. Our emotions and feelings and present moods could also intrude in our lifetime opportunities. We should not also put aside our expectations, illusions and pretentions. I have seen a lot of people missed some opportunities because they were showing signs of anger; full of pride, jealousy, spite and carelessness and lack of humbleness.

Sometimes, it might just be a simple hello to a stranger to start a conversation that we have neglected to do so, that we have missed our blessings at that moment. Or we have simply judge that person already base on few derisory facts that we have dismissed him/her ourselves already. We should always remember that the mind draws in closer what it want. Meaning you as bearing and walking with your mind, you also draw in closer the things that you want and desire including what you need.

There is no recipe in not missing out on our opportunities, but if we simply remained cautious, conscious, attentive to others without prejudicial actions, we may miss few of our opportunities. There is always only one person away to change your future which is the law of two (2) and the law of recognition because you have to recognize the opportunity first. Just like someone 'else is waiting for you to change their lives. Come on now, empowered someone today. Make someone smile and happy. It could just be a simple compliment, or acknowledgment to that person.

Remember that we are living in a world where there is so much division and hate. A world where colors, gender, races are now a determining factors of a qualification of stature and fair treatment. Be mindful to rise your mind above all prejudicial judgment based on those criteria. The mind has no limits nor borders. Everyone and everything is alive depending on how you raise your own mind to become. Let me consider your mind as your child that you have to teach, tender to and protect. You should now realize that as the mind your infant, you have to feed it, bath it, guide it and nurture it. Just as you raise your child to grow and be efficient in society, you should also raise your mind to grow and be efficient in society.

CHAPTER 21

That means you will have to spent time with your mind and do an assessment of growth and test its abilities to survive in the jungle of minds. You know well that if you don't clean your mind of the toxins of the world, your mind will remain corrupt and toxic. So go ahead and flash it out of all impurities from society that you don't like or are prejudicial. This is how you flash it.

Society judges people by their skin colors, so clean your mind of that if you chose to love and put everyone equally without racial discrimination.

Society discriminates about where people come from as a place of birth or tribal belonging, chose not to follow suit.

We know the instinctive rules because they are universally desire by everyone. So adapt to it.

Nobody wants to be killed, so don't kill either.

Nobody wants to be robbed, so don't rob any one.

Nobody wants to be exploited, so don't exploit your fellow man, either.

Nobody wants to be discriminately judge, so refrain from judging others in discriminate criteria.

The truth is that everything and anything, we don't want others to do to us, we shall also refrain ourselves from doing it to others. Before we can complain about how others treat us, it will be wise to consider first how you treat them and others. You can control how you treat others but it is a hard thing to control how others would treat you back in return. Still do not corrupt your mind by entertaining a retaliation when they treat you wrong. Simply move along and change your surroundings or be with people with mindful minds like.

Only worry about yourself and let others worry about themselves as even the fingers of our hands are in different length. Don't expect everyone to understand you because it will be a waste of your time as each mind grow in gradual sequence and will not jump to higher level suddenly just because you want it to. The process of learning and mental growth is gradual and the ability to understand is of a result of so many other piled of related or unrelated knowledge, wisdom, experience, and even good faith. When dealing with others, a lot of things govern and lead to them understanding you.

So you can teach, but do not expect to be understood by everyone at the same time nor at the same pace. You can take your time to guide but not until the one being guided believe in your decisions making abilities to lead to a successful wishful result, you will be sowing on a dry land or a rock. Just know that each mind understanding of any discipline clicks in, in due time.

Do not let yourself be consumed by anger and resentment because others have rejected you. Hold your head up because they are the ones that don't deserve you. Instead shine even brighter so that they would see your light and happiness from afar and they might follow suit.

Not everyone will like you, or love you, nor even acknowledge your presence as each one of us is battling his/her own mind within. You can never determine how sane or insane someone else mind is at a present time, because actual mood and emotions could intrude in any of their actions and deeds anytime without warning. Nice people could suddenly become unreasonable.

Especially do not neglect or under-estimate the mischief minds that want to take you out of your own character for their enjoyment purposes. Therefore I say to you, be mindful of yourself and others by not being quick to judge because the same minds of today will grow in knowledge and understanding tomorrow. Because wisdom comes from within after a long life experience. Wisdom is a good judgment earn from the accumulation of so many other experiences, influential enough to manifest in our life automatically only acquired through

CHAPTER 21

time and could take a life time to achieve. When we train our mind daily, we will instill in it the ability to access wisdom easily only through good faith.

Life is itself a journey. A lone journey that only one will travel through and access all the possibilities that he/she projects to achieve. We have different desires and needs. Each one of us set for himself/herself a mission statement and work in achieving it. We have different mission statements applied to each mind at any given time. Don't be surprised to see some people without a goal or mission for their lives at all. They internally working on some inner greater conflicts emotionally or spiritually that we might have over-looked. Mental health has to be taken seriously in order for the victims of all kind of abuse to join the work force and society without being a threat to themselves and others upon healing.

Some minds want to steal at the moment, and some minds want to help others heal at the same given time. Each mind with its own worries and challenges. So we should always understand that not everyone would want the same thing we want at any given time. Trying to convince one's mind to bend and blend to yours could sometime become annoying and irritating. Therefore leave your worries to yourself and let others worry about theirs. Sometimes the best way to show one's mind how to do things is by doing it while they are observing. Again shine your light to the point that it would be hard for them not to notice it. But under no circumstances should you expect that they will be of good faith to give to Caesar what really belong to Caesar. Good faith is not equally shared among mankind and it is not the preference of many. In fact, no one truly becomes a prophet in his own hometown.

So, in those fine thin notes, I reiterate to you; love your skin color, love truth and justice. Pay good attention about your surroundings and administer to everyone with no regards of their skin color, gender and their place of origin because we all have and share equal rights and equal freedom of speech. And do not be satisfied of a superficial understanding of a book because silence is golden and everything cannot be contained in a book just like you can never really realized and fully ascertain where you came from before being born in this world. A world that only gives nothing else but an avenue to perfect yourself. Just act on what needs to be done and not for the reputation of whatever you did being done.

Just like the Sun, it shines and doesn't worry about any obstacle on its way. It does not care if anybody is paying attention to it; it shines even when no one is looking. In fact, it keeps shining to the point that any obstacle on its way would just feel its presence or the light would just curb to point in another direction, forming a shade. The sun-light is indeed an extension of its being, without caring of any obstacle. Otherwise, then it would create a shadow where there is a barrier which remain still the sun's extension. Surely, the Sun light we see around us from far above to earth is nothing else but its own extension. A powerful light that reaches everywhere.

Therefore, be good, be fruitful and let the shadows worry about themselves as you will always shine your light as an extension to occupy every space where there is an entrance to any small hole to illuminate until time itself moves you around to another dimension. Act like the Sun. Do good deeds for the sake of doing good and not because of the rewards. Take care of your business, even if no one is giving it a damn. Do not seek compliment, just handle right whatever needs to be taken care of. Better yet, do not wait to be instructed to do so; take heed and take the right initiative.

Having said that, don't be a fool because racism and unequal treatment really exist and are alive among mankind. But comfort your heart because every child has been assigned a teacher.

CHAPTER 22
Race, a Divided and Misunderstood Feather among Humans

Race is a real divide within society. As something that can be seen as intrinsic and original to all being making it just like any other species that ever existed including plants and animal world, we have fallen so low that we are now using it as a weapon. We all came with different skin colors like the birds and other animals that also have different feathers colors and skin colors.

It does not take away that we are all the same thing. It's just like a bird could have little birds with different feather colors. One could be brown, black and the other white or yellow. It does not make any difference in the eyes of their mother or dad. They are all of the same family and will be fed and taken care of proportionally without any discrimination.

In our reel society, race and skin color has always been a divided and a center of discord for many years, even centuries. Though we are all made equal and from the same source, we tend to neglect the fact that we are sharing the same womb and are from the same precursor of life.

Neither one of us, as humans could determine the color or tone of the skin of our next to kin. But since we are champions on dividing and conquering, the skin color have been used against our own self fellow mankind that breathe the same air just like we all do.

CHAPTER 22

As a beginner, we first identify with race, which could be normal when all you see around you is the same color like you. And as time goes, the world across all continents were getting closer and closer through migrations, thus the meeting of different skin colors began to sight each other. What was supposed to be amazing at first, became a dividing ground based on superiority complex. Because each civilization had their different abilities to understand and their different knowhow/skills and wisdom, the skin colors became linked to this complex of superiority and inferiority merely with the aim at dividing and conquering.

Some people were fortunate to have an advantage than others, just like in all mankind regardless of their skin colors, we all have different qualities and experiences build over time. Does that make any of the others lesser than you, knowing that each one of us have to live and learn by failure and gain just like the universe intended it to be? A place of learning. A place of growth by experience to guarantee understanding and wisdom of life.

We are all subject to the same rules and same calamities that the natural world throws at us. And being of different skin colors does not mean that we should hate each other merely based on colors. In fact, nobody should be judge first just because they are black, white, yellow, brown or red. The same atom that we are made of is not any different than the other atoms that make everything else in the whole big universe in its own complexity. We share and have 99.9 percent of the same Genes universally.

I have a heart just like you do. You have a kidney just like I do. Could anyone tell which color of the skin a heart or kidney may have come from if they all happens to be exposed outside of their original bodies they belong to? Or, would you refuse the transplant because of hate or discrimination?

A white male kidney can be transplanted in a black man's body as long as the blood type matches and there is no other ab-

CHAPTER 22

normalities. A black female's kidney could also be implanted on a white body to save a life. Not just because in this example, we only need the organs that skins colors do not matter, we should all become color-blinded in life, at work, at the grocery store…

So, why are we still stock on the issue of racial discord when none of us can guarantee his/ her own survival tomorrow? Can you tell me that you will see the next morning for sure by your own strength and mightiness?

We cannot guarantee how tomorrow may looked like after us because if we continue to discriminate on others based on the color of their skin, nothing is a guarantee that you or your kids will not be discriminated in return the next day either. Because if we make a race a center divided, we are then doomed to pay the price as the cycle always turn around and never fails. Just like a wheel, it keeps rotating so that what is high comes down and so forth.

You can be in power today, just to find yourself a slave tomorrow. And that's the circle of life. You can be in power today and find your kids and beloved ones become slaves of tomorrow.

The truth is, no one can come or see God's kingdom unless the love of the neighbor is achieved. Therefore, take heed and love and treat your neighbor the same way you want them to treat you and your offspring. Only this way, that the kingdom of God could open its gate for your accession. And your neighbor does not just limit to mankind only, it also includes the trees and plants; the animal kingdoms, all sources of water and mountains and hills, etc. Remember, race was never the factor nor a factor long ago and never will be. We need to stop being cruel on our animal life and vegetal world as well.

CHAPTER 23
Universal Laws and Rules

Everyone is born free and equal and deserves to always have their right to choose and to move accordingly to his/her will. We have an equal right without borders and territory limits. No one shall be held against their own will unless he/she is a criminal.

We have the same right to play and an equal right to assembly and the right to exercise our duly right.

No one can take the right of anybody else whatsoever the situation and the circumstances away without a due process.

As we have the right to an education, it as to be equal and equal opportunity for all genders and skin colors.

Born in different families and different countries and circumstances, we have been seen on the eyes and our own eyes that there is no more secret to whisper that we are here to co-habit. Made of two hands, two legs and one head, how could you claim to be different?

Cut yourself and flesh; what is it that is bleeding out other than seed and shade of life?

Can we take anything else away or add anything else into it? Besides that your own blood is full of stars stuffs/components making you possessing the same elements and composition as the Stars above.

We are the same product and everything that my eye could see, yours could see, too. What you can also see, I can,

CHAPTER 23

too. So let's cut to the pace and remember that life is beautiful and is worth preserving. And no one can take your right to live away from you either.

Isn't it that everything is vanity? You get born, you crawl, walk and stumble. You grow and get mature then you thought of starting a family to become whole; now you are the cycle, the continuation of life once you have a child.

Everything is vanity. Then we establish our territory to just leave it to someone else after death hoping that they will carry the torches or our names. My question for you is how many names do we have and how many names have we forgotten already individually?

How many other names did we forgot on top of the so many names we have not come closed to remembering? Everything disappears and becomes obsolete in the eyes of the world. Today is present and yesterday is yesterday. Tomorrow never came but let the living tell you how today went down, even though the distinction between the past, present and future is nothing really but an illusion.

At the end of the day, we are all children of the most high and the reunification of all the children must come to past and be a reality. The point of life is to just follow reason and the divine spirit; accepting whatever nature throws at us.

There are just realities in our encounter with others that we cannot avoid. We cannot control or dictate how others will make us feel but we can control how we respond to it. Instead, do not react to circumstances that upset your emotions. The only way to overcome is to not let your emotions get the best of you. Emotions don't escalate nothing; we do give them a room to escalate when we give them an avenue by reacting to them. Our emotions act like when you drop a stone in some water and it shakes the water around. Depending on the size of the stone, the splash of the water would also correspond. There will be some ripples, but eventually, the water calms down when the wave stops.

CHAPTER 23

Meaning our emotions always have an expiration time and when they reach their calming points, we become normal again. If you were feeling, or getting angry or upset, all you need to do is to observe the changing of your moods. Acknowledge those changes but do not react to them as it is clear that you would not stay angry permanently. It is just temporary but the damages from your reactions could be unrepairable. Try to remain behind your emotions always as much as possible.

The question have always remain of how we choose to respond to those emotions by limiting their impact on our feelings. Keep in mind that there is always a space between our emotions and feelings. And by acknowledging those changes that our emotions make us feel, we thereby create a space that is just enough for us to decide either we are going to let the emotions carry us away by reacting to them or remain present while keeping our calm composure. These couples of seconds that we have between the space of reacting and setting off the chain of reaction or just keeping calm completely open our life to working from the space of open awareness according to various spiritual teachers. This process is a guide for the mind to reclaim its natural capacity to remain present at all times when facing the inevitable waives that our emotions bring.

And sometimes we just need to say "sorry," to stop any escalation of any wrong. Saying sorry has a power to disarm others of their anger. Saying sorry amends relationships, soothe wounds and heal broken hearts. A sincere apology prevents further misunderstanding.

So, "I'm sorry," to you if you are reading this book and feeling some type of way. Do not let your Ego get in between you and what is written. Because the ego is looking for something to hold on to in order to have its validity.

I have seen again the three stars among other stars on the night of October 19, 2018. I had not have sight of them for a good while. We had a rain at the previous week and I'm

CHAPTER 23

not sure if it was because of the rain that the sky was suddenly clear at its most, making then the stars more visible or the three stars have their own time of appearances? I'm sure they do have their own cycle and I have been gazing the sky since then with naked eyes and I did not have sight of them. I guess, everything do have its own season.

A lot of things do come in my mind all the time. A lot of concerns that need to be addressed. A lot of concerns that I have gave doors to run through my mind here and there. Some gets suppressed and some get entertained. The reality is, we all pick and choose our own battle. As time goes, we may realize that we have spent time on some issues and life concerns at their specific times that we would not have made them a big deal base on our actual state of mind, after the fact. We grow in maturity, wisdom and understanding. Then you come to realize that some battles are not worth your time, trying to win it. It will just deplete your energy down the road and leave you with nothing for greater and essential battles.

To win, you have to have won it first in your mind. Your attitude and behavior changes on each battle depending on the state of your mind. Some days you just don't feel like putting unnecessary energy out, even though you might have felt some type of way. And some days, it would take just a little bit of someone trespassing you and the battle is on. Our minds are made to survive into different dimensions, just like our soul. They intercept messages from here and beyond so that they could defend themselves and act promptly. You notice I said the minds. Because there is not just one voice that we would hear within our own mind. First, we hear the voice; and second we realize the option to counter or follow suit. If we counter, we still have options to counter again and so forth until the mind gets what it wants. Some people would remain on the middle ground by becoming purely a witness to their own mind and some would keep going and going, still figuring out how to decide. The mind talks to itself and answer back to itself if you really pay close attention to it.

CHAPTER 23

The mind is a powerful thing that could play tricks on you. Especially, when your mind controls you. It has its own ego that yields to no one. We only have no other choice than to take control over it since we have always had choices to make at every decision making. And that's what makes destiny obsolete. Our capability to decide on our next action, thought, deed and intention. When you see the world in a small screen, you can only see yourself and your immediate encounters and all the chaos and miseries. But the day you widen your screen, you will see other things and existence that you were blind to which is the oneness of all things. You would notice that you were surrounded by beautiful beings, species, flowers, plants in an up-scale design.

Self-control is imperative and it starts with you and me. We had a line that we have drawn from our past lives and present. That line is in multi-dimensional correspondence that keeps going into circles until the line links back to where it has started. So, we get back what we put out because the line we may have drawn even 1,000 years ago could just now linking back to us today.

Every action has a return payment. Every deed has a return payment. Every intention has a return payment. Every conclusive thought has a return payment. Everything has to play itself out to complete a full circle until everything is dealt cumulative of our present actions, deeds, intentions and final decisions. That is why the mind is acting crazy. Because it wants to address and handle everything as it needs to close every open case in your life. It will keep bringing past issues and events in an attempt to solve them or escalate them as the mind is also link to its own ego. The ego of the mind wants to be right and win at all cost, therefore, it would keep talking and talking and never would shut up. But you, the listener of your mind should know that you are not the mind. That's why you are able to hear it talk and complain. Just remain a witness, an observer to your own mind when/while it is talking to itself.

CHAPTER 23

Take notice that you are not the mind since truly you could hear it talk. You must have to be outside of the mind to be able to hear the voices in your head. In this case, you are a separate entity, just like a third party within your own body. Therefore, you are the essence of life, you are the authentic Self and the awareness; and you see nothing but beauty in all things and know nothing else but Love.

The truth is that we have no control over nothing but ourselves. We can temporarily control someone, or something, but we cannot indefinitely and eternally control them as they too have time of deliverance and merci. By the grace, we all share a common destiny. The destiny of the returns. We would die and get resurrected once we miss the mark of Love. Then the scale will run into motion to weight and balance everyone's heart and everything out. The scale is impartial and neutral. The scale will not discriminate, nor show favors; it will weight your heart. And to avoid coming back here on earth via birth, you have to achieve true self-realization, or total liberation by being able to control your senses. It is how we experience Grace, Ecstasy and Spiritual Union with God.

CHAPTER 24
The Illusion of Being the Center of the World.

You are not your skin, nor your hair. You are not your rear ends (butt) or skin color. Don't even identify yourself with your car, your house or how much money you have. You are not even your beauty or the age you feel you are. You are who you have always been; Hakuna Matata. Its words in Swahili language meaning No Worries. What your mind is telling you that you are, may not really determined who you are or want to be. Didn't you already been wrestling with and against your own mind? The mind is telling what you can do and what you cannot do. It tells you that you will fail and it isn't even relevant and useful to starting this particular project, or trying to lift yourself up to a better you.

Your mind would also justify and plead its case by pulling into your memory to play the events and various life events and encounter, words in order to be right and contradict your power of choices or your will. Don't forget, there are also times when the mind tells you that you can do it and you just have to take a leap of faith and walk through by making your dreams, a reality. The mind could also lie to you by fooling you to believe that you are better than everybody else and you are the only one that should be in the center of focus. Meaning you would be prone to doing it your way, or no way. Is this qualified here as the Ego of self?

The ego goes something like this. Are you not going to fight back? Isn't it that you are upset, why don't you react to it? Are you really going to keep your cool and not retaliate?

CHAPTER 24

Why forgive, when you are not at fault, or the instigator? What was that disrespect about? We are not letting this thing go; we have to retaliate. I'm bigger and more important than them. I have a better job and a better income. In fact I'm better than everybody-else. I'm black; I'm white; I'm a Jew, I'm Chinese and so on. Yup, this is the identity of the Ego. Always putting itself first and everyone-else at the back. The ego will not accept criticism, nor admit any wrongdoing. Better yet, it would not be capable to say, "Sorry," or to seek forgiveness. The ego would not even acknowledge that it lacks knowledge and need to instruct itself better. It holds on to the primal of its religion, traditions and beliefs because of fear and would resist becoming open minded to facilitate any possible change and to accept new ideas, new teachings or knowledge.

In this situation, the mind is misleading and uses the force of fear and illusion to compromise your relationships with others. Thereby making you a hostile host to others and yourself. Someone in these scenarios that concedes to the ego's pressure would most likely be living in his/her past so often that there is no window to appreciate the present time of life even in places that do not call for drama or hostility. That person seemed to not be able to move pass the past and would always identify people from their past behaviors; making his/her present encounter to them obsolete even if those very people have just done something positive deserving of a positive appreciation. Therefore Move pass your past whenever you can. Think about giving people another chance. This could be a good start to forgiving them and leaving their negative past behind. And there could be no avenue for Love when we keep holding on to our egos and putting ourselves as the center of the universe.

You are not the color of your dress, or the attire you wear either. You are not a gang member, nor limiting yourself to color of clothes to hate or to love someone. Either you are brown, black, white, Yellow or purple, you are not to identify yourself to any color to determine your true being or true Self. Why limit yourself when you can be all things and all presence? Do you want to know how? I'm not your teacher, as no one could teach you to become something that you already are. Continue reading and you will soon realize that you are part of a big plan and every plan that God had from the Beginning and the End. And hopefully, you have already realized it from the previous chapters.

Of course, who has never been hurt before? We have all been there and it hurts. The pain can piled up and change someone's attitude and behavior towards the world. Believe me, the world would kick you to the ground. Hurts after hurt, we become less tolerant, less caring, less self-esteem and to sum it up, we develop a loss of trust and love for the world and its neighbors. We now dress a tall wall and barriers around our Self for self-protection. Living now behind our self-constructed safe zone, no longer being able to trust and be vulnerable, loving and trusting again. But you can start new again by living life present to present. Give a donation to a stranger in need today and you will start living in present. Say Good Morning out loud and listen to it soundly and you are now living in the present. And if you have some extra change in your pockets, give some to a needy one. Do not disturb other people joy even if you are not in a happy mood. Merge your mood with the joy and enjoy the moment of happiness with them.

Today, we give some money to a stranger, tomorrow, we say, "Not today," depending on our own mood and financial stability. Some days, we avoid them when we don't even have change (coins). Suddenly, those days of being generous have just disappeared and you feel now a slight indifference or lack compassion, just to realize later no one escapes handing a hand to a stranger for help. We have all been there when we wish someone would just come and make everything normal again in our life. There is no exact chosen place to seek help, or to ask for forgiveness. It may seemed that there is no way out in your actual life situation, but there are plenty of windows and gates to exit through safely. There is always an angel at the corner of

CHAPTER 24

the street. Just try to keep the same compassion and love for the people you helped, even when you are no longer able to come to their assistance. Look at them like they exist without avoiding eye contact. That's when, your own angel would wait for you at the corner with more blessings.

Do you know what life is? Compassion attracts compassion. Love attracts love.

I tried to answer it, but it seems like life is every day. Meaning that life is defined daily. Even though today is life and we always learn something new every day, we seemed to still have unfinished task and to do list to carry over the next day. Yet life is today, but yesterday never cease to try to catch up with life; which is today and the meaning of life and to be living daily.

Life is somewhat like a new adventure every day. We tend to do the same things over and over. We tend to commit and repeat the same mistakes. A lot of times and most of the times before consciousness, we live life without accountability. We live life without remorse and without appreciation. We pick and judge ourselves by our own standards and privileges. We are the prosecuted and the judge at the same time with what we do or pose as actions. In low key, we truly think we know who we are and the reasons behind our deeds and actions. Because, everything and actions according to us was justified. And we even make decisions sometimes without having all the facts.

Isn't everyday an occasion to learn and grow? I always wonder now. But I never used to pay too much attention to it. I was just living and thinking the best of me. Thinking that I was good overall. But, is the way I think of myself unanimous with what others think of me? I know my motives, but do everyone else knew my motives? Even people that are not close to you might have an idea about who you are without you even knowing of their existence. Anybody you have hurt or transgressed would not give a good report about your conduct. But my mind would justify even my wrongs to legitimate my actions. Not

CHAPTER 24

until you become conscious enough that you would smell your own funk. Remember that words travel and people talk about others behind their back. So people would have an idea about who you are based on what other people said and thought about you, too.

In sum, every-one of us judges or have judged before. Every-one of us have talk about someone behind his/her back and every-one of us have heard of and participated in some-one-else talking about someone on their back.

This is what I call life. We never fully know what others think about us until they tell us. And when they do decide to tell us how they feel about us and we disagree, we usually counter-act with an argument or try to justify ourselves. Imagine then how many words from them, they did not let out during the conversation. Better yet, how many people do you think know and heard about you without you even knowing them or never spoken to them either?

We might be thinking that we are perfect while some-one-else thinks otherwise. At the end why worry too much about that. But once we know what is said of us, then we should be more open minded and really listen with attention. Instead of refusing a criticism, we should remain quiet and care to the concern from others about us. Listen and when appropriate, you could place a few words after you have listened to their concerns.

The road to life and living start with no lack of consciousness. We are there executing our minds and thoughts. We reproduce what we have seen and heard, even what we have experienced. We fight because fight came our way. We always try our best to make ourselves happy and the center of the universe. Having placed ourselves to always have the last word, we go the extra mile to satisfy ourselves either through good deeds or bad. Since we could justify our own actions based on our own limitations, every actions and word said by us, we meant it and had a reason why we acted or behaved so.

CHAPTER 24

At the end of the day, no one would grow old without attending to their emotions, feelings and deeds. We all have strengths and weaknesses. Some people would just hate you because they think that you got it all. Some people would hate you, because they think you are happy, rich, loved, intelligent, smart, honest, loving, without even your knowledge. Yes, they would imagine all kind of things about you that you don't even know about yourself. This is life; we potter and better ourselves every day.

You see, we are in a world of confusion where we are all trying to figure out who we are? We are in a world that we seem not to understand. Why earth? And why Sun? And why Moon?

We see all those events around us and it takes a long time for us to even start wondering why others exist?

Wouldn't it be cool and exciting to learn that a simple cloud could grow as tall in height, thickness and diameter as much as fifteen miles, or over towards the space? I wonder what God sees in you when He looks at you?

Don't Worry and Stress Over the Small Stuff

It is true that life isn't fair and roses all the way. We might have wronged someone along the way or someone did something wrong to us while interacting socially. So many family members are not talking to each other because of a misunderstanding among them. Brothers/sisters from the same blood line are not on good terms with each other, and now they cut any communication and do not care about their well-being. It is common to hear these words, "I do not talk to him anymore; I don't care what happened to him," or "He/she should reach out first." "If he/she does not apologize, I will not speak to him again."

Yes, the elephant is already in the room, so someone should reach out first and I think it should be you. You are the one reading the book, and it makes perfect sense to be the bigger person. Why can't you reach out to your loved ones and

CHAPTER 24

friends that are no longer on good terms with you? Get it done and move forward by clearing the dark cloud of energy that no longer need to hold you down. Even if you believe that they are the one that are supposed to reach out to you and apologize first, and they are not doing so; it becomes ok for you to be the first to act loving and reach out.

If only we could adopt a strategy of life that would allow us to assume and accept that any encounter with someone, the person is here to teach us a lesson. When you are interacting with someone, if your mindset is to understand later what's that person wanted to teach you, you would notice that you are actually paying attention to the person, that you are listening and not letting the conversation become argumentative and stressful. Imagine, once you realize what someone was trying to teach you, their actions will no longer bother or frustrate you. You might even cease to see people's imperfections if you believe that everyone that you meet is there to teach you. In this walk of life, it might be that you need to learn to be patient, to control your anger and temper, to have compassion, to be humble, to show love for your neighbor, etc.

Besides, life should be lived in the present because tomorrow could come with a rain check for somebody else to cash. Reach out to your brothers and sisters, your parents, aunties and uncle to reunite and rekindle the family and friendship relationship. While you are procrastinating, life is going on. Kids are growing up, people are getting older and sick. Some others might be due soon to leave this world, so learn the lesson that was being taught to you and practice compassion by acting first with love to say hello. Consider that life is an automobile, a car, and you are the driver, but it could only be driven from your inside out, your inner shelf. Life will be what you want it to be and where you want it to go. You can practice unconditional love and love and forgive people without putting a condition first before they earn your love. Love them without wanting them to change first or be different. Forgive them and love them just the way they are.

CHAPTER 25
Enlighten and Saved but still Struggling

Living and being part of this world that we have inherited willingly or unwillingly, we will always have time of struggle even after realizing who we are as a being. We would still struggle with our bills, illnesses even loss of loved ones. There would be events in our surroundings or immediate relative's lives that will play against our serenity. We would sometimes witness life events that we don't have the powers and ability to change or remediate. The fact that you know who you are in the divine sense does not mean that life will be easy from there on. You will visit a love one in the hospital. You will still go to your friends' and loved ones' funerals. You may still be homeless, thirsty or hungry. You could still get sick and fall in desperation.

In fact, reaching enlightenment or being saved is not a shield for ending the duality of the universe. Each thing and its opposite will still be part of your life. The difference between you and the others is your ability to understand and cope with whatever life throws in your way. Your ability to accept peacefully everything and any life event either it brings you joy or sadness. Your difference resides on the fact that you have understood that God, the Supreme Being made this world that way and there is no chance for any of us to actually changing the mastermind plan and end. As long as we recognize that there is a Supreme Being with a predestined plan for us that escapes our desires and wishes reach, we would always seek understanding and wisdom from the Supreme Being.

CHAPTER 25

Even having realized that we are made of God Image and that we are actually Divine, we would soon to realize that this journey of earth also have its own purpose and that no one not even the enlightened and saved one could escape its duality. Yet we are saved but would still have to work for our daily bread. Yet we are enlightened but would still be powerless during sickness. And, of course, with the ineluctable and the for sure death of the body in due time. No one is immune to death, sickness, sorrow or lack of basic needs to survive. These are things that are just part of life and will forever exist and shape every-one's life on earth.

Do not fall for the naivety trend, thinking that after mastering the control of your emotions, feelings and desires, life will suddenly become roses and absent from struggles. By being saved and enlighten, it gives you the tools to understand and to possess enough wisdom to go with the flow of life and accept whatever that comes your way without trying to change it. Because if you do so, hopelessness and desolation would come into your life as nothing happened without its due season and time.

You should always remind yourself that life events, regardless of how painful it is to endure, would not last forever, and that just like joy and happiness reigned in your kingdom yesterday, those days will come back again in their own cycle. There could be no summer without a spring season. To say the least, every season has its allocated time until the next season and so forth. The ability to remain still and calm during each season is what makes the difference between the enlightened/saved and the rest of the folks living with no knowledge nor understanding still succumbing on the reflex of their emotions, feelings and different other moods.

In sum, live gracefully and mercifully with in mind that God, the Supreme Being always remains in control and delivers whoever seeks and wants to know God. Always be loving and caring like God commanded us to uphold in this duality

CHAPTER 25

world. And in time of trouble and desolation, we should invoke God blessings and forgiveness on us and to our loved ones. Do not blame God or curse God, because God always makes a way to deliver you even when you least deserve it. God is faithful and trustworthy. God is love, grace and mercy. God shall deliver you in time of trouble and make a way for a worthy adventure on earth when you acknowledge the supremacy that God earns among all existence. Even though God doesn't need or require your acknowledgement and love to exist, by knowing and feeling part of His/hers is sufficient.

CHAPTER 26
The Forty Two (42) Ideal Laws of Ma'at to Live By

MA 'At is an ancient system of laws and a system of morals and values that the ancient Egyptians commonly known as the ancient Kemet / kemp used to guide the thought and behavior of their citizens in order to guarantee justice, equality, peace and harmony among its citizens and its neighbors. It is still being practiced and follow around the world and in many cultures in Africa. These are the laws and directives to follow and to live by.

1- I will not do wrong and will acknowledge any wrong doing and make amends.
2- I will not steal.
3- I will not act with violence.
4- I will not kill.
5- I will not be unjust.
6- I will not cause pain.
7- I will not waste food.
8- I will not lie.
9- I will not desecrate holy places.
10- I will not speak evil.
11- I will not abuse my sexuality.
12- I will not cause the shedding of tears.
13- I will not sow seed of regret.
14- I will not be an aggressor.
15- I will not act guilefully or guileful.
16- I will not lay waste the plowed land.
17- I will not bear false witness.

CHAPTER 26

18- I will not speak against any person.
19- I will not be wrathful and angry.
20- I will not lay with a man's wife.
21- I will not lay with a woman's husband.
22- I will not pollute myself.
23- I will not cause terror.
24- I will not pollute the earth.
25- I will not speak in anger.
26- I will not turn from words of truth.
27- I will not utter curses.
28- I will not initiate a quarrel.
29- I will not be excitable or contentious.
30- I will not be prejudiced.
31- I will not be an eavesdropper.
32- I will not speak over much.
33- I will not act against my ancestors.
34- I will not waste water.
35- I will not do evil.
36- I will not be arrogant.
37- I will not blaspheme the one most high.
38- I will not commit fraud.
39- I will not defraud temple offerings.
40- I will not plunder the dead.
41- I will not mistreat children.
42- I will not mistreat animals.

In another way and in a different order, the forty-two Divine Principles of MA 'At is presented as followed:

1- I have not committed sin.
2- I have not committed robbery with violence.
3- I have not stolen.
4- I have not slain men or women.
5- I have not stolen food.
6- I have not swindled offerings.
7- I have not stolen from God/Goddess.

CHAPTER 26

8- I have not told lies.
9- I have not carried away food.
10- I have not cursed.
11- I have not closed my eyes to truth.
12- I have not committed adultery.
13- I have not made anyone cry.
14- I have not felt sorrow without reason.
15- I have not assaulted anyone.
16- I am not deceitful.
17- I have not stolen anyone's land.
18- I have not been an eavesdropper.
19- I have not falsely accused anyone.
20- I have not been angry without reason.
21- I have not seduced anyone's wife or husband.
22- I have not polluted myself.
23- I have not terrorized anyone.
24- I have not disobeyed the Law.
25- I have not been exclusively angry.
26- I have not cursed God/Goddess.
27- I have not behaved with violence.
28- I have not caused disruption of peace.
29- I have not acted hastily or without thought.
30- I have not exaggerated my words when speaking.
31- I have not worked evil.
32- I have not used evil thought, words or deeds.
33- I have not polluted the water or any source of waters.
34- I have not spoken angrily or arrogantly.
35- I have not cursed anyone in thought, word or deeds.
36- I have not place myself on a pedestal.
37- I have not stolen from or disrespected the deceased.
38- I have not stolen what belongs to God/Goddess.
39- I have not taken food from a child.
40- I have not acted with insolence.
41- I have not destroyed property belonging to God/Goddess.
42- I have not overstepped my boundaries of concern.

CHAPTER 26

These laws of MA 'At are the guide to see if one could past the test of weighing of his/her heart. The weighing of the heart by the scale to find the truth about each petitioner that have resided in earth. Upon passing the test and being deemed by the Goddess MA 'At that the petitioner is in compliance with the laws of MA 'At, then that person passes from the Duat to the field of Reeds (Arus) where Osiris is seating as the gate keeper and the final one. And I will leave you with this eternal quote:

"I'm the eternal. I'm the word. I created the word in speaking things into existence. My voice vibrated and you are the word that I have spoken into existence. You are my vibration made flesh. You are my word and I'm your God, Goddess."

THE SEVEN PRINCIPLE OF MA'AT

1- **TRUTH:** solemnly rest in fact with honesty and integrity.
2- **JUSTICE:** all parties shall have a state of fairness and lawful judgment.
3- **RIGHTEOUSNESS:** a consistent state of good conduct in all matters and actions.
4- **RECIPROCITY:** commonly known as what goes around comes around.
5- **BALANCE:** consist with an equal distribution of weight.
6- **ORDER:** to maintain the correct sequence of thought and action.
7- **HARMONY:** common on one accord coupled with a pleasing arrangement or agreement.

Here is an African proverb to remind us that we each plays a role in the universe affairs. "The world is equally divided between good and evil. Your next act will tilt the scale."

THE SEVEN HERMETIC PRINCIPLES

1. **The Principle of Mentalism**
   "The All is Mind; The Universe is Mental."
2. **The Principle of Vibration**
   "Nothing rests; everything moves; everything vibrates."
3. **The Principle of Correspondence**
   "As above, so below; as below, so above. As within, so without; as without so within."
4. **The Principle of Polarity**
   "Everything is Dual and has poles or opposites; opposites are identical in nature, but different in degree."
5. **The Principles of Rhythm**
   "Everything flows, out and in; everything has its tides; all things rise and fall; the pendulum-swing."
6. **The Principle of Cause and Effect**
   "Every Cause has its Effect; every effect has its cause; everything happens according to law."
7. **The Principle of Gender**
   "Gender is in everything; everything has its Masculine and Feminine Principles"

CHAPTER 27
Parable and Holy Test

When you teach someone how to fish and instead of going about to fish, that person is still content to hand you his hands for fish, what else can you do. If someone lacks the will to execute and to do what is right as a survival instinct but instead that person is waiting for a hand out or outside help, what else could you do? You can remind someone of their duties time after time but if that person remains stubborn and insensitive to their own well-being, what else can you do. If someone comes to you for some directions and you promptly provide that person with the correct information and that person turns around and follows another direction of his/her own, what else could you do?

The saying that a horse could be dragged and lead to the water source, but there is no way to force that horse to actually drink that water remain true and survived time. I have been given so many advice that I did not follow myself. And everyone had carefully listen to an advice, a direction and turned around to do something else at least once to say the least. I'm wondering the reasons behind us doing the opposite of what we were supposed to do if it's actually because we don't trust the advice or the person giving the advice? Are we looking at the hand/finger pointing the direction, instead where the hand is pointing to us to go?

It is sometime like an act of defiance when we actually ignore the right way to pursuing our own ways? Is it that we are committed to see it through on our own way? Isn't it our ego?

For example, if I tell you that there is a hole on the road that you are travelling on and it should be wise to take another route that I actually pointed and you persist to continue on your same road until you fall in the hole, whose fault could it be? If I'm a local of the area and I already travelled that same road to know that there is a hole in advance and tried to stop you from going into that same direction but you insisted and fall in the deep, can we actually blame anyone' else but you?

We can teach our kids the right way and shown them the right actions by our own positive behaviors, but most kids do whatever they want and learn from their mistakes as they grow old. You can be a perfect parent with good deeds and good heart to be surprised to see your own kids enjoying doing evil things with no regards to any morals and virtues that you have taught them. The truth is everyone is indeed the sewer of his/her actions. You can spend a life time reminding someone to turn around from a road that he/she is travelling to realize that it can be exhausting as a burden to wanting the best for someone that care less about himself/herself as much as you do, so you think. The word addiction would only lose its meaning and purpose in life if everyone was living the right way and doing the right things without fail.

For example, if I'm addicted to alcohol, or cigarettes, or drugs and you keep reminding me how bad they are to my health, would that push me to actually stop? If I took your advice and follow suit, isn't it because I recognized my addiction? The fact that I was made aware of the consequences of my bad habits on myself is not sufficient without my actual Will Power to agree with you and initiate the efforts to starting to quit the bad habits within me. It's not like as an addict I don't know what I'm inflicting to myself, it is because of the satisfaction I gain from doing whatever I'm addicted to. What if I just like to punish myself and hurt myself? What was once a pleasure at the beginning could become a necessity for a sane survival because the body and the mind crave for that quick fix to be

CHAPTER 27

satisfied? Yes the addicted person needs your help. And don't ever give up on reminding them that they should stop. Not just the addiction quoted above as an example but also the addicts of sex, lust, lies, thief, fraud, deceit, violence, killings, hate, destruction and those that lacks sympathy towards humanity.

Life is like an addiction. What we do the most becomes our habits. What we say and act the most become who we are. Where and what we spend most of our time doing end up becoming our second nature. So the wise man of today did not just become one out of the blue. He/she spent a life time perfecting wisdom and learning from experiences and mistakes. Just like the fool has no beginning nor an end because anyone could start as a fool and end as a fool without ever becoming wise or learning from his/her mistakes. To say the least we should not rule out that common sense is not the most equally distributed commodity among mankind because some people really lack common sense. We live and we learn; we learn to know who we are as a person and embrace our life purpose. So always remember who you are, and know that you are part of the universe all inclusive. And the universe expects you to also play your role/part in keeping the multiverse including you balanced.

CHAPTER 28
Love, Relationships and What Not To Expect

This world is a world that one has to learn to live into once born. It is a world where you have to analyze. A world where standards of life is defined. Symmetrically a world where nothing is defined. I guess that's why it is a world to learn and to be individually appreciated. To that, does everything has a set of time? Do we have different seasons? Does the world really has an end? What is an end? If not a beginning where there is a cycle and a season to all things. If there is an end, who then is the witness?

Forget about all this and don't get confused. This is the same world, where we all learn and live; then survive and adapt. It is a world where at some points, we all learn to tolerate and be at peace.

We all face the same predicaments. When caught up in love, who doesn't lose his/her sense for a while? When love for someone as a partner is established, reason might get out from the window. At the beginning of each relationship everything is so fine and beautiful to the point that any sacrificed needed is not a burden or hard at all to satisfy. Each partner is eager to go to the extra mile for the other. Being in couple as lovers and wanting to build a future together is a wonderful thing and everyone should try that adventure once he/she meets the right partner to share life and time with.

I did not want to write about relationships but at the end of the day, it is a road and inevitable thing that comes

CHAPTER 28

with life so that we could keep the procreation going. In any situation we each need to find the perfect match for a better and fruitful relationship. Not everyone is made to coexist and share roof with each other even though we all need to be given a chance until proven otherwise. At the end of the day, you need to be with someone that puts a smile on your face and that same person should be able to add something positive into your lives. At least 5%-10% to begin with and thereby work the way up the ladder together in a progressive way. Family structure has to follow and abide by morals and ethics. Kids have to be taught the right way and also made known the wrong way. That's where it becomes a problem because everyone tend to reproduce what he/she knows and believes are morals and ethics, not- withstanding what is the right way or the wrong way. Above all, we should be the first positive example to our children because the kids learn and act by imitating what we do.

We consciously know right from wrong but we all have egos and needs according to different seasons. As parents, we also struggle with who we are and where to go. Adding the pressure from society and extended family relatives influences, even good parents could lose track on raising their kids properly. Besides, don't we need time to be able to coach and properly attend to the needs of our kids? What if at the end of the day, such time and quality essential time is nowhere to be found after a long day at work? Every family needs some financial stability to be able to follow and respond to every needs the kids need. Now that we are talking money, it is important to note that a little bit of financial stability could add a plus in reducing the time spend by the parents trying to make that money just to provide food and shelter for their kids. Leaving more time to spend with the kids and family.

From that point a financial foundation has to be established and make room for a little saving. It does not have to be much. Just a little 5%-10% of every pay-check could come handy in rainy days or during time of emergency. That's another reason to choose your partner carefully because if there is no responsible spending either in a relationship, that beautiful relationship could scramble due to monetary and financial stress. Something that no couple is immune to and it would easily make fragile any strong relationship even based on true love. For my experience, nobody eats love and go to bed. It has to be substantial as really and truly putting groceries on the table, paying bills and taking good care of the kids financially. If not, any relationship will become ephemeral and short lived.

If I'm going to go deep in choosing your partner carefully I think it could be seen as setting a standard when we all know that love has no reason and has no boundaries. Even the wisest men have failed in love just to witness the less intelligent prove to them that love do really exist and true relationship does not cost a thing.

Therefore, what works for me may not work for you because we are different people with different mind-set and needs at any time. You might be with the one you just need for the moment. Like the wise man said, lessons have to be learned and characters have to be built. I have seen rich people divorce just like poor people divorce. I have seen men and women of God even divorce because a time had come to start a new journey. I cannot promise you that even when love exist in a relationship that everything would be all right at all times. Everyone does has a bad day sometime and need consoling and care. Besides the caring for the relationship and the caring for any kids, everyone individually has needs and sometimes just need a little encouragement or caresses even a physical massage or a spiritual tenderness which could be speaking of some ways that are uplifting. Instead of speaking about their flaws and short-comings, focus on the positive side of them. The respect of the dignity and integrity is a must in a relationship that wants peace and understanding among the couple.

CHAPTER 28

The key to love, it has to be reciprocal and absent of any pity retaliation. There should be no room for tit for tat or any revenge at all. Not because your partner did something wrong to you that you also have to do another thing wrong to him/her. Once retaliatory actions takes place, then you should expect a downfall in the relationship. When you suspect that the relationship has taken a tit for tat turn, acknowledge the change and stop the behavior promptly. Communicate with your partner and together move past the downfall and focus on the present giving each other compliments and appreciations.

Do not humiliate or disrespect your partner in public; not even in closed doors. Be the back bone of your partner's insecurities and weaknesses, instead of exploiting his/her insecurities and weaknesses to shut her up or put him down whenever you are in disagreement or angry. Part of your job is to make sure your partner feels safe and secure at all times with you, and to be trustworthy of keeping a secret or a confidence. Remember the old saying that says that the dirty laundry must be washed at the house and not on the street. It just means for you not to spill or gossip your partner's business on the street or with your friends. Do not compete against your partner. And for the welfare of the relationship, do not raise your voice at your partner, nor try to talk him/her down while purposely trying to hurt his feelings whenever there is an argument. This way, you will always respect your partner's dignity as a person first.

Love does not transform to violence; people do let their emotions run them because they become attached to someone just like an object and now fear that they are losing a control. Which means that love does not have to be controlling because the truth is no one no one can control anyone. We could barely control ourselves, not alone contemplating controlling a whole other being full of his/her ability to choose what to do and where to go. Always keep in mind that just like your relationship started, it could finish just as that, because may be it was just time for something else.

CHAPTER 28

One truth is that everyone begin a relationship with a mindset. Not everyone meets with the same reasons or for the same reasons. May be your relationship was the one she/he needed to pass time or get away from a previous one. May be your relationship was the one to pulse that person to higher and precious up-coming relationship. Maybe your relationship was meant for you to learn from your mistakes or to learn from your past practices or deeds; just in another way that particular relationship was for you to learn and grow and get closure from what you have put other people through. Who knows exactly why we all struggle in trying to find love? I guess the answer lays on you to figure it out and learn as you go. Because truly there is no such formula to find love and to keep it. You just need to find the right match. No games and do not under no circumstance lower your standard, morals, ethics and the need for financial stability to force your way in someone 'else life. Do not also cling to anybody because you happen to be feeling lonely. Get yourself together first before you involve someone in your life when your own life is already in chaos. Love has no sorrow and worries involve in it, so don't bring it to your footsteps because you just need someone next to you or you would regret it if only your love was not dishonest and enticed of any malice or calculation.

There is no reason or a slight place for violence where true love is involved. But now, when you become categorized as someone else's property, then that person if not reasonable could mistakenly treat you like an object of his/her own and then later on could inflict pain and suffering upon your body, mind and soul in trying to take full control of you. Then violence could follow as the person is having some fears of losing you or losing control of you as he/she needs to fully enjoy his/her property. Add this to someone that only live by his/her ego and perpetual mental, psychological, and physical abuse is at your relationship door steps at no fail.

CHAPTER 28

At the end of the day, every couple should plan for the future and save a lit bit of money regardless of the hardship. It does not have to be much, it is just for the purpose of financial stability goal, meaning acting like you are working toward something even if that saving is minim. Try at best to avoid retaliatory conducts and set a time and place to eat together in family. Massage and console each other while working together to implement a good communication skills. Hear and listen to each other without interrupting when one of you is speaking his/her mind. Wait and be patient before answering and talking while making sure that any feelings and emotional needs are attended and cared for. Do not just listen to your partner only to respond, listen to understand first. Try at best to support each-others visions and when appropriate, remind each others of the needs for the moments as one has to also be realistic of his/her dreams or long term visions. Any relationship is a work in progress but when true love is reciprocal, the future is full of bliss and happiness just like when you find your match and looking together in the same direction with good realistic plans. Love has no boundaries nor colors and beauty remains at the eyes of the beholder. Know yourself first before adding another into your life.

CHAPTER 29
Happiness and the secret of being present

Happiness is all shared around within all of us. Happiness does not come from outside or external means, it is within. Even though the reason of the said happiness may come from external cause, the effect is always from within. Don't forget, our experience from the past, our own ego and voices within us can dictate our choice to either be happy accordingly or dismiss the cause or good reason for happiness.

The feeling of joy is a sensation arising from our heart leading to a mouth with a smile, a glowing skin and a good attitude. Then from happiness, we swift unwillingly or unconsciously to another mood because other new events in our life or immediate interaction with others may have come along and stole that happiness away leaving us with a different emotion. The key to remaining happy at all times lies in one's attitude towards life. Is happiness something to guard and protect? Isn't it that the idea of expressly guarding it also comes with a burden?

A wise man ones said "You can steal my joy, only if I let you". The truth is that life doesn't change so much as we do. We are accustom to our own expectations based on what we hope to see others act accordingly to our desires, wishes and ethical up-bringing. To remain calm and happy, the question that we should ask is "Where am I? And What am I doing here? And Who do I have in front of me?"

You know everyone is looking for happiness in their own ways and a lot of us still don't know what makes us happy. Even

CHAPTER 29

though only very few have found happiness and learn to keep it at all times, there are a wave of a multitude that still don't know quite what they should do to be happy at last. Every day, everywhere, at any place and moment, there is a probability that the one next to you or the one with whom you are dealing with, is seeking also to be happy.

Now the question is what makes you happy? And what makes others happy? Everyone may be having his/her own vision of happiness. Some people are just happy to be able to steal your joy. Others happy because they have put a smile on somebody else mouth. Not leaving out those happy just because they have satisfied their ego or merely the fact that they have seen another day. Who knows exactly what drives everyone else? One thing to remember is that when life and other people start making you, it could jeopardize one's happiness. So to remain happy, you should have an attitude to making life instead of the other way around. The truth is you can easily change someone else attitude just like other people attitude can change your very own attitude. But at the end of the day, when one decides to be happy, you should be ready to strip yourself of what your very own culture, belief and religion taught you since childhood. Until that time, you finally decided to be, and remain, happy at all times. You should be warned that life will keep bringing events that will not necessarily fit your needs, so endure it, regardless of what life brings into your way. Learn to become tolerant of other people's miseducation/misinformation and forgive them as you go.

Everyone has an ego. The ego is afraid to die. It always wants to be right. Not the least, it always lives in fear. The fear of losing. The fear of achieving. The ego hates to lose an argument and will defend its views to the least argument defensively and aggressively. Human relationships are a mountain of misunderstanding all along. We still cannot live among each other happily all the times without a misunderstanding jumping in between our relationships to others to occasion a mix feeling. This scenario might explain why we are always in conflict with our own mind and others. The mind individually fires the next thought from you to embrace and retain its own thought. It fires that thought because it has heard that the thought from you wanted to quit or express itself freely. So it fires the thought to remain in dominion, to possess the last word. Now the true reason the thought also wanted to quit or express itself is because the thought has heard and believe that the mind was planning and have decided to fire it and take away its freedom of expression. So to also have the last word, the thought manifesting its freedom powers went along first to quit before the mind gets an opportunity to fire it. And ever since the mind and the thought are still not getting along.

That's why we can't seem to make up our mind consistently. After years of not speaking and wanting to see each other eye to eye, one day, finally they were forced by a third party seeking to reconcile them to meet face to face and confront each other. That's when the truth finally transpired. The mind was planning to fire the thought because birdy, one of their companion has told the mind that the thought wanted to quit. At the same time, birdy had also told the thought that the mind was about to fire it (the thought). That's why the thought went along to quit first before it was fire. And that's also why the mind went along to fire the thought anyway. The minute the mind and the thought finally realized that all this time they were avoiding each other for no reason, they came along and embrace each-others. This is the ego playing tricks on us making us confused and inconsistent. That could also translate to our illusion of fear, our illusion of death, our illusion of power, our illusion of the future; our anticipations of things and events to come that might not even occur the way we envision or fear of worse-case scenarios. At the end, it is the back and forth battle of the mind within its own territory yet hostile to itself for illusionary dominion to itself. The only way for you to remain happy even though your mind would always keep talking, is to step back and observe your own mind. Do

CHAPTER 29

not try to stop it or win, just become a witness to it by looking at it as a third party observer and refrain from reacting to it.

Know that if something is going to happen and you don't have the powers or capability to stop it, why worry about it? You cannot change it. Keep a smile and wait for it to happen. If it has to happen anyway, why worry when you know that under no circumstances, you can stop it from happening? Better yet, why even speculate about what has not even happened. So what, you cannot change it, keep a steady joy and a smile still without worrying. Do not let the heavy traffic flow of the future get congested at your mind's doorsteps, while living in the present.

And, if you want to be happy in congested cities in real life? Control then your emotions and feelings on traffic. Look at the road and honk only when necessary. You may speed a little bit without violating the laws and regulations. But, remember that not because you obey the laws that you should also expect everyone to respect the laws. Some people know the codes of the routes and others, not so much or nothing at all. Most people don't have the same ability, nor the same agility to understand what you now might deem easy. It is easy because you have pass the stage but it was harder when you were learning those said codes too. Therefore fill your spirit with understanding and patience. Do not expect people to be good drivers or less aggressive on the wheel. The road is full of angry and impatient drivers already, therefore, do not join the statistic by lacking patience and self-control. After the grown-ups stock on traffic and irritated by bad drivers, I'm going to turn my attention to the youngsters and little ones that also expect so much from us grownups for their own happiness.

Little ones, have you lied before? So did adults. Little ones, have you mislead before? So did the grownups. Never assume anything. If something is not talked about and dealt with, do not assumed that the other party would understand you, regardless of the issue. Double check that all parties involved in a matter are on the same page like you, instead of assuming that it might be common sense; therefore, everyone should know.

Always be eager to wanting to learn and know the History of the world without prejudices. Vulnerable beings, learn to dissertate. Cultivate your critical thinking and try to understand a subject before trying to be the best. To be the best might be an ideal goal but remember the steps on your way to greatness. Climb your ladder, but never forget where you came and started from.

For anyone that wants happiness, be happy and see beauty in all livings. Instead of judging the past, remain at the present. Conquer your ego by being the watcher of your mind as a witness. Try to acknowledge what your mind is trying to tell you. Don't rebuke it as the mind is a form of a boomerang; it always comes back to remind you or tell you something. To finish, your ego is also there to command you and to escalate crises because of its own feeling of fear to be dethroned by you or by somebody-else. It feeds on fears and always wants to have the last word. The key to remaining a witness to the ego is through "observe and report" with no judgment. Just by witnessing the ego's manifestation, we remain in the present while controlling the ego's pulses. That way, happiness may follow.

Happiness is now, not later. Practice and try to forget about the past. Leave the worries for tomorrow to tomorrow. You are not your past. You are not your emotions and feelings. You are a great being of the Now. You are a being of and with the Now power. Your identity is not based on your past life or struggles and successes but your true essence which is that you have the power to be present and be happy regardless of any other adverse circumstances to happiness and peace of mind. Never mind those that always want to remind you of who you are in a demeaning way. Never mind those who would neglect you. Never mind the ones who always want to put you in a box and make you look small and ashamed or insignificant. You are

CHAPTER 29

not defined by any of that. You are not defined by how others think of you or say about you.

You are a happy and lovable person. You are a nice and respectful person. You spread joy and console others. You help your next fellow man/woman without hesitation. You are a pioneer of peace and equality. One of the many that contributes to healing and nurturing our planet started with you. You are divine, therefore happiness is your throne.

Sometimes it is our feeling of time passing and coming by so quick as oppose to our accomplishments that we might be in distress or sad. The pressure of time moving along seemingly faster than our projects realizations that takes our joy and happiness away. Because we feel unachieved or the pressure of not being ready for tomorrow give us stress even though tomorrow has not come yet etc.

What if I remind you that time is an illusion. Forget about time and you will be happy. Live up to your true essence of the Now and you will be happy. Try to be present to the point that you no longer identify yourself with your problems. Try to be present that you no longer identify yourself with your financial burdens and failed projects. Always remember that you are not your problems nor your financial problems. You can move past those emotions and feelings to be present. Your problems and sufferings are not you or who you are. You are the divine Being of the Now present. In the Now present, time has no place including your struggles, sufferings and problems. Time is somewhat what is keeping us from being present and happy. Where there is no more time nor pressure from time, all our problems and worries dissolve and simply vanish. That could represent a growth into a higher spiritual dimension. Never turn back and look at the Salt while on your journey to freedom. Leave your worries and stress behind at the entrance of the timeless zone, where the illusion of time ceases and proceed calmly within to the light.

CHAPTER 29

In Church or temple of God, most of us may have heard this old saying, "Take no thought for the morrow; for the morrow shall take thought for the things of itself". Meaning that your worries and lacks should not be glanced at nor letting them take dominion over your true essence which is stillness and peacefulness. An even clearer quotation that the key to that spiritual dimension/timeless zone resides on the Now moment is "Nobody who puts his hands to the plow and looks back is fit for the Kingdom of God." This emphasizes that whatever that you are going through, however how heavy is the burden and the pain to endure, you could and should still exercise the now moment power by overriding all your struggles and become lovable and amiable so that the godly being kingdom in you may open up. We hear and read those passages in the books but we tend to forget that the messages are meant for us to be lived within their contexts and that is the only way that brings us a profound inner transformation; an everlasting happiness through being present at all times.

The true question for you is that "what are you lacking at this present time?" what is lacking at this moment? The truth is that our past and future blind us from seeing God, from being present as if not now when? Your past is already gone and done. So why let it worry you by bringing it back and letting it haunt you? The future has not yet come but an illusory imagination from the mind. A projection that has not occurred but already lived and felt in advance unnecessary when you anticipate events from the future that are not even reel yet.

The various spiritual teachers and Masters recommend us to be present within our mind. To be present as the watcher, or witness, to what your mind is doing. Be a watcher of your thought and your emotions too. Pay close attention to what they actually want you to do or know. Be cautious of how you react to those thoughts and emotions. Practice it daily and you will realize that living in the present is quite possible. Take a look at your reactions instead of focusing on the situation or

CHAPTER 29

the person causing you to react. Focus on how you reacted and if changes are needed, proceed and make proper adjustments. Now that you have built the space between your thought, emotions, feelings and sufferings by being a bystander observing before deciding, you have already lived in the present. You have then stopped identifying yourself from your mind, your emotions and feelings, now taking control of the Now Present Authority; the key to Happiness.

When presence by remaining present becomes a habit in you consciously, the past and future lose influence over you, kicking Time away from your daily life. You have now activated your timeless essence and all the burden of your past and future will soon vanish and make a way for good health and permanent happiness. In another magic word, "your Sins have forgiven you" when you reach the timeless zone. And you have decided not to let your sins haunt you no-more by not letting your Sins identify you anymore. Because, the truth is, you are not the Sinner, you are Divine and Godly. Be and remain happy now. Save a smile for me while you are spreading joy and happiness smiles to your family and neighbors.

CHAPTER 30
The Divine Code of Human Behavior

The code of human behavior is brought to us by the Kem community that have existed over the past 5000 years and more. It is a gift that we have received from the divine world in order to assist us in bettering ourselves. The code advise us to pay close attention to the human mind as we tend to act and repeat what we have seen, heard or experienced as opposed to thinking that human mind actually invents. Because, the truth is that we do not invent but rather imitate. The intent of the code is for people that wants to better themselves and imitate the divine world way of life. In total, the code of human behavior was given to us in **seventy seven (77) Commandments**. The code must be applied to and by individuals striving to become a perfect human being so that the world will become more perfect, one person at a time. The world we want to see around us must start with us and it is a voluntary endeavor yet a mandatory code for all to live by and abide by in today's world.

1. Thou shall not cause suffering to humans.
2. Thou shall not intrigue by ambition.
3. Thou shall not deprive a poor person of their subsistence.
4. Thou shall not commit acts that are loathed by Gods.
5. Thou shall not cause suffering to others.
6. Thou shall not steal offerings from temples.
7. Thou shall not steal bread meant for Gods.

CHAPTER 30

8. Thou shall not steal offerings destined to sanctify spirits.
9. Thou shall not commit shameful acts inside the Sacrosaints of temples.
10. Thou shall not sin against nature with one's own kind.
11. Thou shall not take milk from the mouth of a child.
12. Thou shall not fish using other fish as bait.
13. Thou shall not extinguish the fire when it should burn.
14. Thou shall not violate the rules of meat offerings.
15. Thou shall not take possession of properties belonging to temples and Gods.
16. Thou shall not prevent a God from manifesting itself.
17. Thou shall not cause crying.
18. Thou shall not make scornful signs.
19. Thou shall not get angry or enter a dispute without just cause.
20. Thou shall not be impure.
21. Thou shall not refuse to listen to words of justice and truth.
22. Thou shall not blaspheme.
23. Thou shall not sin by excess of speech.
24. Thou shall not speak scornfully.
25. Thou shall not curse a Divinity.
26. Thou shall not cheat on the offerings to the Gods.
27. Thou shall not waste the offerings to the dead.
28. Thou shall not snatch food from children and thou shall not sin against the Gods of one's city.
29. Thou shall not kill divine animals with bad intentions.
30. Thou shall not cheat.
31. Thou shall not rob or loot.
32. Thou shall not steal.
33. Thou shall not kill.
34. Thou shall not destroy offerings.
35. Thou shall not reduce measurements.
36. Thou shall not steal properties belonging to Gods.

CHAPTER 30

37. Thou shall not lie.
38. Thou shall not snatch away food or wealth.
39. Thou shall not cause pain.
40. Thou shall not fornicate with the fornicator.
41. Thou shall not act dishonestly.
42. Thou shall not transgress.
43. Thou shall not act maliciously.
44. Thou shall not steal farmlands.
45. Thou shall not reveal secrets.
46. Thou shall not court a man's wife/woman's husband.
47. Thou shall not sleep with another's wife/another's husband.
48. Thou shall not cause terror.
49. Thou shall not rebel.
50. Thou shall not be the cause of anger or hot tempers.
51. Thou shall not act with insolence.
52. Thou shall not cause misunderstandings.
53. Thou shall not misjudge or judge hastily.
54. Thou shall not be impatient.
55. Thou shall not cause illness or wounds.
56. Thou shall not curse a king.
57. Thou shall not cloud drinking water.
58. Thou shall not dispossess.
59. Thou shall not use violence against family.
60. Thou shall not frequent wicked people or places.
61. Thou shall not substitute injustice for justice.
62. Thou shall not commit crimes.
63. Thou shall not overwork others for one's gain.
64. Thou shall not mistreat their/your servants.
65. Thou shall not menace.
66. Thou shall not allow a servant to be mistreated by his/her master.
67. Thou shall not induce famine.
68. Thou shall not get angry.
69. Thou shall not kill or order a murder.

CHAPTER 30

70. Thou shall not commit abominable acts.
71. Thou shall not commit treason.
72. Thou shall not try to increase one's domain by using illegal means.
73. Thou shall not usurp funds and property of others.
74. Thou shall not seize cattle on prairies.
75. Thou shall not trap poultry that are destined to Gods.
76. Thou shall not obstruct water in the moment it is supposed to run.
77. Thou shall not break dams that are established on current waters.

These ultimate commandments are the most blessings one should shower himself in, building a more responsible Being. It is a way of life that enhances trust among humans, if only a lot of people would observe it. It is a choice that one makes to follow the commandments for his/her own benefit in becoming a perfect Man/Woman who could reproduced a more perfect world. You will be the only enforcer of these rules as no one else would do it at your place or coerce you in doing so. Recognizing that good and bad/evil are based on what behavior is, or is not, in line with the Divine Code of Human Behavior set here as the 77 commandments. You should not wait for others to start following the code before starting your journey on becoming a better citizen of the world. Because, you have chosen to live a godly life does not means that you should expect others to follow suit right away. Do it for yourself only and your own light will attract a multitude to follow suit. Consider it and enforce it to yourself as if you had signed a contract with the Gods, and you are the only enforcer of the said contract.

I would also add some laws from the ten commandments of the Bible from the Book of Exodus and Deuteronomy, which instruct us to worship only God, to honor our parents, and to keep the Sabbath day holy and reminds us of the prohibition of idolatry.

CHAPTER 31
The Power of the Mind and how to Reclaim the Power From Your Mind.

The mind is nothing new to anyone, even though it is something I cannot confirm for everyone. I know I have a mind and I also know that you have a mind. The mind is such a powerful entity within us that everywhere we go it is there and manifests its presence by talking to us and giving its opinions about things it like and don't like. The mind within us keep talking at a second but without stopping. It will not even stop when we want it to take a break and let us just be. The mind has a mind of its own and don't give a damn about what us the individual care or want. The mind will not care to contradict itself as it would talk or raise an issue and turn around and answer back and so forth until we get tired of listening to it talking. The mind is a reflection of our karma. It combines our cause and effects tendencies; a chain of reactions.

For some people, it's normal that the mind talks and gets involve in our day to day life; and for other the mind just need to take a break once in a while and let the individual live his/her life without interference at last. I know my mind talks to itself or to me because if I could hear it, it means that I'm outside of the mind. If I could hear it giving suggestion about what my eyes see, it is, in fact, because I'm not the mind, but I'm the Mind hosting the mind. I suppose it is talking to me because no one else could hear it but me. This is how a typical mind talk goes. It is hot; I feel hot. And counter with get up and turn on the fan then; no I'm comfortable in this chair and I don't feel like getting up. I will

CHAPTER 31

just take my shirt off and be just fine. Then the conversation continues; but it is hot, I cannot take this hit anymore. You going to have to get up and turn this fan on and the counter clams back with I wish I could just do some magic from here and turn the fan on. Beside I don't need this shit anymore on, it is going to raise up my electricity bill that I cannot even afford.

The bottom line is our mind talks back and forth to itself or to us like a mad man on the street will do. Asking a question, turning it around, giving an answer to the same question and opening a debate that only the mind would win. This is the mind and everyone's mind is giving him/her nightmares, if you start paying attention to it. Now that you are reading this, I supposed you have already paid attention to your own mind that keeps on talking. Our mind keeps bringing unfinished issues back to the surface to finish the conversation or make closure but is never satisfied.

What will be important here is the part that, it should be a clear acknowledgement that, for you to hear yourself talking inside in your mind, you must be a third person within as a listener listening to someone else talking. The simple fact that you are aware of the conversation that your mind is having is already a step to freeing yourself from its bondage. You can hear your mind going on and on and never to shut up even if you are ready and want it to shut up. Would it take a break? So consider that your mind is someone-else's talking to you to understand what the mind wants and needs. It is nothing new that we listen to the mind sometimes or most of the time thinking it is us that are actually having the madness conversation within. In fact who-else could we attribute our own mind to, if we are walking around with it and it remains a faithful friend even if that friend is just bipolar? But the truth is, the average person pay too much attention and consideration to what his/her mind is saying.

It has been suggested by many teachers that the key to understanding your mind is to become a witness to it. By becoming a witness, what we do is actually just laying back on the side and listening to the mind talk while reframing from taking decisions or letting the mind influenced our judgment. Because if you keep a habit on letting your mind decide for you, chances are your life would be miserable due to the fact that the mind is unstable. Have you realized how quick your mind changes positions or make assumptions or prejudices and after all the mind was totally wrong? Time after time, the mind has proven itself to be like what we could say "crazy". So just become a witness to it by stepping on the side by recognizing that you are separate in your essence and when you actually talk, it sounds different and you know it is you that truly talking; not someone-else in your head. Let's say you say what's up right out loud. You noticed the difference versus the mind? When you speak, it is you and when your mind speaks, you just need to watch it speak from a distance as a witness because your mind is only interested in the cause and effect of your deeds, wants and actions. That's a good cool way to give that space out so that you could make inform decisions on your own because your true mind is unstable and unreliable. The only way to enjoy peace and reclaim your power from your mind is to remain aware of the mind.

For example if you are a Crip and you see someone dressed in Red, what would your mind tell you? Your mind most likely would jump the gun that, that person dressed in red is from your opposing rival gang "blood", but the truth is, anybody could be dressed in red, without being affiliated to any gang or even know of the existence of such gangs groups. The same example goes both ways for the "Blood" gang member encountering someone dressed in Blue. The mind could get us in trouble, if we really don't watch it anytime as a witness without letting it interfere with our decisions. For your information, Crips and Blood are each a gang affiliation in United States that consider themselves to be rivals. And their distinction has been through the difference in colors; blue for the Crips and red for the Blood's. And my humble advice to them is to embrace love and love one another as killing each other would not stop the world from moving or resolve their differences.

CHAPTER 31

The mind; some days it is right and some days it is wrong. But what happened to the old guards? What is beyond the veils? The mind talks. It keeps talking; giving you suggestions. Telling you what to do. Sometimes it even gives you time and warns you. Some other days, it just brings your past to you. Our mind can and always feeds on the energy that we are willing to let it steal. Every unfinished business would be brought for closure, and that's the only way it knows to close that chapter. Every emotion carries its own energy and what is stored must come out. The past always catches up. Whatever we do in the dark will always come to light. The energy in must come out internally or externally. My question is, whose voice is the mind talking from? If not us, then who? You know the voices talk to you and you can hear it. Therefore, where the voice coming from? It seems to know you. It seems to know your past. It seems to warn you. And some days the voice just get us into trouble. Is the voice conditioned to be us? You know we are not that perfect either not literally. Unless, the voice could also be under influence or the influence. But if you hear it, it must not be coming from you. Thinking might be different because you are exercising a will power. Now who else can guarantee where the thoughts and ideas came from? Is it the mind also? But now you should know that it is coming from your true self, your essence. To reclaim your power from your mind, you must become a bystander to your mind; a witness to your mind; a watcher of your mind. Remind yourself always that you are not your mind or the voices you are hearing. Make your decisions from your true essence by analyzing the pro and con first of any of your decisions or choices but do not let the voices influence or interfere with them.

"When you can make your thoughts and your emotions into one, you would say to the mountain, mountain move away and it will move. If the thoughts and the emotions make peace, the person would enjoy peace," said Yesui Christ from the Gospel of Thomas.

CHAPTER 32
The Original Sin

What can I say about the original sin if not what most of us have received as an education, culture, tradition and religion. I grew up in a culture where society placed the man slightly above the woman. A society where a boy is seen in the eyes of almost everyone that he had different role than a girl and that boys are actually more precious than girl. It is also a society, where it is common for people to be wanting so bad to have a boy child than a girl; to the point that having a girl could set a disappointment in some families like having a girl is a curse. And this phenomena exist everywhere at any country as I'm writing.

For starters let's make it clear that it is wrong to be placing a double standard on kids. It is not fair to be judged first once born before the new born even has a name. Boys and girls are all human and possess the same abilities. History has proven that there is no such thing as a job or task that a male can perform and the female cannot do. Man and woman are equal in the eyes of God as there is no distinction because, the truth is we are all the same. The gender difference is for procreation's purpose and also to keep a balance in the universe. An all men world without a single woman would rapidly end life as men would go crazy without support. We are meant to have a world where women are free just like men. A world where everyone regardless of the gender should be treated with dignity, respect, love and equal due process.

So, my friends, get rid of the mentality that men are superior to women because it is not true. We are all equal and if you

CHAPTER 32

want to be healthy, mentally and emotionally, I think the best way is to view the girl as important as the boy since no gender is above another. Get the same excitement when bearing a girl just like you would, having a boy. Raise the kids the same way and give them the same opportunities to succeed in life. Give your attention and care to all of them, regardless if it is a boy or a girl. And we should not forget to remind our boys that they are not superior and they should not expect a special treatment; because from now on boys and girls are equal and have the same opportunity and the same right to an education. No one else is a second class citizen anymore as of now, all gender is equal and no one should serve another because of prejudices like woman belong here and not over there.

In addition, it is imperative that everyone start viewing the world as one unit, instead divided by countries, giving the illusion that you live in another place outside of earth itself. Living in different countries does not mean that you shouldn't care about what is happening on the other side of the world. We only have one earth, one world and the fact that you live in a different country than me doesn't exclude you or me from the same world. If the air quality is not good in my country, chances are it would make it slowly to yours, too, as there are winds that would blow the air all over the other parts of the world. It is one world and the winds systems are connected in one block. The winds that started in your country thousands of miles away could/would circulate to another country and proceed to circle back to the main source. Besides, if the air quality in my country is questionable, the whole world and everyone should take notice because we are all already affected because of the oneness of the globe. We have the same main oxygen sources, including our water sources. By not being concerned about the pollution of our breathing air and the reduction of our oxygen supply, you or me would not be alive long, either, whether I'm in China and you are in United States or Africa.

I think it is time to come back to reality that you are in one world and whatever is happening in Africa should concern

CHAPTER 32

you as much as what is happening in your own country. The different continents divided are nothing but an illusion. Do not let the division of the world in countries make you think in error that you are living in a different place. Someone living in Africa is still inside the world like you living in Australia, or Guatemala, etc. Therefore, we should treat our planet with equal respect and dignity regardless of the limits of our country borders as no country is isolated and standing out on its own. We should behave accordingly as Citizens of the world and not just for one country or your country. From now on, you are hereby Baptized as Citizen of the World moving forward.

To finish, the world should get rid of the illusion of belonging to a race that is different than the other. Color of skin doesn't add or takes away any one's dignity or essence. We belong to the human race as we are all human. It is really time for everyone to realize by now that no race is superior to another. In fact, the race card was only use by society for division purpose in order to be able to sow the seed of confusion is your mind. By placing the race card, it exposed you to feel disconnected to other humans if violence was being inflicted to them. By telling you that you are superior makes you believe that it is therefore ok to close your eyes to the sufferings of the other misconceived inferior races. It was an evil plan that worked for centuries and I think, we can do better now as humans. All it does, is to make you less and less of a human, and farther and farther away from God. As if you let society strips you of your compassion for others, you had just opened the door to the darkness. It is godly to be able to treat people equally with respect, love and dignity regardless of their skin colors. Try it, you will feel better and it is a free health therapy for mentally dysfunction people. Once you can treat people without discrimination nor prejudice, it becomes easier to respect their religion, tribal and cultural systems. That's only when you will be close to seeing God; The Light.

There is also an ego that has been instill in us without our consent that made us believe that our religion or languages or

CHAPTER 32

culture was superior to others. It made us pick a side as far as my religion was better than yours and my religion was the only way to salvation. Mine only was right and yours wrong because you were not believing the same thing as me. Therefore, your religion and everyone that believes in it, would go to hell. Another one concerns languages and only mine could be considered a language and the rest are primitive dialects and therefore inferior and spoken by inferior or savage people. You could notice here how we have been screwed up by society and by our loved ones over time at an early age. It would take a desire and an effort to rewire the brain to accepting that all religions are equal; that all languages and cultural aspects of different groups of people are equal as well. All along, it was the work of the ego and we should go beyond ego and realize that there is not a wrong or right when it comes to religion. Making yourself right and others wrong is a mental dysfunction that needs to be addressed by letting go of the ego of superiority. No single beliefs system possess the absolute truth or sole proprietor of the truth without love for all living. And we all know by now that we can only find truth within us instead of through ideologies, set of rules, doctrines or stories. They are just a combination of thoughts that might point to the said truth but will never be the truth itself. The truth is inseparable from who you are. You know that you are the truth? Right. If you keep on looking for it somewhere else, you would be deceiving yourself. Love is your truth.

In sum, it comes down to each person to rewire their brain and mindset, making a total U-turn from the way most of us were brought up since childhood to adulthood. Most societies only taught national, tribal patriotism, instead of Global patriotism. This rewiring of the brain is an exercise that is a must for anybody that wants to rise above the different divisions and discriminations around the world. Better yet, anybody that aspiring to be a God like has to love the world with everything in it first without prejudices, nor discriminations.

CHAPTER 33
Daily Proverbs, Thought and Wisdom for the Soul

"The snow falls, each flake in its appropriate place," is a Zen saying.

"Do not think that you can please God with prayer. You will please God by submitting to Him. Prayer is just a reminder for you of who you are and what the purpose of your life is."

"You can call God by various names, you can avoid His name altogether, but you cannot avoid accepting His existence. Nothing exists here if God does not exist. All I know I know because there is God, and I know Him because He gives me the knowledge of everything. Let us think about God, remember Him, and talk to Him as often as we can." –Epictetus

"The essential meaning of every religion is to answer the question "why do I live, and what is my attitude to the limitless world which surrounds me?" There is not a single religion, from the most sophisticated to the most primitive, which does not have as its basis the definition of this attitude of a person to the world.

At the heart of all religions lies a single unifying truth. Let the Persians bear their taovids, Jews wear their caps, Christians bear their cross, Muslims bear their sickle moon, but we have to remember that these are only outer signs. The general essence of all religions is love to your neighbor, and that this is requested by Manu, Zoroaster, Buddha, Moses, Socrates, Jesus, Saint Paul, and Mohammed alike. – Edward Flugel.

CHAPTER 33

"Every person has his burden. One cannot live without the support of other people; therefore we have to support each other with consolation, advice, and mutual warnings." – From the Book of Divine Thoughts.

"It's important to strive to do good, and even more important to strive to abstain from evil. Abstention should be a habit in your life; it should support you in your virtues. For he who is resolute in goodness, there is nothing that he could not overcome." - Lao-Tzu

"Kindness is necessary in relationships with people. If you are not kind to a person, you are not fulfilling your major obligation. You have to respect every person, no matter how miserable or ridiculous he or she may be. You should remember that in every person lives the same spirit which lives in us." – After Arthur Schopenhauer

Buddha said, "A man who starts to live for his soul is like a man who brings a lantern into a dark house. The darkness disappears at once. You have to be persistent in this, and your soul will have this light."

Christ expressed all His teachings in His last commandment: "Love each other, as I loved you. Everyone will see that you are my disciples, if you love each other." He did not say, "If you believe," but "If you love." Faith can change with time, because our knowledge is constantly changing. Love, on the contrary, never changes; love is eternal. Jesus Christ religion is love to all living beings.

"Some of your friends praise you, and others blame and criticize you; be closer to those who blame you and further from those who praise you." – The Talmud.

"When an arrow does not hit its target, the marks-man blames himself, not another person. A wise man behaves in the same way." – Confucius

"Beware of false prophets, which come to you in sheep's clothing, but inwardly they are ravening wolves. Ye shall know them by their fruits. Do men gather grapes of thorns, or figs of thistles? Even so every good tree bringeth forth good fruit; but a corrupt tree bringeth forth evil fruit. A good tree cannot bring forth evil fruit, neither can a corrupt tree bring forth good fruit. Every tree that bringeth not forth good fruit is hewn down, and cast into the fire. Wherefore by their fruits ye shall know them." –Matthew 7:15-20

"Love for other people gives a real feeling of good, and it unites you with other people and with God. –A wise man loves not because he wants to profit from it but because he finds bliss in love itself. –Do not regret the past. What is the use of regrets? The lie says that you should regret. The truth says you should be filled with love. Push all sad memories away from you. Do not speak of the past. Live in the light of love, and all things will be given to you." –Persian Wisdom.

"They asked a Chinese man, "What is science?" He said, "Science is knowing people." Then they asked, "And what is virtue?" He answered, "Virtue is loving people."

Just as a mother puts her life at risk to guard and save her only child, so every person should guard and save in himself love for every living being.

The fearlessness, calm, inner peace, and joy which are given to us by love are so big that all other things in the world cannot be compared with them, especially for the person who understands the real blessing of love."

"I and God are the same," said the teacher. If you think that my spiritual being is God, you are mistaken. But my real self is close to God, and to other people. In order to understand this part of myself, you should elevate the man inside of you. When you elevate the man inside of you, then you will see that there is no difference between him and any other person on earth.

CHAPTER 33

It only seems as if we differ from each other. A flower on a blossoming tree can think that it is a separate being, but all flowers are parts of the same blossoming of one apple tree, and they all come from one seed.

We live a short period of time in this world, but we live it according to the laws of eternal life. –After Henry David Thoreau.

"Kindness is for your soul as health is for your body: you do not notice it when you have it."

A person becomes happy to the same extent to which he or she gives happiness to other people. –Jeremy Bentham.

"First think, then speak. Stop when told "enough." A person is higher than an animal because of his ability to speak, but he is lower than an animal if he cannot properly use this ability. –Muslih-Ud-Din Saadi

"Nothing can support idleness better than empty chatter. People would be better to keep silent and not speak the boring, empty things they routinely say to entertain themselves. How can they endure it?

The person who speaks much will seldom fulfill all his words in his actions. A wise person is always wary lest his words surpass his actions." –Chinese Wisdom.

"Ye have heard that it hath been said, an eye for an eye, and a tooth for a tooth: But I say unto you, That ye resist not evil: but whosoever shall smite thee on thy right cheek, turn to him the other also. –Matthew 5:38-39

"He who is really skillful in communicating with people is usually a humble and quiet person. This is called the virtue of nonresistance. This is called harmony with heaven. –Lao-Tzu

"Our biggest desire is to live forever. But when we are freed from this body, we will not wish to come back. Is there such a child who, once born, would like to return to the womb of his mother? Is there a man who, freed from prison, would like to return to it? In the same way, a person should not be afraid about the future liberation from his body, if he is not connected too closely with this material life." –Tables of the Babids, a Muslim sect from Persia.

"A person is not afraid to die only after he understands that he was never born, that he always existed, exists at present, and will always exist.

"A person will believe in his eternity when he understands that his life is not a wave, a period of life, but the eternal movement which is manifested in this life only as a wave.

"Those who believe that their life has not begun with their birth and will not end with death find it much easier to live a good life than those who do not understand or believe this."

"The feeling of compassion for other living beings reminds me of the feeling of pain in our body. Just as you can become less sensitive to pain in your body with time, you can become less compassionate to others.

"The first condition to bringing religion into your life is manifesting love and pity toward all living creatures." –Chinese Wisdom

"Compassion for animals is closely connected with character type. You can say with confidence that he who is cruel to animals cannot be a kind man." –Arthur Schopenhauer

"When the suffering of another creature causes you to feel pain, do not submit to the initial desire to flee from the suffering one, but on the contrary, come closer, as close as you can to him who suffers, and try to help him."

"Faith is not true faith if love is not in harmony with it.

"The door to heaven is opened to you to the same extend you want it. Get rid of your troubles and problems, and direct your soul to spiritual things. Be attentive, and

CHAPTER 33

fulfill your duty without thinking about the consequences. You should not guide events, but be guided by events." – Indian Wisdom

"What doth it profit, my brethren, though a man say he hath faith, and have not works? Can faith save him? If a brother or sister be naked, and destitute of daily food, and one of you say unto them, Depart in peace, be ye warmed and filled; notwithstanding ye give them not those things which are needful to the body; what doth it profit? Even so faith, if it hath not works, is dead, being alone.... Ye see then how that by works a man is justified, and not by faith only.... For as the body without the spirit is dead, so faith without works is dead also." –James 2:14-18, 24, 26

"Nothing more can be considered as real merit for a person than his effort. Only in his effort is a person shown in his real light." –The Koran

"When one understands life's law, one manifests the part of God which lives inside him.

"Every man, from the king to the poorest pauper, should seek his own perfection, because only self-perfection improves mankind." –Confucius

"False faith is the major cause of most of our Misfortunes. The Purpose of a human life is to bring the irrational beginning of our life to a rational beginning. In order to succeed in this, two things are important: (1) to see all irrational, unwise things in life and direct your attention to them and study them; (2) to understand the possibility of a rational, wise life. The major Purpose of all teachers of mankind was the understanding of the irrational and rational beginnings in our life.

"We should be ready to change our views at any time, and slough off prejudices, and live with an open and receptive mind. A sailor who sets the same sails all the time, without making changes when the wind change, will never reach his/her harbor." –Henry George

Accept the teaching of Christ as it is, clear and simple; then you will see that we live among big lies.

"The real purpose of Christianity is obvious to all, and it is stronger than lies which try to pervert it. We should separate the religion that was taught by Jesus from the religion whose subject is Jesus. Then we will understand the real meaning of the New Testament and follow it." –Henry Amiel

"Family and motherland are but two circles that are part of the wider circle that is humanity. Those who teach morality and who limit one's duties only to family and country teach a selfishness which is dangerous for all of us.

"The understanding of one's unity with all of humanity comes from the understanding of the divine beginning in us all, and gives all our greatest good. True religion creates this understanding, and different prejudices interfere with it – prejudice of state, nation, and class."

"Our understanding of ourselves as discrete beings separate from each other grows out of conditions of our life in time and space. The less this separation, the more we feel our unification with all other living creatures, the lighter our load, and the more joyful our life will be.

"For the body is not one member, but many.... And if one member is honored, all the members rejoice with it." –I Corinthians 12:14, 26.

"Time is behind us, time is before us, but in the present there is no time.

"I consist of spirit and body. Time affects the body, but the life of the spirit has no meaning, either in the past or in the future. All is concentrated in the present." –Marcus Aurelius

CHAPTER 33

"Time does not exist. There is only a small and infinite present, and it is only in this present that our life occurs. Therefore, a person in this present time should concentrate all his/her spiritual force only on this Present."

"Above all, do not lie to yourself. A man who lies to himself and listens to his own lie comes to a point where he does not discern any truth either in himself or anywhere around him."
--Fyoder Dostoevsky

CHAPTER 34
Alternative Techniques to Improve Energy and Balance Emotions

- **Reflexology of Fingers and Massage of Hands**

    The massage of hands improves health. Massaging the hands alleviates pain and improves the blood circulation and moods. You don't have to wait to fall sick before massaging your own hands. It would be a wellness attitude to have by frequently massaging your own hands or have someone massage them for you.

    The fingers of the hands possess a secret that greatly balance our physical energy and emotions. Each finger is connected to two (2) organs according to an ancient Japanese knowledge called Jin Shin Jyutse. Each finger is also connected to an emotion. And by holding and squeezing each finger for three (3) to five (5) minutes, you will greatly get well and increase your energy flow while improving your moods and emotions at the same token. And while squeezing your fingers, take also deep breath in and out as you continue massaging your fingers.

    The thumb is linked to the stomach and spleen and may presents emotions such as anxiety and depression. The physical symptoms involve stomach pain, skin problems, headache and neurosis.

    The index finger is attached to the kidneys and bladder. The emotions present are disappointment, fear and confusion. The physical symptoms are muscles pain, back pain, toothache and problems with the digestive system.

The middle finger is connected to the liver and gall bladder. Its associated emotions are anger and indecisiveness. The symptoms presented are blood circulation problems, menstrual pain, tiredness, frontal headache and migraine.

The ring finger is tied up with the lungs and large intestine. Sadness and negativity are the associated emotions. Respiratory problems, asthma, digestive disorders and skin disease are shown as physical symptoms.

The baby finger, the last of the five fingers is linked to the heart and the small intestine. The emotions connected are anxiety, nervousness, worrying and lack of self-respect. Its physical symptoms are heart ache, throat pain, bone problems and stomach bloating.

It is a technique that consists of holding each finger at the time and squeezing it gently for 3 to 5 minutes at a time while taking deep breath. It has been in practice way before the era of Buddha, Jesus, Moses and Kojiki.

I have tried it myself and I was impressed how quickly my mood and emotions changed from stress, worries, irritation and unhappiness to just relax, calm and happy with increased energy within. Take note that you can just put pressures on your fingers without taking the big breath in and out. I took the liberty to add it up.

- **Reflexology of the Feet.**

Our feet also hold some healing secrets when pressure is applied to specific points to increase healing. The feet are also linked to their specific organs just like our fingers. There exist reflex points corresponding to our organs and by pressing them, it provides real good benefits for the person's health. The reflexologist uses the feet as a map because each foot corresponds to a side of the body. The left foot are in alignment with the organs found in the left side and the right foot to the organs on the right side. But some parts of the feet share link to the same organs and other part of the body as well.

The benefits of foot reflexology are multiple. It relax and calm the mind; Increases the energy flow within and helps activate the natural healing ability of the body. It reduces pain, ameliorates health concerns and contributes to healing of a specific unhealthy organs. Aids in post-operative recovery and can address mental health issues, too.

Reflexology has been used thousands of thousands of years and is still a must go-to, as it will always be relevant to our well-being. Just by randomly massaging your feet regularly would keep you away from incurable diseases. And just like eating food every day, I will recommend that you make it a habit to do your own feet massage weekly whenever you can, even daily. It will reduce your daily stress, anxiety and other psychological symptoms. Keep in mind that each organ in your body is connected to a specific point under your feet and by placing pressure on those points, you will increase the energy and organ health in connection. The energetic connection between organs improves greatly after the massage of feet and it is worth noting that reflexology takes its roots all the way from Ancient Egypt and Ancient China. Here are some of the reflex areas and their corresponding body parts:

The tips of the toes reflect the head and the ball of the foot governs the heart and chest. The liver, pancreas, bladder/gall bladder and kidneys are in the arch of the foot while the low back and intestines are located towards the heel. Reflexology can address those health symptoms: stress, migraine, headache, arthritis, insomnia, hormonal imbalances, menstrual disorders, digestive problems and even multiple sclerosis.

And in addition to massaging your hands, fingers and feet, you should know that you can also improve your internal health by massaging your ears, elbows, joints, wrist, forehead, neck, head and knees regularly for a duration of 3 to 5 minutes

CHAPTER 34

a session. You should massage your butt chicks or rear ends too because of the fact that we constantly sit down on them and the butt also has a vital connecting role to our overall health.

- **The Benefits of Drinking Water**

    Water is one of the vital resource that keep humanity alive. Without water, we would surely all die of thirst. In addition to the regular and basic drinking of water when thirsty, water can be used to cure so many diseases. Expert underline now that water is indeed an effective way to prevent and treat diseases. It is preferable to drink eight (8) to twelve (12) glasses of water daily. A glass would be about an eight ounces holder at least. Drinking water prevents kidney stones, and drinking 12 glasses of water a day helps treat kidney stones for your information. Water treats urinary tract infection by flushing harmful bacteria from the bladder through urination. It reduces fever, treats cough, colds, sore throat and respiratory infections. Good for diarrhea by slowing down and preventing dehydration and reduces heartburn. So far, water is life and health that cannot be replaced or skipped.

    In addition, water keeps you alert and energetic, thereby reduces stress, anxiety, fatigue and confusion. Make water your best friend daily and you will be full of life and health. It prevents constipation and alleviates any constipation complications. The drinking of water in a regular basis and in enough quantity can even help reduce weight by drinking a glass or two before you eat. Meaning that in that process, you will be filling up the spaces of your empty stomach first with water before eating causing you to eat less consequently. Drinking water produces miracle wonder. Among the wonder of drinking water regularly are: migraine, headache, skin conditions might easily get treated simply by drinking water. It is recommended to drink a glass of water before going to bed because while you are sleep, your body is still working and it is good for the heart too, as it prevents the individual from having a heart attack. Therefore, you would have to make it a nightly routine to drink water every night before going to bed. It is a must also to drink water when you wake up in the morning to flush the toxins that have built up during the night and refresh the organs. During the day you should keep drinking water before you actually feel thirsty. At the end, drink even more water when you are sick or pregnant even though you might not feel like. Do not wait to be thirsty, first, before drinking water. Water is life and by drinking more and more water, we would keep our life as well.

On this note, I have to inform you that water should be treated with care and love. Water is alive and has a memory that registers and adapts with any condition that you put it through. Water senses our vibes and automatically conforms to them. Happy thought and positive vibes will be registered on the water memory as well as unhappy emotions and negative vibes. Water changes its molecular structures when exposed to our emotions, feelings, and intentions. Therefore the water in your cup might conform itself to your moods and state of mind already before you even drink it.

In sum, the very water you are drinking may behave differently and present different molecular structures in someone else's hands and therefore present different health benefits. That's why it becomes necessary to make water your best friend to reap all of its health and medicinal benefit and properties.

- **The Benefits of Turmeric**

    Turmeric is a good source of energy that contributes in balancing the energy of the person that consumes it. It is a natural anti-inflammatory and increases the antioxidant capacity of the body to tackle diseases. It helps balance the brain energy systems by regulating and improving the circulation and connecting the system of nerves to the other parts of the body; thereby improving the communication via messenger cells more efficient and quick to and from the organs.

CHAPTER 34

Turmeric can also be consumed when in chronic pain or any type of physical ache including skin diseases, wounds, digestive ailments and liver conditions. It balances the whole body structure as it would clear any and all blockages within arteries and veins, joints to improve the blood flow and oxygen flow as well.

Turmeric should be readily available at your household just like salt and pepper never lacked in your kitchen cabinet. It is good for Arthritis, and possesses manganese, iron, potassium and vitamin C that the body needs daily. More reason to always have turmeric handy is that it protects against pancreatic cancer, prostate cancer and multiple myeloma. For patients with diabetes, turmeric strengthen the liver and actually stops your liver from being damaged by toxins or from side effects from powerful drugs and modern medicine. Helps cleanse your kidneys and align your digestive and circulatory systems. You can consume a tea spoon a day with tea or food when needed for a short term and retake after a break and so forth. You can also chew the raw fresh roots to benefit the same health potential. They sell it in almost every grocery store.

- **The Benefits of Ginseng**

Ginseng has been used for many centuries and survived time because of its powerful medicinal properties. It boost energy and balance the energy system for positive moods; reduces stress, lowers the blood sugar and cholesterol levels. Ginseng is full of antioxidants and anti-inflammatory properties that can even help cure cancers, fight fatigue, eczema, treat **diabetes** and improves symptoms of **erectile dysfunction**. We should all have some ginseng readily available as its importance in our well-being and of those of our family members call for it. It strengthen our immune system so that we could fight diseases effectively and enhance our brain functions (memory, behavior, mood, Alzheimer). Ginseng is a must have if we want to keep our family healthy and happy. You can eat it raw, mix with tea or as tea; put it in your food as spice at will.

CHAPTER 34

- **The Benefits of keeping your Heart Open at all times**

Keeping the heart open without closing it has been the secret and teaching of the great sages and enlightened people throughout the world. The secret behind it is that, it keeps the energy of the body flowing in and out, without getting blocked at any part of the body. You also know that blockages within the energy system will eventually cause you to get sick, or feel uncomfortable. When the energy cannot circulate because you have closed your heart, you will get sick. And you know when you have closed your heart, or opened your heart. We actually tend to open and close our hearts whenever we want or feel like it. When someone do something to us that we don't like, then we close the heart at that time and open it later when we are happy. We also close our hearts in places or events where we don't feel secured, reassured, safe or convinced. We even close our hearts to our own family members when they disappoint us or make us upset.

Anytime you close your heart, you are blocking the energy from circulating and getting in and out. Your heart is the receptor and the distributor of the energy. And the energy is going to the heart from the universe as we are also made of energy. The more your heart is open, the more energy rushing in to your heart from the universe. Always keep your heart open, at any given time, no matter the situation or circumstance; that way, you will see that your health will improve rapidly and you will enjoy an abundance of energy flowing through your heart throughout your whole body. With the abundance of energy flowing out of your body freely, you will also heal the people around you as well including your family members. You realize now that the simple task recommended is to never close your heart again and try to keep it open at all times whenever you can, so that you can heal yourself and your loved ones. You know very well when you close your heart and you also know very well when you open it. if someone gets you irritated or upset, just take a minute to remind yourself that it is not worthy for you to close your heart. Just remember that there is nothing worth closing your heart for. Always open your heart to remain healthy all the time.

- **The Misuse of Time**

    The misuse of time will deplete your body of energy and make you unhappy. It consist on focusing or putting your attention at everything else except being present. You misuse your time when you are anxious about the future. You misuse your time when you are constantly or reliving the past. You are also misusing your time when you caught yourself regretting old mistakes, just like trying to relive or reliving the yesterday's life.

    Misusing the time is something common to all of us, or has been everyone's path before awareness. It is just like a rite a passage where the only way is to become aware and alert when there is an act of misuse of time. It is hard to find someone that has not been on that road before. A lot of us even know what being present consist of, but still find it hard to just not worry about or anticipate tomorrow. Do not resist change. It is even harder when we have to race against the clock with so many deadlines to meet at work, or a project that must be done within a certain time; or try not to agonize or languish over our life's circumstances and situations when facing difficulties(financial, sickness, loss of self-esteem). What to remember and retain here is that all these misuse of time, whatsoever one, depletes the energy of the person and would cause sickness and depression. These are in sum what consist of misuse of time:

    – Being anxious about the future and pulling it close. Mostly, the result of pulling the future closer would undermine our present focus and would require some energy that is needed for our present situation.

    – Reliving the past by holding on to it dearly. By dragging the past heavy luggage on our back every day with its weight and pain.

- Regretting old mistakes and not forgiving yourself. Letting past decisions and actions regain power to disturb our feelings and emotions.

- Anticipating tomorrow while not living in the present; such as rendering a final decision on events that have not taken place nor been decided or situated. With questions like; what if?

- Racing against the clock; burning and dispensing excessive energy to complete a project or work.

- Reliving yesterday; when your mind is replaying constantly unfinished or unresolved issues of the past or yesterday for you to act on them now and you bought into it like you could go back on time and changes. Instead you let it upset you again and set a chain of emotional reaction taking your focus away from the present.

- Resisting change by complaining; knowing what is best but not following instructions. Staying closed-minded with no attempt to become open-minded. In some cases, just happy and satisfy being and remaining ignorant.

- Languishing over your life circumstances. Such us nagging, complaining, giving up hope, excuses, blaming yourself or others and being ungrateful and selfish.

- **THE IMPORTANCE OF SLEEP AND GETTING ENOUGH REST**

    Have you ever wondered why we sleep or why is it even not an option not to sleep? When the body is tired, it runs out of energy to afford any more physical effort needed. It just becomes weak and your mind simply stops properly functioning. If you keep trying not to rest, your body will soon give up on you, force you to take a break or induce you to go to sleep. Sleep is very important for our health just like good healthy diet and clean water.

CHAPTER 34

You should make sleeping enough hours a habit if you are planning to live longer. Research have shown that getting enough good sleep at the right time would help protect your mental health, physical health and the quality of your life. It is during sleep that your body heals itself while supporting a healthy brain function. I'm sure you have experienced it yourself that the more rest and sleep you get, the better you function when taking care of your business. When you get enough sleep, you are full of energy, pay more attention to detail, smile more and interact better socially without being grumpy; you even think better, concentrate better and remain more alert when your body and mind are well rested. You become more likely to be patient, less irritated and can socially show some love and understanding.

On the other hand, sleeping less would increase the risk of obesity, weight gain, heart disease, high blood pressure, memory problems and stroke. Sleeping less is also linked to inflammatory bowel diseases and the increase of disease recurrence.

Since sleep affects our glucose metabolism as well, sleeping less adversely affects blood sugar and reduces insulin sensitivity, eventually leading to type II diabetes. It is then very crucial that you sleep at least seven to eight hours a day/night to increase your health and your productivity in life. Studies have also shown that people who sleep less hours are more likely to be depressed, anxious, and less effective at work. They have a lack of tenacity and lack of good quick judgment (less alert). Besides, getting at least eight hours of sleep daily improves your immune system and help fight diseases and heal your body and mind. It helps you recover from the day's activities; it helps your body heal the damaged cells and recharge your heart and cardiovascular system for the next day. Sleep also help us solidify and consolidate memories while balancing our emotions and attending our spiritual needs or growth through dreams.

At the end of the day, your priority besides eating healthy, exercising, sleeping enough takes the third place. The good news is that keeping up with your sleep would help you fight cancer and your heart diseases. Adults need about seven to nine hours of sleep per night, one year olds need approximately eleven to fourteen hours of sleep, school age children between nine to eleven hours and teenagers between eight and ten hours sleep per night. So, once I publish this book, I will make sure that I sleep at least eight hours a night. But, do not worry if you only sleep 4 to 6 hours a day. As long as you exercise, meditate and eat healthy with a sane mind, you should be alright. Our life project and creativities would probably not see light, if we all consistently sleep 8 hours every night.

Even though we have missed some sleep already, the best way would be to remain consistent with our sleep pattern with a healthy routine that guarantees at least eight hours of sleeping per night since you could not just log in many hours of sleep to make up the sleep less days. Eating raw garlic would help you sleep faster because of its high concentrations of sulfurous compounds like allicin that naturally promote relaxation. Walnuts, almonds, spinach, kale, collards and onions will also induce sleep including meditation and mind relaxation.

- **If you Don't Tell me, How Would I Know?**

If you are used to drinking alcohol and want to take it easy, you can chose to fill your glass with water after couple of glasses of alcohol. Reduce the number of glasses of alcohol and continue filling your next glass or glasses with water and drink the water as well. You will feel the difference and it's actually not something that you cannot do. As drinking becomes a habit, you would just need as much quantity of liquid in your stomach for your brain to register satisfied.

Water falls from the sky, goes under ground and some of it goes back up. The water that rose back up will come back

CHAPTER 34

down to the ground, thereby some of that water will rise back up again and so on.

The hit from the Sun come down to the ground and some of it goes back up. And if the cycle stays true to its own cycles, then some of the hit from the ground will also rise back up and come down to the ground and so on.

So, water comes down and goes back up. Sunlight comes down and goes back up. Everything extended whatsoever its distance to us comes down and goes back up. And, at the same time, on earth here, we have a slogan, "What goes up, must come down," and I guess we forgot, "What goes down, must rise up."

Now the Sunlight and solar wind come down on earth and move winds and air around. Evaporated water meet a piece of air and they commune to the sky and give birth to some water that comes down pouring. All is governed by the Sun. Now, what controls the Sun and so forth? How far can we really see with our eyes, intuitions, telescopes, dreams and visions above?

The eye looks at what the mind dictates at a second. The eye releases energy or light that could be peaceful or upset, a gentle touch or burning. It can even invade someone's privacy or cause harm. The eye can glance, look a little and run away. This is why I say, "Thank you, God, for the food, bless the hands that cooked it, take any impurity out of the food and provide for those that don't have."

Everybody recycles. When you drink some water, the water nourishes your body. Some of the unused water or the ones that evaporated though the pores, skin goes back up and comes back down and so on. We eat and subtract the needed nutrients and throw some of the digested food processed out back to the nature. So, water, urine and poop fertilize the soil and food grows that we later eat. Isn't it clear that we need each other? If you do something behind my back and don't tell me, how would I know? If we don't talk, how would we know? Now, we have some people that cannot speak, just like they

CHAPTER 34

had their tongue sealed up. They want to talk but they can't. For some, they chose not to talk and for others, they just never have been able to talk or just happen to lose their voice upon living. We really cannot tell and be sure about what is going on in your head. Once you open your heart, the energy of the universe will flow through and reach out to people and back. The machine of the body grinds until the wheel goes out.

It's now 1:01 a.m., November 27, 2019, a different day. I should inform you that in ancient Egypt, Greece, Rome, people used to drink their own urine for therapy and to help cure a series of diseases. Little I know, people in China, Mexico, Africa and some other countries, the use of urine for therapy is widely acknowledged. Many people all over the world actually drink urine to remain healthy. A British naturopath in his book called *The Water of Life: A Treatise on Urine Therapy* claims that urine could cure all major illnesses. He stated that people who are in near death situations would benefit from eating and drinking nothing but their own urine for several weeks and have a urine massage daily into their skin.

It is claimed that drinking urine may treat allergies, acne, cancer, heart problems, infections, wounds, stuffy nose, rash and other skin ailments and stings. In Nigeria, some cultures and traditional communities up to today still use urine as a home remedy and therapy for children with seizures. Even though there is no scientific evidence to support what has been said above, it might look like there is not an effort either to discredit the advantages and health benefits of Urine Therapy as a means to cure diseases. The list of ailments it can help cure is: adrenal failure, arthritis, candida, eczema, herpes, cancer, diabetes, eye infections, infertility, hepatitis, multiple sclerosis, psoriasis and dandruff. In China, there is a village that have the most oldest and healthier people in the world, and their secret, is that they all drink their own urine as needed and regularly. That it boost their immune system, replace lost nutrients and can even support thyroid health. By the way, did you know that

CHAPTER 34

long ago, doctors used to taste patients urine by mouth in order to check if the patients had diabetes?

I'm just relaying a piece of information here and to each its own because it is hard to tell someone who is blind and deaf what to do. But usually when people run out of options, drinking urine to gain their health back, would not be a problem. You should also know that urine contains some bacteria and can present traces of medications, pills, drugs or alcohol if the person take pills, do drugs or drink alcohol that could contaminate the urine. A study involving 100 children attests that there was antibiotic-resistant strains in their urine. At the same time, researchers have also found very small quantity of hormones, vitamins, minerals and antibodies. Urine is a powerful diuretic and we also know some people use diuretics to lower blood pressure.

Its 1:57 p.m., the afternoon of the same day, and pain is my subject of the day. If you don't share your pain, who would know? Even if you try to explain your pain, is there any words that could really sum it up in a sentence or level of pain? Pain can be unbearable and yet tolerable as time goes by. You can try to tell someone how painful your pain is, but nobody else can really felt it and made it his/her own. We can relate and understand a pain, but can we really expressly feel to the same degree someone' else pain? When someone endures an extreme pain, any other pain that would come later, if not to that same exact intensity or more pain, that very person can somewhat become immune to it as it is lesser pain.

Pain is an energy that enters the body, mind and soul. Once it gets in, just like any other energy that goes in, it must come out. The energy from pain usually comes out screaming just the way it entered the person. It somewhat makes you vulnerable to retaliation and insensitive to people, thereby leading you to be less tolerant and forgiving. Pain could blind you and make you want to see pain for self-satisfaction, if you don't pay attention and remain in close communion to your feelings from your emotions. Can you really be joyful and peaceful, loving, when all you know and experience is pain and deceit? Those that have understood and made peace with themselves have used their pain as a stepping stone to help others and to move forward with love and kindness in their hearts. Some would actually advocate for more strategies to avoid others to ever become victims. Therefore, I would encourage anybody, no matter the pain that has been afflicted on them, to use that energy to do something positive. Deceit can also be painful, that could lead someone to self-preservation and distrustful impulse.

Sometimes, we can also deceive ourselves. The ones that wants you, you don't want them. The others that don't want to have anything to do with you, they are the ones you run after. It's Thanksgiving Day, you get an invite, but you don't really want to go there. You force your way to go to where you want to go and they don't want you in their company either, or are not as excited.

Your friend made you a plate at the Thanksgiving get-together and informs you to come get it, but you are on the mission to hunt for a plate from your other friend who actually doesn't have time and would not make you a plate. Isn't that life? Each thing and its opposite. And if we ever calm down and slow down, we can learn from life and accept what the universe is throwing at us. Pay attention to your blessings because they just show up to you uninvited.

Some hearts are sensitive and some others are already hardened. We have the ones in between and here and there soft heading to hardening, if they don't pay attention. So, protect your heart from hardening to become less sensitive to life. Become courageous enough to talk to someone and share your pain and feelings. Doing that in itself will give you a relief and closure toward your healing. Never hesitate to seek help.

- **Balancing of the Chakras**

    The balancing of the chakras is a technique used for thousands of years to balance human emotions and feeling with

CHAPTER 34

the objective to improve health and the energy flow within the body. The balance of chakras came along because within every living body, there is a spiritual realm where there are a series of energy fields working just like generators. That's what is called chakras and the word come from the Sanskrit word meaning "Wheel." They are like and conceptualize like wheel as it spin around much like it. They each have different and specific color and in a number of seven. The major chakras are as followed:

- The Root Chakra or Base is located at the base of the spine comes with a color Red. It represents our grounding to the earth and to our physical plane.

- The Naval Chakra or Sacral located is between the base of the spine and the navel with an Orange as color. It is the chakra that represent our sexuality, our sexual impulse including our creativity.

- The Solar Plexus which is located at the solar plexus area about 2" (5cm) below the navel. It is the seat of our personal feelings, emotions including our feelings of personal power, anger and hostility. It is where we gets the gut feeling and our intuitive instinct. Its color is Yellow.

- The Heart chakra is located at the center of the chest with a color Green. As we all know, the heart is the center of love, harmony and peace. It is the chakra that manifest in us the desire to wanting to settle down and to feeling loved. It is the center and the connecting part from the upper and the lower chakras in communion moving up to the Crown chakra to complete the total union of Chakras.

- The Throat Chakra, of course located within the throat is the center of all communication, self-expression and judgment. Its color is blue and by coloring your throat in a blue color, it will improve your communication skills and remediate any problems with communication.

- The Third Eye chakra, or the Brow Chakra, is the chakra that helps us answer the questions of our purpose on earth. It guides in directing and finding answers to our spiritual questions. It responds to the spiritual nature of our lives as it stores our inner visions, and inner gifts. All visions and dreams are held in this chakra and it is from where we get our gift of clairvoyance, wisdom and perception including the gift of interpreting dreams and visions.

- The Crown Chakra in a form of a crown seating on top of the head in a Violet color. This chakra opens our way to the world of God. It is the doorway to the divine and the beyond or transpersonal chakras. It is represented as the chakra of destiny and divine purpose as it balances out interior with our exterior in order to bring all parts into harmonious voice and union. The transpersonal chakras could go beyond and beyond in an unlimited number according to each person individual connection with God, the divine and those are our true connection with the divine as well as the connections between masters and teachers. We become as one with God and are indeed in communion with Him as one, as He is in us.

Now the balancing of the chakras are possible by means of Meditation, Concentration, Prayer, Intercessions, the use of Hot and Cold Stones, by Spiritual Works and Incantations, Exercises, Reiki, Aroma-therapy, Forest Bathing, Ecotherapy, Yoga and various Sports aimed at the Realignments of the body Standard Posture, Massages, physical Therapies and Acupuncture including the Mastering of the movements of the Chi (Energy flow within the body) and various other techniques throughout the world and ancients civilizations. All of which includes the balancing also of the Meridians that are parts of the Spiritual Anatomy. Hot Stone massages balances also our emotional disturbances and is good for pain when the stones are directly applied to where it is hurting. Mucus-less diet healing system can also balance the chakras and meridians while at the same time helps cure a lot of diseases including weight loss.

CHAPTER 34

- ## MUCUSLESS DIET HEALING SYSTEM (Dr. SEBI'S SAMPLE LIST)

Mucus-less diet has been proven to cure a lot diseases and possibly all kind of diseases. It consist of a progressively changing your diet from mucus making foods to non-mucus making foods. According to prof. Arnold Ehert, "Every sick person has a more or less mucus-clogged system, such mucus being derived from undigested, un-eliminated, and unnatural food substances accumulated from childhood on."

It is understood that mucus clogs the intestines and colon and most of the time glue itself pile after pile to the point of obstructing normal conditions for a good digestion. Mucus also accumulates over time and adds up every time we continue consuming mucus causing foods thereby causing constipations, worms' friendly environment and diseases. In most-worse cases, the walls of the intestines and colon get lined up with a crust of hardened feces, a sign that the intense accumulation of mucus over time could rendered the intestines and colons inefficient. The system has been clogging up with mucus forming foods since childhood and that is why in order to remediate and get your health back, a mucus-less diet has to be considered.

Mucusless diet consist of fresh, ripe fruit and starch less vegetables. Fruits, green leaf and starchless vegetables do not have nor contain the pasty, gluey mucus substances and are natural foods. When considering the approach of mucusless diet healing system, the patient should be gradually changing his/her diet progressively by replacing mucus-forming foods with mucus-less foods followed by intermittent fasting. It is a system that cleanse and rid your body of the accumulated toxins and dirt build up in your body over time. And by gradually switching to fruits and green leaf and starchless vegetables, you will be cleansing your intestines, your colon including your whole digestive system before mucus clogs all the system that

CHAPTER 34

usually is the cause of all sickness. You can practice it one, two days at a time while progressively adding more days to your mucus-less regimen. Some would prefer a one meal a day to start and the remaining of the hours from that day spend eating nothing but fruits and vegetables.

Here is a list of some of **mucus-forming foods** form **Dr. Sebi**: Fish, Butter, Cornmeal, Milks, Yogurt, Bread, Kefir, Buttermilk, Processed Meat, Fast Foods, Dried Convenience Food, Packaged food, Frozen Food, Alcoholic Beverages, Soft Drinks, Ice Cream, Vinegar, Coffee, Tea, Cocoa, Candies, Jellies, Baked goods, Marshmallow, Sauces, Chips, Plant Based Butter, plant Milk, Vegan Whipped Cream, vegan mayonnaise, all types oil, chili powder, curry powder, vanilla extract, pepper, black pepper corns, chili, avocados, corn, white potatoes, sweet potatoes, beans, rice, sugar, carrot and broccoli etc.

The **Mucus-Free Foods** from Dr. Sebi are: Arugula, Dandelion leaf, turnip, lettuce (all types except iceberg), cucumbers, Kale, Onions, Green Onions, sea vegetables, tomatoes, Endives, Dill, Zucchini, peppers (green, red, and yellow), Squash, Apples, Black Cherries, Cantaloupe, Grapes, mangoes, Black berries, banana, watermelon, sweet cherries, Strawberries, papaya, peaches, pears, Dates, Figs, Coconut water, fruit jellies (without sugar added), plums, prunes, raisins, raspberries, Sprout, Leafy Herbs, (parsley, Dill, basil, thyme etc.), Garbanzo beans, mushrooms, Nopales Cactus, Wakame, Dulse, Arame, Hijiki, Okra, Olives Tomatillos, Watercress, Purslane (Verdolaga), Izote Cactus Flower and Leaf, Dates, Curants, Limes, Tamarinds, prickly pears, Sour sops, Soft Jelly Coconuts, Oranges etc.

According to Dr. Sebi, you can consume in moderation those moderately mucus forming foods that are: Pasta, chick peas, Nuts, Seeds, approved flours, olive oil, avocado oil, avocados.

For your information neither of the list above is final and exhaustive. There are plenty of more mucus-forming foods and

CHAPTER 34

mucusless foods that are not in Dr. Sebi's lists; I just thought his sample lists might guide you in starting your journey in Mucusless Diet healing system for your personal well-being.

Dr. Sebi continued to bring us the laws of eating in rhythm that between 5am to 12 noon, it is best advice to eat fruits, herbs and water so that the body could easily flush and cleanse the toxins out. From 12 to 3pm, it is recommended to eat vegetables to replenish the cells and feed minerals, chlorophyll, melanin, and carbon to the body. Finally, between 3pm and 8pm, since it is evening time you can eat more solid foods but definitely no more eating after 8pm.

Random list of vegetables include, Garden Asparagus, Celery, Cabbage, Spinach, Cucumber, Sprouting Broccoli, Lettuce, Brussels sprout, Curly kale, Garlic, Turnip, Carrot, Okra, Cauliflower, Onion, Tomato, Parsnip, Potato, Collard, Pumpkin, Radish, Watercress, Jicama, Kohlrabi, Radicchio, Arugula, Artichoke, Endive, Avocados, Eggplant, Taro, Ginger, Sweet potato, Chard, Water chestnut, Black Mustard seed, Turnip greens, Tomatillo, Chayote, Pea, Fennel, Bell pepper, Bok Choy, Mushroom, Leaf vegetables, Horseradish, Elephant Garlic, Lemongrass, Nymphaea nelumbo, Mung bean sprout, Galangal, Jerusalem artichoke, Wax gourd, Celtuce, Fiddlehead fern, Napa cabbage, Water spinach, Dandelion, Beetroot, Maize, Rutabaga, Celeriac, Yam, Parsley, Green bean, Bamboo shoot, Chives, Dill, Garden rhubarb, Snow pea, Snap pea, Bitter melon, Pineapple, Broccoflower, Daikon, Alfalfa, Cantaloupe, Romaine lettuce, Olive, Apple, Banana, Iceberg lettuce, Spaghetti squash, Zucchini, Leek, Pepper, shallot, Arrowroot, Amaranth Leaves, black eyed peas, black beans, Lotus root, Nopal, Salsify, etc.

- **THE IMPORTANCE OF BREAKFAST**

Breakfast is the important meal of the day. It is not just another meal like we might think. It is actually the meal. At morning, you just wake up from sleeping about 6 to 8 hours the previous night. While you were sleeping your body kept using and burning energy and in the morning, your body is ready to be fueled. And it is important that you fuel the body by eating breakfast. We might have built a bad habit of skipping breakfast but it is a healthy habit as every time you skip breakfast, you run the risk for your body to convert the amino-acids from your muscles as fuel. Rewire your brain and start eating breakfast again as it is the most important meal of the day. Regardless of your choice of diet either healthy or unhealthy, mucus-making food or mucus-less food, breakfast remains an important meal not to be skipped as it recharges your body with energy for you to start your day with vitality and strength.

CHAPTER 35
Breathing techniques/ Breath control / Breath of life

There is an acknowledgment from different cultures and belief systems that a universal life force exists. It is the universal energy that permitted life in all things existing in the universe. This universal life force is the one that gave birth to that materialized world in a form of physical matter surrounding us.

In some systems this vital life force can be controlled and manipulated to induce and improve health, healing and happiness. This universal energy has been called different names such as Prana in Hindu Yoga, Qi/Chi in Chinese tradition and Ki in Japanese but in practice they all share the same techniques on how to control it and it resumes to breathing control.

Prana is the energy that the soul uses. It is in the air but it is not the air, or even one of its chemical constituents. Prana reaches where the air cannot penetrate. It is the essence of all life forms and things even inanimate objects.

In Chinese tradition and other cultures around the world even in far centuries back in Africa, the universal life force (Qi) is regarded as the source of health, harmony, creativity and courage. The more energy you possess, the healthier you are and less of it would translate to sicknesses. Here are their different breathing control techniques:

Prana Breathing exercise

The philosophy behind it, is that prana/the life and vital force comes to us freely through the air we breathe in. That's why, when we breathe prana, we charged ourselves with the basic force of all life that is in all things.

To start, do this practice twice a day, for a period of five minutes. Through both nostrils, breath in, hold it and count to four then breathe out.

Now, close your right nostril; breathe in through the left nostril and count to four. Close your left nostril and breathe out, completely, through your right nostril, keeping the left nostril closed to a count of four. Now, keeping the left nostril closed, breath in trough the right nostril to a count of four. Close your right nostril and breath out, completely, through your left nostril, while still keeping the right nostril closed to a count of four.

Repeat the exercise alternatively from left to right nostril as instructed above. As you become familiar with the technique, you may increase the counts for inhalation and exhalation to eight, ten, and so on depending on your ability to do so.

You should practice this breathing technique to recharge your soul of the energy of life also called the breath of life, the essence of all things so that you can regained your health, heal your mind and become happy again. A session could be 3 to 5 minutes and even more.

Qi/Energy Breathing Exercise.

Lie down, totally flat on a comfortable flat surface face up. Relax for a second or two. Now breathe in deeply through your nose. Push your belly up while taking the air inside. Stick your chin on your chest and watch your belly rise. When you have taken in as much air as you can hold, stop and hold your breath. Try holding it for five, ten or twenty seconds. Then breathe out slowly and completely.

CHAPTER 35

You can practice this technique daily for five to fifteen minutes also and prolong the duration accordingly to your own ability. At first it may feel strange but once you get use to deep breathing and with your eyes closed, you will eventually feel and sense the rhythm of the deep breath you are taking. You will therefore feel energize and relax. You can do it at home, in the park or at your office.

This breathing technique is believe to increase the amount of oxygen the body can use to burn out disease and improve your health, while re-establishing the Qi/ energy flow within the body. It also increases your body and spirit vitally and strengthen your mind for higher creativity.

Since we are living a busy life, besides practicing this breathing technique whenever you want and daily, if possible, it could be best and easier for most of us to do it before getting up of the bed during mornings and at night while we are getting ready to sleep.

A Basic Relaxation technique

First, choose a quiet place where you won't be disturbed. Turn off your phone and any electronics at your possession. Start with some gentle stretching, bending and flexing exercises to relieve muscular tension.

Make yourself comfortable sitting down or laying down. Breathe in slowly and deeply, in a calm and effortless way. Gently tense then relax each part of your body starting with your feet and work your way up to your face and head. Now that you have focused on all part of your body, think of warmth, heaviness and relaxation.

Even though it may be hard to stop thinking or being distracted, push those thoughts to the back of your mind and imagine them floating away. Stay there and simply relax. Let your muscles relax. Let your mind go empty.

Relax, relax and relax again for about 10 to 20 minutes. When done, remain at your position, either sitting or lying down for a few moments before getting up to avoid getting dizzy. You can also do this technique anytime and any day preferably in the mornings and evenings or after a long day at work.

Tips for Health and Wellness.

Remove clutter in your house/room or office to facilitate the flow of chi energy. Clutter blocks the passage of energy making it stagnate and, at the same time, blocking the positive energy from coming into your life and work places.

Feng Shui suggests that it is vital for our health and wellbeing to surround ourselves with souvenirs, artworks, images, books and anything that would further nourish our spirit. Keeping in mind that the philosophy behind Feng Shui, less is always more and the space used does not have to be spacious as long as it all belongs to you and it's regarded as your special place, a place where you can dream and find peace.

It is also recommended and important to create an environment that promotes health and wellness such as clean, fresh, moving water, good air quality, a balance of dark and light and soft and hard surfaces all towards the facilitation of a good flow of energy chi.

Feng Shui strongly suggests that we let nature back in into our homes and offices because Feng Shui is all about harnessing the power of nature to bring health and good fortune for our family well-beings. Bring in indoors plants and flowers, fountains or fish tanks to bring fresh new moving energy. Throw open the blinds and curtains of windows to let the sun shine in daily when it is morning and throughout the day. Crack your windows or doors to let fresh air in and out.

CHAPTER 35

A Good Practical Habit to Keep.

A good habit to keep at all times is to always remind yourselves to drink water every morning and anytime you wake up from sleeping.

In addition to that, you should drink water every time whenever you can before taking a shower, bath, exercising, even before you start working.

Of course, it is automatic to drink water after a meal but a lot of people fail to do so. Always know and remember that juices and other soft drinks cannot replace water. Drink water always shortly after a meal to improve your digestion and avoid constipations and stomach aches. Never drink water or any liquid during meal while still eating unless necessary.

Water is what the body needs to promote health throughout our organs' system and cells. Overall, make water your best friend to never depart from as it restores our daily water burned out. It helps our body system run well while keeping us healthy and pain free. Make time for yourself to get plenty of rest every day.

One more thing to know and to keep up with your health is the fact that after a meal we always burp or fart and both at the same time. That's a normal process of our body functions. It is how our body machine works. When you start noticing that it becomes harder and harder to enjoy or get a burp or fart and both following a meal, then it is wise to start refocusing on how you treat your body. It is then advice to revisit your diet list and make sure to add daily exercises techniques such as stretching, bending and flexing to your daily work out notwithstanding all of the above breathing techniques.

It will not hurt to also start paying attention to yourselves to be sure that you actually urinate, or take a piss while, during or after a shower because it also can give you a warning on your overall health status. It is normal to piss specially right after you finish taking your shower. Because during the act of showering, you were actually spending and burning energy. To keep us clean, we use our hands to rinse all parts of our body, reaching out and bending while staying steady and balanced. During shower time, all our body systems are at work simultaneously, and we tend to also be more focused on finishing the task of keeping dirt out of the skin pores. That's exactly why you should drink water before getting into the shower to help the body get rid of the toxins build up over the days out.

After shower or a bath, it is just as a reboot of our system and reenergizing the body. That's why it is a good habit to make sure we drink water before every shower in order to have enough water to burn through and take out the dirt and toxic from our organs and joints. It is also recommended to take a shower with cold water.

Cold water shower boost the energy and the immune system, thereby getting us more ready and alert to start our day arm with courage and determination.

It is also advice and recommended to drink water before we go to sleep or to bed for a better circulation of the body organs systems and to avoid cardiac arrest or heart attack and heart burn.

Additionally, a quick advice about the type of simple headache that we commonly get and wondering what to do before seeking medical attention is to remember those 3 types of headaches.

When the pain is in the front of our head or forehead, it could mean that we need some sleep. Mainly, we need to catch up on some sleep for the body and mind to rest.

When the headache resides on the top of our head, it just means that we need to drink a lot of water and get some food to eat. Remember the body has so many other ways to talk to you when the signals at the stomach level fail to get your attention.

CHAPTER 35

Finally, the third type of headache is the one hurting from the back, or the back of our head. That one encourages and require us to get some rest. It is recommended to stop all activities if you can to lay down for couples of minutes or hours for the body to reenergize in full force in productivity.

To end this section, add a fruit and plants based diet to your life. Eat a lot of fruits daily as much as you want and try when you can to reduce your meat consumption to improve your health and increase your energy. Stay away from alcohol beverages at all or consume it with real moderation to keep a healthy kidney and liver. Don't even start smoking cigarettes to be safe and avoid lung and throat cancer. And for those that are addicted to alcohol and cigarettes or drugs, the intake of Carbon(charcoal from wood) would help you quit all those bad habits because Carbon would attract the positive ionic charges of toxins and poison (when poisoned) and escort them out of the body. Carbon is also very good to treat all colon diseases, oral health, and gently benefits the intestines especially when you have bloated stomach with gas. It detox, assist the kidney function by filtering out undigested toxins and drugs, and you only need a tea spoon of Carbon (charcoal powder from wood) in some clean water to drink daily for a week or two depending on how addicted you are. Always consult your physician first. Think before you talk, breathe before you respond.

Daily Exercise While on the bed or on the Street.
(Tatieta Physical Therapy Formula)

Lay down on a flat surface on your back and start by raising your arms high at chest height like you are holding a wand or stick chest level. Next slowly push your arms outwards in front of your body to the point that your elbows become fully straightened. Then, return to the original position. Repeat ten (10) to 25 times while holding your arms at each position for 5 to 10 seconds. No equipment needed for this particular exercise but you can instead use a wand or stick or hold on each hand a warm hot stone in which I recommend.

CHAPTER 35

Now with your arms at your side while still laying down, draw up your hand by bending at the elbow and keep your wrist in a neutral position at all times. Repeat the drawing of your hands 5, 10 to 25 times or desired number of hands movements. (Still holding the warm/hot stones)

Proceed then with your left hand kept elevated above heart level on pillow and open and close left hand 5, 10 to 25 times or at please. (Squeeze hands when done together with the hot stone for couple of seconds). Conclude the arms and hands exercise by interlacing hands together resting at your lower stomach; hold for a minute then slowly raise arms above your head to touch the flat surface back far away from your head back and forth 5, 10 to 25 times still with your hands interlace.

Now put your focus on your feet and legs. With your ankles, point them out; hold for 5 to 10 seconds then flex both ankles slowly 5, 10 to 25 times up and down. Repeat until satisfaction. You can also add squeeze and release of your toes with repetition.

Remain in laying down position and Squeeze your buttocks tightly; hold for 5 to 10 seconds and release. Repeat squeezing your buttocks 5, 10 to 25 times or till satisfactory number of times.

Next keep your heels on the flat surface; draw up your leg by bending at knee while sliding the heel of your operated leg towards your buttocks as far as you can. Hold for about 5 seconds then slide your heel back down pressing your knee back against the flat surface. Repeat the flexing and bending of your legs at knee level 5, 10 to 25 times or until on both legs.

Finally open your legs out to the sides. Keep your knee and foot pointed toward the sky or the ceiling, then move your leg back in side-ways and out 5, 10 to 25 times.

Keep legs open flat, straighten your knee to lift your foot off the flat surface or bed. Lift your foot up, Hold for about 3, 5 to 10 seconds and slowly lower your foot back and repeat exercise

CHAPTER 35

about 5, 10 to 25 times on both legs. Complete the session by twisting your ankles and the wrist of your hands 5 times from each side left and right taking turns or at the same time.

Remember that everyone have been there lacking the motivation to even try to lift a finger. But nonetheless, we dig inside of us and find that fire still barely burning in us to wanting to exercise and proceed one day at a time.

Once you complete all steps with repetition and consistency after several session or if you are up to it, you can now graduate to the bicycle ride upside down by adding it to the previous techniques. Remain on the flat surface and end your session by lifting up both legs up and act as if you were riding a bicycle by pedaling on the air 5 to 10 times forward and 5 to 10 times backward and you may increase gradually the numbers of pedaling at your convenience. You have now became a master of your domain. Keep practicing and never stop exercising daily.

This exercise formula will strengthen your muscles and back bone by pulling joints back into their sockets thereby realigning your standard posture for a healthy flow of oxygen, nutrients and improve the circulatory systems while reducing any risk of heart attacks and diseases. Now you can think clearly and act within a right state of mind.

(Good exercise at all ages, including kids and teenagers, mostly adult, elders and those confine in bed or with hips and back problems. Even for those lacking motivation to live and be productive again. When done and in pain pass the hot stones throughout your body and massage every part of the body with the stones.)

Next step, after you have successfully mastered the first exercise techniques, you can add or exercise in a separate session at will.

Lay down on your back with your hands at the back of your head, arms spread out flat on the floor left and right; interlace your legs together so that one ankle/foot is resting on top of the other. Now slowly rock yourself from the legs to the waist left to right, right to left. Move your legs and foot both together at once from left to right for about two minutes or more.

Stop and flex both feet up and down at ankles level for about 30 seconds to a minute, then twist them left to right and back and forth for another 30 seconds.

You can now swish legs and foot still crossing at the ankles and repeat the same movements. Proceed to put your legs next to each other and relax for couple of minutes. Finish the session by raising up yourself from the head up to a seating position while keeping your legs on the ground or the flat surface. After you get up, keep your legs straight and cross them together for 30 seconds, then twist your ankles and flex them up and down for another 30 seconds at ankle level. Swish legs and remain at the crossing position and repeat the same cycle like above. Release and let go all tension by taking big deep breath in and out for another 30 seconds to a minutes.

Lay back down flat on your back, raise up both feet up at waist level perpendicular to the flat surface, hold them up for a minutes while twisting feet up and down, side to side at ankle level for about 20 seconds or more and you are ready to go back running and dancing as usual. Apply the hot stones. Massage whenever you are in pain, or feel that your emotional state is disturbed, or you feel confused, disoriented, unhappy, stress and restless or lacking sexual drive.

TATIETA BALANCE OF ENERGY TECHNIQUES

Bend over by your waist with your eyes looking down to the ground. Then use your hands to massage the back and front of your tibia, massage your thighs, massage the back of your knees and your knees, and massage your ankles and feet. Pretty much by the time you realized, you have given yourself a whole leg massage while in a bending position by your waist; apply a little

CHAPTER 35

bit of pressure if you need to, during your legs massages to better improve and facilitate the circulation of blood and oxygen. You can also do this exercise while sitting down with your two legs together straight flat touching the floor.

Remain in bending position and reach out and hold your toes. Try squeezing them, one by one, each for few seconds. Get up and stand straight for a couple seconds; then bend back over by the waist again and repeat the massaging of the ankles, tibias, knees, back of the knees, thighs, feet and toes.

Stretch while using your own imagination. You can make any stretching position and move's you desire for about five minutes. Try to remain 10 to 15 seconds at a time on each stretching position.

Now sit down like Buddha sits with your legs crossed like you are about to do a sitting for a meditation. Or just sit on a chair, if you prefer. Remain seated and proceed by holding your fingers and squeezing each finger, one at the time. Give it one good squeeze, one at the time, while rotating fingers. Meaning use your right hand to squeeze your left hand fingers thoroughly and switch hands. Repeat three times. Squeeze gently hard, hold for a couple of seconds, then release and proceed to the next fingers at least 10 to 15 seconds apart.

Remain in meditation seating position or on your comfortable chair, do three, five to ten deep breaths from each breathing technique. Take a deep breath in, hold it for couple of seconds, then breathe out through your nose. Breath in deep through your nose, hold the air in your chest for couple of seconds, then breathe the air out through your mouth. Use your hand and close your left nostril and breathe in deep through your right nostril; hold your breath for a couple of seconds. Now, close your right nostril and breathe out completely through your left nostril. Then, close your right nostril and breathe in deeply through your left nostril; hold it, close your left nostril and proceed to breathe out through your right nostril. Your session is over, and it will be very beneficial to your long term health to practice daily at your convenient time during the day; or at least three times during a week period.

Eat less and fast regularly because your body and brain work better when your stomach is empty. Let your stomach be empty for 2 to 3 hours here and there for any purification and correction to happen within your body. Allow 6 to 8 hours in between meals for a healthy and smooth digestion.

What to ask for the Next Time you see Your Physician.

At certain age in our life, just about after 35 going up, both males and females should insist on having the following tests done and follow up.

- A chemistry panel called "Chem 20" – a battery of 20 blood tests.
- A complete blood count with differential
- A urinalysis
- A thyroid profile
- An RPR to R/O syphilis or herpes, hepatitis, profile and HIV, if and when sexually active at least ounce
- A baseline chest x-ray with result
- Women should have a Pap smear and a mammogram and ask your physician to also use a "thyroid guard" for health safety.
- Men (40 and above) should have a digital rectal exam and a blood test called a Prostate Specific Antigen (PSA).
- Both women and men should undergo a yearly eye and dental exam at a regular basis to help determine your overall physical health.

And at that age, we are also susceptible to more exposure to all the types of diabetes which will be important for us to be familiar with their differences.

CHAPTER 35

Type II diabetes is caused by a genetic predisposition to the disease or and including a diet with a lot of refined food couple with less physical activities/ exercise. Type II is linked with excessive production of insulin. We also know that the insulin job is to keep the glucose level balanced in our blood streams in its normal working condition. So when there is an excess of insulin in the body, it is because something is wrong. The body is not letting the insulin do its job. There is insulin but restricted in eliminating the glucose on the blood stream.

Now we have a situation where the level of glucose becomes way too high in the blood (blood sugar), thereby causing additional health complication, such as high blood pressure, obesity, heart diseases and cancer.

According to Dr. Atkins, "All the millions of early-stage diabetics who are eating meals high in carbs and taking medications that may stimulate insulin production are quite innocently on a path to self-destruction."

This makes one understand that to tackle diabetes and control the level of sugar in the blood, food with less carbohydrate is recommended. While controlling your carbohydrate intake, you should also eat foods with so little glycemic impact so that you can normalize your blood sugar without ever worrying about the disease getting out of control.

With this note, I think it becomes imperative for us to know the difference between the two types of diabetes. You already know that the type II diabetes is caused by a genetic propensity for the disease which means that if someone in your family tree have ever had a diabetes disease, it becomes now a genetically probability that you too could become diabetes by a way of inheritance. Just by simply belonging to that family or that race or group of ethnic descend. Or you can also eat your way up to the disease, even if no one in your family has ever been diabetic type II based on your choices of food thereby setting up your next generation to be more likely to be diabetic also.

Type I diabetes usually happens at early childhood age or adulthood stage and is not related to food or diet or any genetic predisposition of the disease. It is an auto-immune disease or disorder. The mind of the person or the control systems have stopped working properly and the body mistakenly attacks the pancreas. The pancreas is the organ that produces insulin to regulate the glucose level in the blood. Now that the body has lost its mind and largely or totally destroyed the pancreas, there is no more capacity for the body to produce insulin again whatsoever. The conclusion is type I diabetes patients needing insulin at constant and regular basis to balance sugar level in the blood streams.

Other than that, type II diabetes is mostly a diet-induce based on how we feed ourselves. We actually eat our way up to type II disease and can be prevented with a proper diet especially if you have had loved ones already within the family suffering or have suffered with type II diabetes.

Diabetes is insidious. It exists and takes a long time before manifesting itself. As pre-diabetic stage, it could lay dormant usually for several decades meaning more than 10 years and so on. So to avoid an unpleasant surprise down the road years later, a simple **glucose-tolerance test** (GTT) can establish its presence or not. Take heeds my friends and ask for a GTT test on your next physician visit, because type II diabetes can be defeated when we act promptly in advance.

Diabetes Foods and Supplements

Type 2 diabetes can be prevented and reverse with proper diet and exercise. The diet must have a fresh fruits and vegetables, whole grains and legumes including a high quality protein to induce weight loss and helps prevent with weight gain. 90% of people with diabetes are type 2 whereas, about 5% of diabetic patients are type 1.

In addition, eating food with high level of magnesium would help considerably. Note that low levels of magnesium

CHAPTER 35

are usually associated with poor blood sugar control and in a lot of cases, the beginning of the diabetic complications.

Foods high in magnesium are almonds, avocado, beans (dried), greens, peas, pumpkin seeds, tofu; and supplementing magnesium (250-500mg daily) can help. Also, check chapter 8 for more food and vegetables rich in magnesium.

Coenzyme Q10 assists and aids with carbohydrate metabolism while also protecting the patients against any diabetic complications. Food sources with CoQ10 include broccoli, eggs, and red meat, spinach, wheat germ and whole grains. You can also take a supplement (120mg daily).

The patient or preventing diabetes should add a Vitamin E supplement (400 IU daily). Vitamin E improves the glycemic control and prevent any complication. Food sources for Vitamin E are almonds, broccoli, greens, kiwi, mango, peanut butter, sunflower seeds and wheat germ oil.

Garlic appears to have substances that are anti-diabetic and also possess the ability to help prevent diabetic complications. You may take two to three fresh cloves of garlic daily or incorporate it into your diet daily (2 cloves) or a supplement dose about 2,500mg of the two fresh garlic daily. For those that are not yet diabetic could start cooking with garlic or add it to their diet at a regular basis.

How to Decalcify/Cleanse your Pineal Gland-third eye for Higher Performance

- Use fluoride filters to reduce or eliminate your fluoride intake from public water but most of the shower water we bath with is fluoridated.

- Stop drinking public water containing fluoride. In USA, at least 80% of the public water is fluoridated.

- Stop using toothpaste that contains fluoride in it

- Use alternative toothpaste that do not have fluoride in it
- Stop taking calcium supplements with synthetic calcium in it. Synthetic calcium is bad for the pineal gland and your health.
- Avoid using nonstick cookware with PFOA and PFC
- Eat more and more organic whole grain and food (support your local farmers market.)
- Cook your own food with organic ingredients to know for sure what you are feeding yourself
- Meditate for couple of minutes and exercise daily
- Turmeric is excellent for the pineal gland detoxification
- Shivaji; Activator X; Fulvic Acid; Chaga Mushrooms (King of Plants); Raw Cacao; Tamarind; Raw Apple Cider Vinegar and Boron are also efficient at cleansing the pineal gland.

Food rich in Boron are: avocados, almonds, bananas, beans, beets, chickpeas, dates, hazelnuts, prunes, raisins and walnuts. Raw apple cider vinegar is a natural metal remover and detoxifier. It kicks heavy metals out of the body while providing at the same time some natural vitamins, minerals and enzymes that nourish the body and strengthen the immune system. Raw apple cider vinegar is great for your pineal gland detox and also helps cleanse the lymph nodes, allowing a better lymph circulation which is necessary for removing toxins and improving your immune system. Tamarind increases the excretion of fluoride in urine and can even possibly reverse the effects of skeletal fluorosis caused by ingesting fluoride. Chaga Mushroom provides the individual with phytochemicals, nutrients and melanin. Chaga is an efficient anti-tumor agent as well as antiviral. It has potent effects on the immune hormonal and central nervous systems confirmed by hundreds of scientific studies across the world. The Chinese call the Chaga

Mushroom the "King of Plants," in Siberia it is called "the Gift of God," and in Japan the "Diamond of the Forest."

Iodine consumption assists the thyroid gland in regulating hormones and it would tremendously take out the heavy metals from the body. Iodine is mineral found in sea vegetables like seaweed or kelp. It chelates heavy metals such as mercury, lead, cadmium, aluminum and of course fluoride. While taking iodine, be sure to add foods rich in calcium on your diet simultaneously.

A calcified pineal gland impairs your sleeping patterns, cognitive abilities, reaction time, judgment, perception and performance all together leaving the individual defenseless and vulnerable. It is clear that when you have a limited perception, you are bound to have a close mind thereby reducing the chance for any internal growth be it spiritual, emotional, insight or mental. Now you might understand why fluoride in your neighborhood public water? The third eye helps you see the supernatural and spiritual world putting you in connection with the spirits, previous masters, God, gods. It also help you communicate with the spiritual world and receive messages from above. It is clear that if you are blind, you cannot see; and by having your pineal gland calcified, it is as you being blind because you would lack your third eye to connect with God and the ancestors. Therefore, you are blind if your pineal gland is calcified. And if you never cared for your pineal gland, chances are you must be blind by now. Besides, the pineal gland is in charge of producing melanin that provides the pigment for our skins, hair and eyes. It uses the melanin to help shield us from the Sun ultraviolet light.

The third eye, also known as the pineal gland, is represented at the Brow chakra, just above the center of the eyebrows. It holds great powers and its opening gives you access and connects you with almost everything existing and present in the Universe. When your third eye is opened, it increases your intuition and you can see upcoming events before they happened.

Your tolerance level also increases and most likely a change will soon happen urging you to make conscious choices about your diet and the way you treat others and the things within the Universe. You will start seeing the other worlds and dimensions we are sharing the life with, at the same time your psychic powers would increase and you will start having lucid and vivid dreams. But most importantly, you will remember your dreams and vision and possibly gain the insight to interpret them.

People would noticed the change in you and it is okay to progressively open your third eye so that you won't get confused and scared when you start seeing other beings from different dimensions. The cool part about the third eye is that it would afford you to have a new perception by changing your thought patterns and will increase the feeling of your connection with everything that exist in the Universe regardless of their dimensional level.

Overall, it gives you the ability to sense the warning signs for your next actions and everything in your world seems to have a better synchronization as things and events work and line up for the better good. Be sure to have a guide while your third eye is opening so that your transition from blind to seeing would be smoother because it could be scary and strange to new comers since the third eye is the very sensitive part of the body that let you see the unseen. The eye is truly the lamp of the body and resides within the midst. The ideal is to have a gradual third eye opening so that you will become known to other worlds as well, since the eye will give you access first to the fourth dimension with other beings that necessarily are not all pleasant or nice. At the end your third eye holds the keys to heaven and everyone should thrive to open theirs and lead the way for others to follow. Remember that the kingdom of God is in the Midst. And some of you might not see it, unless you are willing to be Born Again. The third eye opening may not be for you if you are not ready to see beauty and love in God's creation.

CHAPTER 35

Tips for kids

First of all, educate your children, regardless of their gender. Teach the children how to climb trees; how to put a thread into a needle hole. Teach them how to swim and how to fix their own clothes with a needle on minor wear and tear. Let them be kids and learn to play by themselves when other kids are not around. Teach them how to read and write and increase their desire in mathematics, physics, chemistry, Literature, Art, History, philosophy, agriculture, engineering, art and science. Guard and protect your kids from making your same mistakes, otherwise they will repeat the cycle as you know, the apple doesn't fall far from the tree. Your kids will have relatively your same strength and weakness in almost all emotions and feelings, therefore try your best to teach them slowly by time, now that you know better how to overcome those short comings that can make a difference in life at any moment.

Protect your kids thinking and thoughts by telling them what is right and what is wrong. Do not hesitate to correct a kid when he/she is wrong. Learn to become an impartial judge to your kids with no emotions and flexibility attached if they are at fault play. Understand that your kid is a soul, a spirit that have his/her own mind and will, freely thinking and doing whatever things he/she wants. Guide them right so that their thoughts will not harm them as a consequence of how they carry themselves, mentally and spiritually, in those spiritual and mental dimensions.

Your kids could only think for themselves and by themselves, so please make sure they know their boundaries not to cross between right and wrong; and make it an imperative rule that everyone has a right to be respected, loved and treated equally among all the other kids.

Always remember that your kids are souls just like you and also have visions, dreams, nightmares...

CHAPTER 35

Your kids are subject to the same laws and rules into the spiritual world. And we know that the insane and the sane minds are all living into the spiritual worlds along with your kids' minds and spirits.

Therefore, teach them how to avoid and detect the traps set by the enemies. Warn them to be aware of the evil eye and to avoid unnecessary confrontations with other kids and adults. The evil eye by many cultures can simply be any look with envy towards the envious subject not necessarily with an intention to do any harm but could end up bringing bad luck, and sicknesses to the person being gazed with the envious eyes. Symptoms connected to the evil eye are desiccation, diarrhea, constant crying, and dehydration even death, not forgetting that some look with the eye could have been with evil thoughts and intentions to start with. Having said that, the word evil eye could be misleading as it is simply an unintentional curse from the eye gazer to the subject envied. Adults, livestock and other possessions can also be affected. Not just kids but also adults can become victims of the evil eye. Advise them also not to be envious of others as they could be the ones pointing the evil eye to someone else, which carries its own consequences in the Karma law.

It is then a must for you to teach them how to guard and protect their own emotions and feelings. Because the kids also have the right to a stress free world and a balanced mind. Help them grow stronger and wiser by helping them to confront and overcome their fears and weaknesses.

See through them and remain attentive to them so that you could protect and teach them right by anticipation to prevent them from falling into a pit that they have dug for themselves a while back. Talk to your kids and provide them with the proper tools and knowledge to survive and be independent into the society. Let them know gradually the laws of the land and the laws of the universe. Encourage them

CHAPTER 35

to follow the news and always remain informed. Help them grow consciously by increasing their awareness to the natural life and stars and moons. Emphasize the communion and relation to all living and how everyone and everything depends on each other to remain alive. Introduce them to the trees, water streams, Earth rotation, mountains, ocean, lakes and animal life so that they would know of other existence and learn how to respect the nature. Make sure your kids get to know the different seeds of the fruits and trees and actually learn how to sow and all the procedure that involve the farming and harvesting. Every kid should gradually be introduce to a hand skill so that he/she would learn how to use tools and work with his/her hands.

As a survival kit, everyone should have a basic knowledge of how to make fire and cook; how to climb a tree to get its fruits; how to get fish that live in the water and how to hunt and climb hills and mountains; how to use the cardinal points for the sense of direction.

The lesson here is that, there are some things to never depart from as it is a basic survival kit under all circumstances as the world evolves and changes. Regardless of one's civilization and modernization, those shall be kept at all times from generation to generation to avoid any gap where the need would be and there would be no one within that generation to teach.

I just realized how of a challenge this could be done easily but it is one step at a time and besides who-else could be the best teacher ever if not parents, your friends, their friends, the community, the environment, the work place, the entertainment places, your classmates, your casual friends, your buddy's, your random encounter, your interest and you and your state of mind and moods.

Life evolves and need changes but one thing remains, it takes a village to raise a child.

CHAPTER 35

The Reason why you Should Meditate or Learn How to

Try to recollect how much stress you have possibly accumulated throughout your life until this moment. Have you been in school? If yes, did anything during school give you stress? Homework, , exam tests, surprise tests, finals and the pressure from teachers, professors and other classmates? Was there a time when you really felt pressured and stressed out because of a school project that you had no clue how to start, or who to turn to for explanation? What about the time limit sets for each test or exam that you had to hurry and do the best you could to finish the test before the time was up? If you answered yes to any of the questions above, it means that you have been through stressful moments.

Now, if we add the stress of looking for a job, or an internship, you probably realize by now that stress keep accumulating, time after time. The stress of getting ready for school, work and the traffic or the time spent waiting for a bus that could come late, is all stressful. Paying the bills, the rent, the insurance on time and getting food could all become stressful as time goes by.

When in a relationship with an abusive partner, or with someone who really doesn't understand you, that alone could induce an extreme stress throughout the duration of the relationship. The break ups and the disappointments, the lack of money to go on a proper date or to the grocery store, come with a lot of stress. Figure, you are still in school and you have not even started the real life, per se, as adult with children.

For adult with children, imagine how much stress they accumulate daily. From dealing with the children, each with their specific needs to entertaining their partner. Taking the kids to school and back, then go to work in stressful traffic to end up dealing sometimes with an unpleasant boss or co-workers. The pressure from the extended families, your in-laws, friends when they need help or your services or your time,

CHAPTER 35

time that you barely have. The stress that comes when one of the kids is sick or your partner, the fear of losing them and the vulnerability of not being able to do anything to help besides a doctor; to make matter worse, when you lose a loved one. Life is full of stress that we endure daily and let it accumulate. I will not even go in details, how hard it is to maintain a healthy family financially and the stress that it brings. It is time to meditate to start wiping away the accumulated stresses built up over the years.

There are so many other reasons that you could complete on your own. The truth is, no-one is immune to stress and besides, stress cannot be avoided as it serves as a boost for creativity and innovation. You just need to learn how to control and balance your emotional Being.

HOW TO MEDITATE

You probably need only ten minutes a day to meditate so that balance could see light over your life. You can either seat on a chair or on the floor comfortably in a quiet place to start with. When on chair, sit straight with your neck and back straight (spine) with your feet flat on the floor. On the floor cross-legged, you will need to have knees below your hips and place your hands on each knee with a straight spine and neck.

Close your eyes preferably, but you don't have to, and diagnose your body. Scan your body from head to toes and from toes up. Proceed now to breathing through your nose, and breathing out through your mouth. A series of thinking would happen inside your mind. Acknowledge that you are thinking by being aware of your thoughts, and proceed calmly to refocus on breathing. Again, breathe in through your nose and breathe out through your mouth. Don't try to calm your mind or try to stop yourself from thinking, just focus back and forth on your breathing in and out and enjoy the sensation of the breath. Of course, at the beginning, your mind will keep wandering away in to thought, but when that happens, remain aware and acknowledge that you are thinking and proceed back to focus on your breathing. When you practice, time after time, you will be able to meditate without your mind interfering through time and might experience the silence that everybody is talking about. A place with no thought, just emptiness.

When you meditate, your brain grows in size that naturally enables you to balance your emotions and stress, while opening you up to more Love and Compassion to share with your loved ones. And meditation is all about consistency and frequency not about the length. You should try as much as possible to meditate regularly to benefit most of its fruits. You can start from five minutes to ten and so on whenever your time allows, but do it every other day of the week, better yet every day. You would reap the benefits of a healthier body with a stronger immune system, a more emotional well-being with less stress, anxiety, anger, fear and depression. It would reduce your blood pressure and make your heart healthier. You would enjoy better sleep and rest. Meditating would improve your blood circulation, lower blood cortisol levels, slower your respiratory rate and, most importantly, you will feel relaxed, calm, patient and peaceful. Then, you can say bye-bye to your accumulated stresses over your life time gradually as you keep meditating daily. You can also do a little bit of stretching, bending and flexing before sitting up to strengthen and smooth the muscle for a prolonged meditation session. Stretching loosens your muscles and increases the blood flow allowing more oxygen delivery. Walking couple of miles at least 3 times during a week period would also help strengthen your muscle.

WHAT IS LIVING IN THE MOMENT, BEING PRESENT?

When you pick up your phone and answer, "Hello," is living at the moment. At that instant time, you are focused on the conversation at hands alone. To live in the moment is to focus only in the present time. Whatever that we are doing,

CHAPTER 35

we should just focus on that alone and not worry about any outcomes. This is not implying for you not to plan for the future, it just means, be here at the moment, at each instant consciously and aware of what is going on.

It means that you are conscious and aware of what you are doing and that you are not letting your past interfere with your present moment. Your moment only has your undivided attention. You are not worrying either about the future, you just seize each moment in your life and enjoy every minute of it. When you come in contact with your neighbor, you don't just brush over him/her, you actually give everyone some attention as you embrace every moment of your life. Even when you are resting, allow yourself to just focus on resting. Clear your mind of worries and from regrets to just rest fully for a minute. Living in the moment means leaving your stinking attitude behind at every encounter. Starting fresh with an open-mind and ready to learn from everyone you are going to deal with. Living in the present is learning to stop spreading anger throughout the whole day. Yes, someone made you angry, or you are upset, your job is to acknowledge the anger and try to calm down, instead of going about your business, angry at everybody else that had nothing to do with the cause of your anger. When you are conscious of yourself and surrounding, everybody you meet will start with a good attitude and with respect, even if you had a three days' notice to vacate your apartment prior.

Staying angry, upset and worried are considered living in the past. It means that you have not learned to let go of your painful experiences, perceived wrongs and difficult times. Do not let your experience with society determine how to treat others. Because you are hurt, you should not go around hurting other people. Besides, do not let rejections from society get attached to your self-esteem, to a point that you are retaliating your pain to others.

Doing so, you set yourself up for failure in the moment time where your full attention is needed. It means you might miss the present value as you already tainted it with your past emotions and feeling or your worries from the future. You cannot change the past, but you can make amends with it and move on. You cannot anticipate the future and let it already stress you out when life is going on at the moment. In finish, you miss everything as you no longer cannot claim the past as it is gone and should not be relieve, you failed to value your present moment or present encounter by being present with your bad attitude. Therefore, make every moment count with a positive attitude and see how pleasant it is to fully be aware at each instant and live it fully with open-mind and open-heart. Remaining positive and optimistic will always attract positivity and good opportunities into your live.

When life becomes hard and full of worries and stress, just take a moment and just Breathe. Breathe again and again, in and out. Breathe in, and breathe out. Breathe in through your nose and breathe out through your mouth. Learn to be still, without doing anything for once. Take a break and breathe. A lot of people need to learn not to do something. It is okay not to be doing something once in a while and focus on your breathe to remain at the present. It is ok to let the dirty dishes sit at the sink so that you could get some rest after a long day of work. Stop always looking for something to do, or somewhere to be, when you can just seat at home and relax your mind, rest your body and reenergize your soul.

The truth is life unfolds and we need to live more in the moment with mindfulness and learn that it is okay to take a break from life and just Breathe and relax.

CHAPTER 36
It is Okay to Talk about Money in our Families and Communities

Money is the least subject talked about in most of the households everywhere in the world. Most of us have made it to adulthood life without being told how to manage money. At least for me I don't think someone ever expressly tried to teach me about how to control my finances or even how to make it grow as a mean of investing. Even most books that talk about money would literally not break down how we can manage our day to day money and expenses. We have all made bad personal choices when managing our personal finances with or without a family.

Money problems are made to be believed that it is only your personal issue and no one wants to hear it, or even needs to; because everyone has one and won't bother to discuss it with nobody. We have been subconsciously programed by who I don't know that money should not become a topic of discussion anywhere even at home. So we grew with this stigma that talking about your money problems with someone-else's is a taboo. Beside we are not even sure if someone would bother listening to our personal finances issues since on the back of the listener, he/she might be thinking that next you are going to ask to borrow some money that he/she doesn't even have. A very large number of the world population is struggling with money, because money is scarce and not enough to tackle basic life needs. So, a lot of us are playing games with ourselves, trying to show a positive facet that money is not an

CHAPTER 36

issue and truly we are all struggling financially and one, two, three pay check(s) away would send most of us to the street. In truth, no one wants to be blamed and lashed out for poor money management skills. Everyone is bad with money. That's why we don't like or want to talk about it. So you would know that I'm bad with money and think that I'm irresponsible and that I should be ashamed for not having my finances together?

For example, how would you feel if someone ask you how much you have in your bank account? Would you put the person in his place that it's not of his business? Or volunteer to frankly answer? Do you even really know how much is left in your bank account with the exact numbers right now?

To come back on some of the stigmas surrounding money is the fact that we mostly don't know anyone else's salary, or weekly pay. Nobody discloses none of that matter. Brothers don't know how much their sisters are making; kids (teenagers) don't know how much their parents are making. Even true friends for life don't know how much money their friends make. I'm exaggerating now, because not everyone that you will tell your business to. So, we are surrounded by family members, friends that are struggling financially separately with no one to talk to about. Even though everyone surrounding us have the same denominator, we simply prefer to keep our money problems to ourselves. There is a need to break this stigma and start the discussion instead of judging each other. I'm not sure if I'm ready for that.

So, I could relate to you that you are struggling by yourself with no sound. I could relate with you with your stress and depression when money is scarce and bills need to be paid. I could relate with you not going to the family reunion because money was scarce and you could not possibly have told your loved ones that it was because you didn't have money. I could relate to you when you are at the restaurant, not being able to really order what you want, because money is an issue. Yes, we have all settled for less not because we don't love ourselves, or want the best for ourselves, but truly, we didn't have enough

CHAPTER 36

money for the best. So, we play humble and conservative. But, in reality, it is because of lack of money, but no one has an ear to listen to you complain about your finances. There are also a lot of people that are living humble even though they are financially stable. Regardless, we are going to keep a lot of stuffs to ourselves anyway.

How can we Move Past the Difficulties and Stigma Surrounding Money?

Have an open discussion with your family and disclose how much you are making when working. That could also discourage those that always ask for loans and end up upsetting your own financial stability flow, not to bother asking you for money. You know when money has to be stretched and someone that you cannot refuse to help ask you for money; you may help that person regardless just to find yourself with less money now to survive.

So, instead of making it look like you are bowling when you are really not, just admit that we all have money problems and disclose it to your loved ones so that it becomes clear that most of us are among the said population without enough money to live. The truth is, a lot of our brothers and sisters are sleeping in their cars nowadays and low key on the streets, or in technical homelessness. Their family members and friends are not even aware of it. The truth is a lot of our sisters are struggling to put real organic and healthy food on the table for their kids daily and a lot of them are on the streets with their kids with nowhere safe to go when it's dark. The reason is not because there are poor in managing money; it is not because they are dumb, naïve or irresponsible, it is simply the fact that the money they earn is not enough to stretch and cover all the necessary expenses or bills and address any other necessity as far as allowance for the kids, snacks for the kids, a subway sandwich for lunch at work, to the basic needs to be able to have something to cook and roof over the kids' heads.

CHAPTER 36

It might sound like in a movie, but that's what most of us are dealing with every day. Deciding which bill to get an extension for and which one to cancel because we can no longer afford it. Once you come to realization that this is what truly is going on in almost every household in America and everywhere, then you will see the need to face the money problems with its stigma. What is the real reason that causes you to run out of money?

This is not an issue of a race. This is not an issue of black or white or brown, it is in almost all household that the struggle is real and leaves no race behind. Not that race has nothing to do with it either. It is time to stop pretending and face the money lack problems within our families. No more need for fake bling-bling to appear as you are successful. No more need for expensive jewelries and cars, while the rest of your family is struggling to eat and stay mentally healthy. It is no one fault that a large number of the world population lives below poverty rate, it is a system and there are ways to not let your family and friends suffocate and chocked to death when we all stop pretending and face the reality about the systemic economic segregation upon all of us.

Do not spend too much money on vacations, clothes, parties and furniture you cannot afford. I hear you saying, "I don't do all that but I am still broke."

I understand the reality we are living in today's world. It is mostly not because of bad spending or bad money management; it is just a fact now that the incomes are no longer enough to meet all of our basics need to survive. The rent is high; the gas is high; food prices at the grocery stores are high; utility bills are high; taxes are high; interest on loans are high etc.

Two incomes in a single household cannot even guarantee a sustainable and healthy life when everything you need, you have to pay for it. Now imagine how even a miracle cannot make it any easier and better in a single household with only one income?

CHAPTER 36

Teaching our youth sexual responsibility will protect them from having kids at a young age when they themselves are not even able to take care of their own needs financially, let alone adding a baby to feed and to protect. It should be mandatory that you make sure your daughters are familiar with their menstrual cycle and how it works and what having their periods monthly means. They should be taught how to avoid getting pregnant when being a teenager, or a young adult, not ready to raise a family. Part of the problem is that we have too many young men and girls that end up with kids that they were not ready to raise, even to provide them with their necessary needs.

Teen pregnancy is a barrier to a lot of teenagers not being able to pursuit their dream careers and to finish their education. This can lead to endless financial problems that could be prevented by teaching them what it means for girls when they start seeing their menstrual cycle; and what it means for boys when their girlfriends are having their periods as both gender bear a responsibility for not having babies when they cannot afford to raise them. This cycle needs to be broken to give the next generation a chance to have more healthy and stable families.

In addition to not spending too much money on expensive stuff you cannot afford, you should avoid buying something just because your friends have it. Do not spend on unnecessary things just to be in style for the season and later regret it because you are broke now. Do not think that things and objects you are to buy are going to lift your self-esteem. Attaching self-worth to material achievements is not healthy for you financially because you will be spending money in an out of control manner until you reach your ego's satisfaction. And we know that the ego never gets satisfied. If the ego wants, it thinks it shall have, and it is your problem down the road, if you are broke. The ego already got what it wanted. So think twice before making any financial decisions based on competitiveness and entitlement feelings otherwise you would end up biting your own butt later and possibly in debt now. Not because so and so have a Cadillac that you should break your neck to get a Cadillac. Do not compete with others when it comes to you spending your hard earned money. Especially, do not try to live beyond your means.

It would be a great financial move to start tracking your money. Whenever you spend, mark it down at least for a whole month or two so that you can diagnose your own financial foundation. When you go and pump your gas, keep the receipts and add them to your expenses to get a clear idea of how much you really spend on gas approximately every week. Keep any receipt for the food take outs, the money given to the kids as allowance, the cost of bringing food to the table every week. You should at least have an idea on how much you spend on food when shopping at the different grocery stores for bargain prices. Once you submit yourself to that financial scrutiny for a whole month, it should become clear to you on how much you truly spent all together each month besides the emergencies spending here and there. Then you could know exactly how much money you need to make or have to make it through the month. This exercise would make you avoid making unnecessary purchases, thinking that you might have some extra money left to cover that purchase and just focus on paying what you need since you already know how much you working with every month compared to how much you are making.

When taking a loan, you should be focusing on the interest rate because it all adds up and can become burdensome later down the road. Sometimes, we really don't have a choice but to take the highest rate offered. Be sure to pay more than the minimum payments whenever you can so that you would reduce the principal more and more, thereby reducing how much interest you would end up paying.

And we should be open to discuss our money foibles with our kids and family members so that they, too, will learn from our mistakes and maybe by doing so, we can in return be given

CHAPTER 36

a better technique in how to do better with money. Money talk and its issues should not be a taboo anymore. At least not for a married couple.

Let's start becoming more open to discussing money when we are with our trusted family. It would not be easy at the beginning because it is a subject less talked about and no one is really prepared to be open minded. So let's join the other people that have broken the barriers of this stigma and boot the taboo label on it out of our communities and families. If we don't start, the next generation will continue with it and we are all aware that there is a need to change so that tomorrow might be better. Be more open-minded and you will see that it was a big deal to start with.

Besides, having financial difficulties and stress all the time lead one to have some mental issues. There is a thin line between money (poverty) and mental health. Poverty bring with it some stress, anxiety, loss of self-esteem, self-incrimination, fear, confusion, doubt, anger, resentment etc. that affect people health. You cannot be constantly broke and in needs for basic necessities to stay alive and be healthy at the same time. Maybe with some few exceptions.

Mental health could also be linked to poverty. Some people are just unsocial because they are broke. Diseases are linked to poverty, due to the fact that your glands release hormones all the time every single time you are stressed. See previous chapters when I talked about the consequences of an elevated Cortisol level and it's linked to destroying the glands. When the glands are overworked, they can give up. And when the pancreas gives up, the person becomes diabetic and insulin dependent because the job of the pancreas is to also create insulin to regulate the glucose level in our blood. Note that elevated cortisol over some time at a consistent basis will keep producing glucose that leads to an increase and elevated blood sugar levels in the blood. Therefore, I could easily conclude that poverty, coupled

CHAPTER 36

with extreme and chronic stress at a consistent basis could lead to diseases, high blood pressure, traumas, anger, obesity, malnutrition and mental health issues. Which makes it a mandatory mission to lift our people out of poverty today and put your money where your mouth is. Put your money in the bank that support your community and race and spend your money in places/shops where you matter and where you will not be racially profiled or discriminated against.

The lack of financial stability has destroyed so many families and dismantled communities. So many heart broken and so many sad faces are the paint on a lot of people's faces everywhere with a fake smile just to camouflage the pain and suffering within. Let's make life happier again by making this family and community uplifting possible and bring back the joy of life in our households since we lost it thousands of years ago.

CHAPTER 37
Egyptology Health 101

Our ancestors, the ancient Egyptians, inform us that earth is alive. Its entirety is an integrated and living organism. In our ancestors' understanding, the multiple atmospheric sheaths is also part of the vital part of the living organism. In this note, the ancient Egyptians understood that all phenomenal effects in nature are all part of the bodily functions of Ra (God) commonly known as the breathing of Ra through expansion and contraction. Until these days, the Dogon in Africa confirms that the thunder lights when it's raining are paving and making way for God to pass through; and that the actual roar is the movement of God moving from mountain to mountain.

In fact, the universe breathes just like every other being on the planets. It expands and contracts in fluctuating cycles. When you consider Earth, it breathes in the form of volcanoes, earthquakes and various other natural phenomena. By the same token, the Sun breathes through the sunspot cycle and the solar wind. The sunspot affects our weather system as well just like the solar wind that I covered already in a different chapter. So the Sun is equipped with a regular cycle of sunspot activity that always reaches its zenith every eleven to twelve years. In that process, it shoots down some powerful electricity or intense electrical phenomena to the point that it could cause volcanic, earthquake movement on Earth and force a change to our weather pattern. Now it becomes a fact that earth responds to external influences just like how a man's aura can be affected by external influences. The universe, in its process of breathing, creates seasons and when the pressure from external and internal influences are too strong, it could cause the earth's crust to flex. Adding some extreme radical change in response to the earth's altered ionospheric tension, it could cause whole continents to rise or fall. Ancient records prove that there were continents in the Atlantic, Indian, and Pacific Oceans. It is now accepted among scientists that earth undergoes periodic ice ages and places like Antarctica covered with nothing but ice will periodically become sub-tropical climates in due time.

The breathing and contracting of the universe can also be noticed during the process of the Great Year or Annus Magnus. Our ancestors, with their advanced science and mathematics, have recorded that during the Great Year, the Sun passes through the zodiac signs, one at a time, every 2160 years. At each progressive 2160 years, the Sun reaches different zodiac signs without fail at every cycle. Our Galaxy (Milky Way) itself also turns around but on its own axis, very slowly compared to our solar system. The Milky Way turns once in a complete orbit, roughly every 230 million years and, at the same time, within that period, our solar system would complete nearly one hundred Great year cycles. To refresh your memory, it takes 25,920 years for the Sun to complete its full cycle after travelling around all the twelve zodiacal signs.

The ancient Egyptians, or Kemet, have noticed that during the sun's process of completing its cycle, it passes through twelve great stars before its full complete cycle. So the kemet gives names to each star of the zodiacal sign, which consist of Nile, Amon-Ra, Mut, Geb, Osiris, Isis, Toth, Horus, Anubis, Seth, Bastet, Sekhmet. Take note here that only the Nile was not a god or goddess; the rest of the other names are from the Egyptians' gods. Our modern zodiacal signs have different names but borrowed the same reasoning about the Sun cycle. They are: Aries, Taurus, Gemini, Cancer, Leo, Virgo, Libra, Scorpio, Sagittarius, Capricorn, Aquarius and Pisces.

CHAPTER 37

With their advance knowledge in astrology and astronomy, they have divided their day to year calendar in twelve equal months of thirty days each, which leaves out five days in a 365 days year. The five extra days "Epagomenal" are called the "festive days," especially separately dedicated to the gods Osiris, Isis, Nephthys, Set, and Horus, the Elder. It was not just randomly done. It is in connection with the 25,920 years of the Great Year. Since each year was short of the astronomical year, to compensate and make 365 days, the five extra days was added. This system of calendar was first created and introduced to and by the Egyptians as early as year 4200 B.C. and by the year 3300 B.C. they knew how to write down a number as high as 1,422,000. From 1850 B.C., the Egyptians knew and created the exact formula for calculating the volume of a quadrilateral pyramid.

For the ancient Egyptians, our ancestors, intelligence is the objective expression of spirituality. At the beginning of new cycle, or (zodiacal) age, the gods will reappear in person to always provide the new impulse and sense of future direction. This is according with divine purpose, in correlation with the advancement and human intelligence at its globalism. And the gods are not birthed by any human contact or sexual intercourse. They are "self-born," one after another, by mental self-projection. They do not need or require any help from anybody; simply through mental self-projection without the aid of the commonly known human birth process.

EGYPT, A BLACK AND HUMANITY HERITAGE

Egypt is a part of Africa and belongs to the African heritage. Ancient Egyptians were black- skinned and African. White Europe and others tried to deny Africans from claiming their heritage by trying to manipulate the international communities that the Egyptians were either white or red. In about 1830, mainly because of the rise of modern European imperialism in a form of a "new racism" against Africans, it was inconceivable for white Europe and others to accept that black people were equally intelligent, and actually were more advanced in almost of all the subjects. Therefore, most of all the noses of the Egyptians statues, proving the obvious pure blackness, were chopped off and many thousands others were vandalized and destroyed.

The Atlantic Slave trade actually took off in about 1630 as disdain of the black race by whites and others, Black people from Africa were captured by force and brought to America and other countries for forced and free labor that lasted for 300 years. After the 300 years of inhuman enslavement, whites came out with an idea that instead of capturing Africans in their counties of origins, it was best now to keep them in their countries, strip them from their own lands and force them to farm their own lands for only whites' consumption almost for free.

So slavery and colonization have destroyed Africa, Africans civilizations and the stability for a decent life as a human and first man ever to walk on earth. The slave capturers and colonizers were destroying the general Africans heritage and cultures. They stole and destroyed sacred books, scriptures, secrets, anything that came out as treasure. While destroying families and tribal structures, they were also colonizing information, secret knowledge and scientific advancement. Basically, by the time slavery and colonization ended, Africans were stripped of almost all their able-bodied men/women in the   millions, their wealth, health, strength, knowledge, gold, gods and important sacred document as old as 10,000 years old.

It is proven with historical and scientific facts that Roman history is Greek as well as

Roman. Both Greek and Roman history are Egyptian due to the fact that the entire Mediterranean was civilized by Egypt. Egypt itself borrowed some of its history from the rest of other parts of Africa, especially in Ethiopia and Nubia. Therefore, humanity has benefited from the advance knowledge and wisdom from the Egyptians. With the decline of Rome, the western Europeans' empires have seen daylight after absorbing the already borrowed Egyptians' knowledge from Rome. Plato himself in the Timaeus tells us that Greek's aspirants to wisdom visited Egypt for initiation, and the priests of Sais used to refer to them as "children in the mysteries". It is also proven when Prof. Cheikh Anta Diop, an Egyptologist on his book "the African Origin of Civilizations" attests that ' the Pythagorean mathematics, The theory of the Four Elements of Thales of Miletus, Epicurean materialism, Platonic idealism, Judaism, Islam and modern science are rooted in Egyptian cosmogony and science'.

After the Golden age of Egypt, it had suffered l several devastating invasions; especially from the Kushite invasion in 751 B.C. coming from within Africa; and the Assyrian invasions from western Asia (called the Middle East now) starting in 671 B.C. The Egyptians' glorious days and history came to a pause in 332 B.C. when the Greeks conquered Egypt, and formed their own dynasty that nearly occupied and ruled Egypt for 300 years until the turn of the Romans in 30 B.C.

Egypt was subsequently under the Romans' control in 30 B.C. and was declared a province (Aepytus) belonging to Rome and remained a province under the Roman Empire until the year 476 C.E. During the seventh Century, Egypt came under Arab control when Rome itself was susceptible of being invaded. Egypt was nearly under the rule from foreign invaders for almost 1000 years.

During the seventh century, Egypt fell under the control of the Arabs that will conduct the most brutal and inhumane treatment on Egyptians and other Africans known as the "Arab Slave Trade" from seventh century until the wake of the Atlantic Slave trade to America. So, in 652 C.E., the organized cruel slavery of Africans began by Arabs invaders that lasted until the eighteenth century just about the time the Europeans started to colonize Africa, which had resulted in another three hundred years of slavery in America and the beginning of the colonization of the African continent by Europeans dominated by France, Germany and Great Britain. By the year 1914, ninety percent of Africa had been divided between seven European countries with the exception of Liberia and Ethiopia that remained independent; even though African countries regained their independence in the 1960's.

In sum, it looks like for about twenty-five hundred years (2500), Africans and people of African descent have not been stable and have been under the subjugation of another group of people.

For your information, Egypt, before and after all these invasions and occupations from foreign invaders, was a distinct black African Nation. The nation of Egypt was also populated by Africans and as a result an African heritage. Even the Greek writer, Herodotus, who visited Egypt and other parts of Africa between 484 and 425 B.C., confirmed in his writings that Egyptians were dark-skinned with wooly hair. He continued by affirming that Egyptians have the same tint of skin as the Ethiopians. Therefore, Africans and African descents should be able to rightfully claim their heritage and connect back to their Ancestors' great civilizations and cultures.

Having gave you the rundown of Africa overall and her general struggle, you should know that during the glorious days of Egypt and other African civilizations of the Nubians, Ethiopian etc., other people in huge numbers were also forced to slave on the Egyptian lands as well for the profit of the pharaoh. This piece of writing is aimed to refresh your memory of how deep our health and the world health is rooted in insanity. Imagine a little bit what humanity is going through and that there is a real need to address the world mental health issue to facilitate our individual healings.

It could be necessary for you to also know that white people have also been slaves as well as the Arabs and the Asians; not

CHAPTER 37

forgetting about the Indian's Slavery and the Latin-American's generational struggle for freedom and liberty. There is no race from this world that has not been affected by slavery and other inhuman treatment by others. Our collective mental state needs to be checked and individually we should give another look at the world because there are still states' violence on people, countries' violence on people. It is still like back in the days when the strongest and most powerful countries behaved as savages by devastating other countries, families, ethnic groups, racial groups, political groups, religious groups to force them to accept an ideology. Indeed, the world has not changed a bit. As humans, there is a need for us to become sensitive again to world cruelty and barbarous behaviors upon its own people.

Children are dying in huge numbers of famine all over the world. Families are still being separated from their parents without any court order nor a due process, black people are being put in jail on a massive scale or gunned down on the streets everywhere by racist and mentally blinded police officers. There are more than ten wars going on around the world as of December 21, 2019 that have already killed millions of innocent people just for an ideology to stand out. Powerful countries run the world as thugs with no respect for human dignity and its society under the hypnotizes of their respective country people that think their leaders are destroying other countries to guarantee their food, safety and their life style by naiveté. But, in truth, there is room and enough food and water for everyone once we stop being greedy and heartless.

At the end of the day, every race have borrowed trauma and chronic stress from their ancestors that sadly will be handed down to the next generation if care is not provided. Every race has inflicted pain and suffering directly or indirectly to other races, including its own kind. The pain is global and the majority of the world population are negatively affected mentally, physically and spiritually. Hopefully, you have made closure with your pain, stress and the past in order to pave the way to your self-healing by letting go of the excuses, the blames and the feeling of being wrongfully victimized. Because, frankly, everyone is already walking on your shoe without you even realizing it. The truth shall indeed set you free.

GENERAL KNOWLEDGE ABOUT FEW AFRICAN QUEENS WARRIORS

"Queen **Nzinga** with her full name Nzinga Mbande was one of the fearless queens in the seventeenth century who fought cleverly to obtain the freedom for her kingdom and her people. She fought the Portuguese, who were trying to colonize her and her people. She ruled the Ndongo and Matamba Kingdoms of the Mbundu that are now in the country of Angola. With her astute diplomacy and her visionary as a military leader, she resisted the advancement of the Portuguese invasions and slave raids for over thirty years. As a Queen with advanced military skills, she fearlessly fought against the slave trade and European influence throughout the African continent. Her father, who was the King before her, started the fight against slavery and Europeans' invasions among so many other Kings and Queens who were resisting to protect their people with their life. Countless warriors within their respective kingdoms resisted the attacks from more than ten European countries on each side from north to south and west to east.

Names of other Queens that have put their leaderships and lives on the line against foreign invasions are: **Amina Mohamud** in the sixteenth century and ruler of Zazzau in Nigeria took over the fight as a queen and a Hausa warrior from her late father King Nikatau. She became the twenty-third ruler to continue the fight against slavery and to free her people. **Yaa Asantewaa,** (1850-1921), was the only woman appointed as Queen mother of Ejisu to rule the Ashanti Empire in Ghana in the late 1800s. She fought and led her army in continuous battles against the British, until the time she was captured in one the deadliest battle ever in an attempt to free her people and stop the British army from capturing the people for slavery. Before her capture, with her warrior and military skills, she waged wars with acute skills and helped the Ashanti keep and maintain their rightful independence from England. Queen **Nefertiti** was one of the queens in ancient Egypt. Her name in English translation means "a beautiful and strong woman has come". Nefertiti had earnestly worked to reunify Egypt, which was split between Upper Egypt and Lower Egypt before her reign. She succeeded in bringing peace by ending the war between the upper kemet and the lower kemet, by challenging the status quo, thereby reuniting the nation and their sons and daughters again. She was raised on the rank alongside with other prominent and noble queens like Nefertiti and Cleopatra as Egypt's most important three queens. She left a legacy of beauty, strength, peace and power.

Names of a few queens who have ruled parts of the African continent are **Queen Makeda of Sheba** in Ethiopia (mentioned in the Bible along-side with King Salomon), **Queen Nandi** of the Zulu kingdom and mother of Shaka Zulu in South Africa, and **Princess Yennenga** (the mother of the Mossi people and one of the founder of the Mossi tribe in Burkina Faso.)

EGYPTIANS' TIPS FOR YOUR HEALTH

"Far from being a self-indulgent fixation on the past, the examination of ancient Egypt is our wisest option if we intend to plan and create our cultural future." Pr. Cheikh Anta Diop

'The heart is the main motor of the human body, the starting point for the irrigation of the whole organism.' These writings were found in the Papyrus Ebers, page 108. The Egyptians wrote this during the ninth year of the reign of Amenophis I between 1557-1530 B.C. The text from our ancestors in translation reads: "Introduction to the secret lore of the doctor: knowledge of the heart's movement, and of the heart." It says, there are vessels inside the heart leading to each member.

CHAPTER 37

Thus, when any doctor, surgeon (literally, priest of sekhmet), or exorcist places his hands or fingers on the head, on the back of the head, on the hands, on the position of the heart itself, on the limbs or any other part, in so doing, he, in fact, examines the heart, because the heart's vessels lead to each of the (patient's) members. In other words, the heart speaks within the vessels of each member.

You can notice here that over 3500 years ago, Egyptians had already mastered a scientific knowledge of the heart, an anatomy and physiology with accuracy that paved the ways for our modern medicine we know today.

The text continues to state: "The vessels whose special function it is to supply vascular fluids to the members originate in the heart." Indeed, in our modern science, which has borrowed the knowledge from the Egyptians, confirms that the principal arteries among the vessels of each limb start in the heart. And, in fact, those central arteries are the aorta and the pulmonary artery. Therefore, thousands of years ago, the Egyptians had extensive knowledge of medicine and sciences. They explained the purpose of laying the hands on the patient's body member was to take the pulse, and to sense body pulses coming from the heart beats.

Notice that our ancestors are telling us that the heart speaks. And it speaks within the vessels of each member (body part). They are reminding you that pulses transmit and communicate the rhythms of the heartbeats to all your body parts. That is why doctors of even today's world, regardless of their specialization, have to first check the heart's communication to the rest of the other parts of the body. I think everyone, or every head of family or community, should learn the language of the heart. Become the first doctor of the family in order to prevent heart attacks and partial paralysis of the body.

The Papyrus Ebers that was discovered in the Egyptians' pharaoh's tomb, was humanity's first medical encyclopedia.

CHAPTER 37

It also contains the first reference to the taking of the pulse. Egypt, in those days, was the only country that had authentic, professional medical documents without referencing gods, demons, divination, or astrology. Over 3500 years back, way before our modern civilization, the Egyptians already invented the instrument for counting and taking measurement of pulse beats. A small portable Clepsydra was found by the archeologists while doing excavations in Gaza Palestine. They discovered the said instrument that was used long ago by the Egyptians to take measurements of the heart and pulse beats. The Clepsydra (a portable water clock) found was bearing the name of the nineteenth Dynasty pharaoh Min-Ptah.

In sum, the medical science and advancement in technology have planted the seeds of knowledge which eventually crossed borders to Greece and Rome. Due to the many invasions of the Egyptians by the Persian, Greeks, Roman and Arabs, this knowledge was planted in these lands as well.

The temples of Memphis and other medical schools were subsequently looted and important books stolen away by each subsequent invader. For example, the first thing Alexander the Great did, when he successfully invaded Egypt was to take over and grab possession of the Royal Library in Alexandria; and to make the Egyptians land Alexandria, into a Greek city, and a Centre of research; and Alexandria became the capital of the newly created Greek empire.

The paragraph 855 of the Papyrus Ebers deals with heart malfunctions and their impact on the health of the liver and lungs. It reads, "Regarding the weakness, which attains the heart, it is a tumor all the way to the lung and the liver. He (the patient) grows deaf, his vessels having collapsed." In a situation like this, pulse beats can no longer be felt because the vessels of the heart have grown mute.

The Egyptians' medicine was so sophisticated and holistic that many dimensions, where the body and mind, illness and tradition, individual, community and society, were all interconnected in a context of a holistic healing. That is why, besides being a veritable medical practitioner, the person would have to also be a magician, (not the magician of today in entertainment), an exorcist, healer, witch doctor, medicine-man, an interceder etc. He would have the use of the power of words, the potency of speech, and the efficacy of ritual motions. The Egyptians' culture and healing tradition, add the trust in amulets, talismans and medals of all sorts for protection from the evil eye and negative charges/energies coming from the natural world and people.

In other words, scientific, medicinal, magical and religious practices are combined to guarantee and afford an effective therapeutic system of healing, established well over 2500 years before the time of the era of Aristotle (384-322B.C.), Hippocrates (460 B.C.), Herophile (300 B.C.) and Jesus Christ.

To refresh your mind, even before 1550 B.C., our ancestors have possessed the knowledge of medicine as shown in the Papyrus Ebers. The world had already been presented with its first medical encyclopedia accumulated over previous years and Dynasties. This knowledge had been handed down from generation to generation with improvements from each generation's era, until the instability and different invasions disturbed and cut the cycle of stable continuity.

During Egypt, healing also took a form of priestly vocation, where the Sekhmet specialized in the administration of therapeutic cures, under the divine patronage of the gods and goddesses. The gods and goddesses are Thoth, Osiris, Isis, Horus, Neith, Hathor, Bes, Thoueris, Khnum and Hekhet. It was also in ancient Egypt, that aromatherapy was born. Aromatherapy is the use of plant essences for treating diseases. They used such aromatic plants as myrrh, incense, etc., to enhance intuition capacities, foresight and "direct vision." This was to reach a good psychosomatic balance. The animal and vegetable kingdoms were also the sources for the Egyptian pharmacists from which medicinal remedies (ingredients) were created.

CHAPTER 37

In addition, our ancestor's medicine use a lot of garlic (Allium Sativum) and onions (A. Cepa). Garlic stops the blood from clotting, preventing heart attacks, heart diseases and thrombosis; it also possesses tonic and antiseptic properties. Whereas, onions were even considered a sacred plant due to its richness in sugar, minerals and vitamins. Onions are good for the nervous system, the liver and the kidneys. It has disinfectant and antiseptic properties. Therefore, in ancient Egypt, onions were used to treat heart ailments and Hydropsy. It slows down the beating of the heart and, at the same time, strengthening the heart contractions. By doing so, it improves the blood circulation in the kidneys and liver. The practice of yoga and meditation also began there in Egypt before spreading to India, Asia and so forth.

In conclusion, Egyptians did not see illness as a form of punishment for your sins from God, nor the result of moral and personal disorder. They understood early on, that a human being is a combination of organic, mental, spiritual and divine energies.

This is how they viewed man's composition. First, we have the body, along with the body's organs and the body's instincts, which is called "khet". Second, we have the "ka", the vital force that gives the body life. Ka is in sort the astral double of the person representing the essence of the person's ego. In third position, we have the "ba" —the divine energy. It is a principle of divine origin in a higher rank than the first two, the khet and the ka.

In the Zarma of Niger, there are two approaches to illness. The first type of illnesses are the ones that affect the body, the "ga/khet" and are purely somatic ailments. The second type is mainly concerned with behavioral ailments that are connected with the "bya/ka," which is the astral double of the person. To cure the second type of diseases, it requires a whole array of ritual practices. In the socio-cultural system of the Mitsogho of southern Gabon and in most African healing tradition, healing proceeds in two phases. The first important step is you have to call the errant spirit back to the person's body. The second challenging part is the healing of the spirit, now back in the body. In those situations, a specialist from either gender have to be solicited to intercede on behalf of the patient because it requires knowledge of human beings in their physical, emotional, and psychic aspects, including their spiritual aspects as well combining the patient's past and future beyond this earth' dimension.

The Egyptians know and reaffirm to us that humanity is divine. Human beings as gods get born, live, suffer, die and remain connected to the Demiurge, connected to all and everything in the universe. So, in the art of healing, a lot of strategies have to be employed. A combination of drugs, medicines, oils and fragrances, ritual and sacred ceremonies are exploited to secure health. We also have the development of mental powers, ancestral myths, magic, religion and natural science. It was understood that medicine was for men and women's use, in consideration that we are multidimensional entities, within our individual, family, social, tribal, special affinities, cultural, historical, astral and cosmic systems. In short, the total environment has to be considered as a whole to guarantee total health of the sick person.

Ancient Egyptians doctors were highly skilled and specialized in various definite domains just like the different specializations existing in the twenty-first century. Throughout African kingdoms and tribal heritages, we still have the same systems of healing handed down from generation to generation. The territory of old Buganda, now located in actual Uganda, was known and famous for the various specializations of their doctors called bosawo baganda. The Bosawo Baganda were general medical practitioners. Next to them, we have the ones with specializations: the musawo we musole with a specialization in the treatment of snake bites; the mukozi we ddagala, which is the pharmacological expert that is specialized in the concoction and prescription of medicines. The list is long, but the musawo muyunzi, the bone doctor, is

CHAPTER 37

one of the prestigious specializations, responsible for fixing and treating any type of fracture, regardless of the complication. Today, their techniques to treat fractures are even in use in our modern hospitals.

One of the western doctors, Dr. R. W. Felkin, reported that in 1879, he witnessed a caesarian operation done by a "native" surgeon of the Kingdom of Bunyoro-Kitara, an operation that was successfully done.

In the 1550's B.C., the Egyptians had already invented a pregnancy test kit. They knew how to detect sexual hormones in the urine of pregnant ladies to indicate pregnancy. They could determine the sex or gender of the fetus still in the womb.

A formula written in the Kahoun Papyrus in about 1200 B.C. was giving instructions of how to determine if a woman shall give birth or not: "Arrange to have a clove of garlic wetted; (peel it, insert it as a pessary,) stay a whole night until dawn, in her flesh (vagina). Check the next day. If the odor of the garlic rises into her mouth, then she shall give birth or conceive. If it does not rise to her mouth and smell of garlic, she will not give birth or be able to get pregnant...

Ancient Egyptians, as also noted in the Papyrus Ebers, 1557 B.C., presented several formulae based on resin and mineral substances for filling cavities in teeth. There were twenty passages, or instructions, on the digestive system: flatulence, swelling and extrusion of flesh under toes and fingers, vomiting blood, the passage of black blood through the anus, appendicitis, and uremia. The same manuscript, the Papyrus Ebers, also contains a hundred prescriptions for the treatment of eye diseases. They also had specialists for ear and nose diseases, rheumatism, and special doctors for gynecological ailments.

African medicine, in general, is Egyptian medicine and Egyptian medicine is African medicine. The way of medicine in African cultures remained similar to the ancient Egypt attitude toward medicine and illness in general. From ancient Egypt to ancient Ethiopia and ancient Nubia, the whole African continent have kept and maintained some, or all, the medical practices, medicinal skills and approaches to illness from thousands of years ago. The African medicine is filled with know-how and has paved the way for modern medicine. Until tomorrow, the African medicine will still have its place and is actually an immense treasure house of science to explore by Africans and persons of African descent. African medicine has healed its sons and daughters throughout the old age to this new age. It will continue to take care of the future generations, regardless of the different struggles for freedom to end the superficial colonialism.

CONCLUSION:
"After Being Washed, the Blind Went Home Seeing."

"You are the light of the world and in the world. Do not wait, or seek for a role model before shining your light. You are the role model of others, therefore, shine your own light instead. Sow good deeds. Help feed the hungry. Help clothe the homeless. Help protect and care for the motherless or fatherless children and the weak. Pray for one another and forgive one another. Be kind and merciful and assist the poor at your best ability.

Above all, praise God and seek his mercy and her glory. Try and live godly while acknowledging your own struggle. See beauty in all things and remember that we have been created in God's image. Love mankind and understand that every soul has been deprived of the truth involuntarily and would need to be reintroduced back to the truth. In short, follow God.

And remember to protect the newborn. Shield them away from your own emotional distresses and dysfunctions. Always remain patient when dealing with newborn babies as they are not yet to understand and even know your customs, traditions or moral standards to quickly adjust to your will, desires and wishes. Stay calm and attend to them as they are still learning to adjust to your world. To make you understand better the gap, ask yourself how many days old are you? Not how many years, but how many days old. If you are twenty-five years old, you have only been on earth for 9125 days and 100 years give 36,500 days. Do not break the Golden Rule as it truly takes a village to raise a child. Allow your family members and friends to help you educate and teach your children the values they will need to stand up for you and for the whole family.

Sometimes, our ego gets in the way and blinds us when what we only need, is a cup of tea to calm ourselves. In this game of life, we don't have to win all the times. It is not even about winning or losing. It is about understanding that we become disinterested in participating in certain games of life as we grow wiser. Freedom to live without barriers becomes toxic just like freedom without purpose would become obsolete. Without any good communication between freedom, barriers and purpose, the game of life cannot be solved. Once an ethic of life has been breached, emotions run through it and take control of someone's behavior, attitude, mood and sense of communication. Ethic here could be the moral behavior Code, or society's rules and personal responsibilities. You know that emotions can dictate the way we walk, talk, think, act and do; therefore, give yourself a self-diagnosis, emotional check list to see which ones of all the emotions you feed the most. Is it anger, impatience, self-hate, jealousy, etc.?

Take note that there is always freedom amongst and within the barriers of life when the barriers are already known. Our survival cannot be guaranteed without the respect and applications of ethics of society. Only in those conditions we will have justice. Also, you cannot guarantee your own freedom, if you keep falling on the traps of your emotions and ego. The same goes with breaking the ethics of life that would lead to nothing else but guilt, self-destruction, stress, lack of self-respect, and indifference towards the world and your immediate environment.

Because, foremost, one has to be honest and ethical to be fully free since the world would not change itself without the prerequisite that we first change ourselves. God bless you and yours.

I will conclude the book by reminding you of your purpose on earth. Your purpose is to seek God and to serve God by loving

CONCLUSION

and caring for God's creation by the means of knowing thyself first. Just like Eckhart Tolle said, and I quote, "You are here to enable the divine purpose of the universe to unfold."

I will add a prayer from the last three SURAH from the Holy Quran that you can use anytime, any day.

"God is the One and Only, He is the Eternal, Absolute; He begetteth not, Nor is He begotten; and there is none Like unto Him."

"I seek refuge With the Lord of the Dawn, From the mischief of created things; From the mischief of Darkness as it overspreads; From the mischief of those who practice Secret Arts; And from the mischief Of the envious one As he practices envy."

"I seek refuge With the Lord and Cherisher of Mankind, The King and Ruler Of Mankind, The God and Judge Of Mankind—From the mischief of the Whisperer (of evil), who withdraws (after his whisper)—(The same) who whispers into the hearts of Mankind—Among Jinns and among Men."

(Jinns are some intelligent spirits of lower rank than the angels that are part of the unseen creations. They have the capabilities to transform themselves into a human or animal form at will and manifest themselves physically on earth. Jinn can also possess humans and animals. The rebellious Jinn leads men astray. They have free will just like mankind. They make their own choices. There are good Jinns and bad Jinns like we also have good and bad people).

Note from the Author to you:

Now you have heard there is a god in you that constitutes your true essence, don't you start thinking that you are already one, regardless, if you have not achieved enlightenment? Even though we are made in His image, we should not let our ego already start claiming the highest title just to satisfy the ego. God's particles are in all living things in the planet. And since you are part of the planet, God's particles are in you, too. So, now you know that there are ways to awaken your divine Being, but do not forget that is everyone else's purpose, including you. There are so many people that have reached that divine level, but you would not even know, or see them, when you cross their paths. Because they are very humble, down to earth, living the simplest and happiest life ever in silence.

You could know them by noticing how they have mastered the art of self-control and self-restrain; and by how it is practically impossible to get them angry, jealous or bitter. Those that are awaken and conscious are able to let go of their worries, regrets, mistakes and are constantly living in the present. In truth, they don't worry nor regrets anything. They are not impressed by the past, nor by the future. They can control their emotions, impulses, thoughts and their sexual desires. They recognize that only Love is the solution, so they are peacemakers and forgive anyone instantaneously that transgress them. They are not violent, and pray for peace for humanity.

You would know them by their fruits because they would not seek retaliation, nor contribute to a start of a conflict. Because they have control over their minds, their egos, any decision or act they do is without discrimination, or prejudicial to others. They understand that all life matters and should be treated with dignity and respect. They know that self-defense should not be justified and we should not let anything and anybody make us start killing each other, or disliking each-others.

They remind us that we should see beauty in all creation because the same God particles in us are also in all things. God is love and not revengeful. God doesn't punish. God does not seek retaliation, nor gets angry over anybody. In God's eyes, we are all equal, and we are all part of His extension. God is always happy to have you come back to Him. God is ecstasy and does not complain, nor set anyone up for failure. He does not hold grudges, nor waits at the corner to inflict pain and suffering on anybody. God is love and will always love you, regardless of what you have done with your life. He will embrace you with love, whenever and

CONCLUSION

however, long you take to go back to Him. And by you acknowledging that you are divine, you should be able to show love for God by loving all His creation without discrimination.

In truth, who then could claim to have possess all and every available knowledge? I cannot and you can't either, unless you are among those who have an ego as big as the Mount Everest and Kilimanjaro combined. In my search of knowledge, I have exposed myself to my own ignorance. The more I learn, the more I realize what I don't know. The width of my ignorance is widening every time I come across something new. It makes me wonder if there were someone who happened to have known everything about everything. Even though I don't want to cast any doubt out there and assume due to lack of knowledge, I would speculate that such a Man/Woman would have been quite a super human. I know the average person barely uses about 5% of their brain but, for someone to know everything, that person used 100% of the brain and possibly borrowed some other brains.

For that possibility to even exist, someone else had to teach that person and so on. So, it could not just be one super Man/Woman. I'm going to admit that chances are, no one on Earth possibly could have known everything. Due to the fact that Earth itself is very big, knowing everything implies that you are also accustomed to all the different other cultures and civilizations. That simple fact is quasi impossible because there are some communities that have preferred to live in isolation out of sight of the world.

We do have advanced Beings from other planets that have a lot of skills and knowledge. Even those ancient civilizations that have built the pyramids all over our world, we can also agree that they were advanced compared to us. Therefore, it is fair to assert that they knew a lot more than we do. We are a work in progress and hopefully, we will get there some day. I guess, that's why it takes a lot of people working as a team to build and create something extraordinary like building a plane,

CONCLUSION

or a nuclear reactor. It takes a team always to bring something new to the world.

When you consider an eye, its composition alone and its location signifies its role and importance. Let's you and I imagine how it all came about that it is necessary for us to be able to see. Was it during our creation or after our creation? The Bible says that we were created in God's image. Now does that means that we were created to resemble god or to have the qualities of god? If we were created to physically be like gods, does that mean that gods have two legs and two arms also with one head? If that is the case, what or who created the moon, Sun, Stars, Mountains, Earth, which visibly have nothing in common with a god with two legs and two arms. So God cannot possibly look like us because then God would have to also look like the rest of other Creations individually. In a way God is looking like his/her creation because there could not have been nothing in existence to copy besides being Himself/Herself. If there is nothing prior to everything, it implies that everything is out of God and from God and possesses God's particles in it, regardless of its significance and size.

So, everything is God in so many units and different components. Therefore, when I look at you, I see God in you. Likewise, there is God in the trees, animal life, mountains, sun, moons, and stars, including the ants, bees and insects. Basically, everything belongs to God and is not separate from God because no one can stand alone, except with Whom that created all of us.

God loves you and I love you, too. Trust in God only. Never say never; and sleep in a flat surface/terrain. When in company with other people, watch your behavior and your tongue. When by yourself, watch your mind and your thought. And watch your temper when you are angry.

"With a fraction of Myself, I invest in the Universe. Yet I remain (a part)." God the Supreme

BIBLIOGRAPHY

- Ahmed Y. Tatieta (2017) *Soul Pathway to Total Health*
- John Gordon (2004) *Egypt, Child of Atlantis: a Radical Interpretation of the Origins of Civilization*
- Carolyn Collins Petersen (2013) *Astronomy 101*
- Chuck Missler (1999) *Cosmic Codes; Hidden Messages from the Edge of Eternity.*
- A. C. Bhaktivedanta Swami Prabhupada (2004) *Bhakti-Yoga; The Art of Eternal Love*
- Dan Brown (2009) *The Lost Symbol*
- Robert C. Atkins, M.D. (2002) *Dr. Atkins' New Diet Revolution*
- Dr. Les Parrott (2003) *Shoulda Coulda Woulda: Live in the Present/ Find Your Future*
- Marcus Aurelius (175 CE. Printed 2017) *Meditations*
- L. Mike Henry/ K. Sean Harris (2002) *Jamaican Herbs & Medicinal Plants and their Uses*
- Betty R. Price (1982) *Through the Fire & Through the Water: My Triumph Over Cancer*
- Pema Chodron (2013) *How to Meditate – A Practical Guide to Making Friends with your Mind*
- Astral Books (2010) *The Evil Eye – Protect yourself against the terrors of the Evil Eye.*

BIBLIOGRAPHY

- Holy Bible (King James Version)
- Quran
- A. C. Bhaktivedanta Swami Prabhupada (1972, 1983) Bhagavad Gita – As It Is
- L. Ron Hubbard (2007) Scientology- A New Slant on Life
- Stefan Chmelik (1999) Chinese Herbal Secrets (the key to total health)
- Denise Whichello Brown & Sandra White (2001) Alternative Health Therapies (the complete guide to aromatherapy, massage and reflexology)
- Barron's (2nd Edition 2004) Anatomy and Physiology (the easy way)
- Paula R. Hartz (1993) Taoism (world religion)
- Theresa Cheung (2006) The Elements Encyclopedia of the Psychic World (the Ultimate a-z of Spirits, mysteries and the paranormal)
- Satguru Sivaya Subramuniyaswami (1993) *Dancing With Siva (Hinduism's Contemporary Catechism)*
- Michael Philips (2008) *The Undercover Philosopher*
- Osho (2004) *Buddha (his life and teachings)*
- Christmas Humphreys (1962) *Zen – A Way of Life*
- Kendra Sims (2018) *I'm Saved But I Struggle (a realistic view of salvation)*
- Eckhart Tolle (2008) *A New Earth (Awakening to Your Life's Purpose)*
- Deepak Chopra (2004) *The Book of Secrets (Unlocking the Hidden Dimensions of Your Life)*

BIBLIOGRAPHY

- Leo Tolstoy (1998) *A Calendar of Wisdom (Daily Thoughts to Nourish the Soul)*

- Ernesto Ortiz, LMT, CST (2009) *Hot Stone Massage Therapy (A Guide to the Total Mind-Body Experience)*

- Deborah Mitchell; Foreword by Hunter Yost, M.D. (2009) *The Complete Book of Nutritional Healing*

- Gaby Dun (2019) *Bad With Money (The Imperfect Art of Getting your Financial Shit Together)*

- Richard Carlson, PH.D. (1997) *Don't Sweat the Small Stuff and It's All Small Stuff*

- George G. M. James (1992) *Stolen Legacy (Greek Philosophy Is Stolen Egyptian Philosophy)*

- Robert M. Schoch, PH.D. and Robert Bauval (2017) *Origins of the Sphinx (Celestial Guardian of Pre-Pharaonic Civilization)*

- Theophile Obenga (1990) *African Philosophy* (The Pharaonic Period: 2780-330 B.C.)

- Cheikh Anta Diop (1974) *The African Origin of Civilization* (Myth Or Reality)

- Cheikh Anta Diop (1991) *Civilization Or Barbarism* (An Authentic Anthropology)

- Mckay Hill Buckler (1988) *A History of World Societies* (Second Edition- Since 1500)

www.ingramcontent.com/pod-product-compliance
Lightning Source LLC
Chambersburg PA
CBHW021052080526
44587CB00010B/225